90 0164904 9

This book is to be returned on
or before the date stamped below

31 AUG 94

3 0 APR 2001

1 1 MAY 2001

UNIVERSITY OF PLYMOUTH

ACADEMIC SERVICES
PLYMOUTH LIBRARY
Tel: (0752) 232323
This book is subject to recall if required by another reader
Books may be renewed by phone
CHARGES WILL BE MADE FOR OVERDUE BOOKS

D1422545

Edinburgh Law and Society Series

Closure or Critique

New Directions in Legal Theory

Edited by

ALAN NORRIE

EDINBURGH UNIVERSITY PRESS

© Edinburgh University Press, 1993

Edinburgh University Press Ltd
22 George Square, Edinburgh

Typeset in Linotron Plantin
by Koinonia Limited, Bury, and
printed and bound in Great Britain
by The University Press, Cambridge

A CIP record for this book is
available from the British Library

ISBN 0 7486 0445 6

Contents

Acknowledgements

The idea for this book, and the great majority of the contributions within it, stemmed from a seminar series held at Warwick Law School under the auspices of the School's Legal Research Institute in the academic year 1990–1. Warwick seeks to further the contextual understanding of law, and, to that end, its Legal Research Institute provided a grant to meet the expenses of a number of speakers who gave papers in the seminar series. I am very grateful to the School and the LRI for this financial assistance. I would also like to thank all the speakers who gave papers at Warwick during the year, and, most especially, those colleagues and postgraduate students who attended the seminars and, through their participation and support, made the series so successful and rewarding.

I would also wish to acknowledge the judicious advice and ready assistance during the editorial process offered by the Edinburgh Law and Society Series editors, and the patience and helpfulness of those at the University Press with whom I worked.

Versions of chapters 8 and 9 have appeared in the *Oxford Journal of Legal Studies* (1990) 10, pp. 539–58 (MacCormick), and in A. Sarat (ed.) *The Fate of Law* (1991), University of Michigan Press, Ann Arbor (Fish).

Finally, I would like to thank my wife Gwen and our children, Richard and Stephen, for their support throughout the project, and particularly in its final stage.

Alan Norrie
December 1992

List of Contributors

ANNE BARRON, Lecturer in Law, Department of Law, University College London

DERYCK BEYLEVELD, Reader in the Philosophy of Law, Centre for Socio-Legal Studies, University of Sheffield

ROGER BROWNSWORD, Professor of Law, Centre for Socio-Legal Studies, University of Sheffield

ROGER COTTERRELL, Professor of Legal Theory, Department of Law, Queen Mary and Westfield College, University of London

ROBERT FINE, Senior Lecturer in Sociology, Department of Sociology, University of Warwick

STANLEY FISH, Arts and Sciences Professor of English, Professor of Law, Department of English, Duke University, North Carolina

PETER GOODRICH, Professor of Law, Department of Law, Birkbeck College, University of London

NICOLA LACEY, Fellow, New College, Oxford

NICK LAND, Lecturer in Philosophy, Department of Philosophy, University of Warwick

NEIL MACCORMICK, Regius Professor of Public Law, Centre for Criminology and the Social and Philosophical Study of Law, Faculty of Law, University of Edinburgh

W. T. MURPHY, Reader in Law, London School of Economics and Political Science, University of London

ALAN NORRIE, Senior Lecturer in Law, School of Law, University of Warwick

Introduction

ALAN NORRIE

The last ten to fifteen years have witnessed an astonishing and exciting flowering of legal theory. This has resulted, on the one hand, from the development of critical legal studies movements in Europe and the United States and, on the other, from the insurgence of a general culture of postmodern and critical theory and its impact on thinking about law. As a result, the previously rather staid field of jurisprudence has been hit by a variety of new theoretical perspectives which have been but slowly and partially absorbed. The old oppositions between natural law and positivism, between realism and formalism, and between 'legal' and 'sociological' approaches have given way before the realisation that law and legal theory are deeply implicated within a more complex and sophisticated philosophical tradition that, depending upon one's position, has its most significant roots either in the Enlightenment or an earlier, but avowedly 'Western', set of sources. However one looks at it, the old categories and certainties have been seriously undermined by these new positions, and it is the purpose of the essays in this volume to present, to examine, and to seek to locate these new developments on the social, political and philosophical terrains of which they are a part. They start from the view that current critical concerns about the character of law as a liberal institution and about the implications of the many *impasses* of modern(ist) thinking have crucially impacted upon our understanding of the nature of law at the deepest levels.

The primary focus of the essays is claims about the nature of law and about its moral character. At stake are classical Enlightenment views of the value of legal justice, and about law's ethical foundations on the one hand, and modern claims about the very possibility of law as a rule governed enterprise on the other. Is law morally based and is legal system theoretically possible? Both questions ultimately hang upon the nature of 'reason' and the way it is understood in the Western philosophical tradition. It is reason that is variously conceived either as the basis of moral authority or as the 'cement' which holds legal rules together. It is accordingly the relationship between law, legal and ethical reasoning and moral authority which is subjected to critical scrutiny. As many of the contributions to this rich and diverse collection indicate in their titles and content, the possibility of legal or ethical closure and (/or) the need for critique constitute central theoretical issues in modern legal theory. This is as true for those who in different ways locate the problem of law in the nature or development of the rationalist tradition of the Enlightenment (Beyleveld and Brownsword, Fine, Norrie, Murphy) as it is for those working within a postmodernist approach to questions of legal theory (Barron, Land, Goodrich). It also remains central to the debate about the possibility of legal closure, its terms and conditions, that emerges in the chapters by Norrie and Lacey, and which is joined with vigour by MacCormick, Fish and Cotterrell; and, as Lacey makes clear, questions of both ethical and legal closure along with questions of critique of law and its implications are crucial to a progressive political project such as that offered by feminism.

How is one to understand these diverse debates with their common themes? In organising the text, two possibilities presented themselves. One was to seek a deeper synthesis of the issues raised, and to present them as part of a common intellectual trajectory. In this way, the chapters would appear as part of a logic organised under the editorial hand. The other was to allow the contributions as much as possible to stand by and speak for themselves within the collection, and to limit editorial intervention to a minimum. The latter course was the more attractive given the strength and the free-standing quality of the individual chapters. In this introduction, I therefore do no more than outline the major themes, and leave the reader to pick and choose between them. In the first chapter, however, an attempt at a theoretical synthesis of the different approaches is offered, in which it is argued that a historical dialectic underlies the dispersion and variety of theoretical perspectives on offer within modern legal theory.

The collection starts with Alan Norrie's analysis of the emergence of the Enlightenment conception of the synthesised nature of the relationship between law, reason and morality, a synthesis that breaks down under the weight of the historical development of modern western society. The emergence of a positivist tradition within legal theory is the product of the breakdown of the modern classical tradition of natural law. The result is a fragmentation of theoretical strands that stand in opposition to each other, leading to a situation of conflict in which antinomies such as that between closure and critique thrive. In the process, rationalist theories face irrationalist ones, and positivistic accounts of law face sceptical and critical challenge. It is these conflicts emerging from the disruption of Enlightenment thought that underlie the different chapters in the present collection.

Deryck Beyleveld and Roger Brownsword defend the need for a 'strong' moral foundation for law based upon categorically binding moral judgments. They set out Alan Gewirth's argument for the existence of a rational Principle of Generic Consistency, and defend its more controversial elements against criticism. They identify their position with the Kantian aim of establishing a supreme *a priori* moral principle as necessarily binding on agents, and therefore locate themselves as resolute defenders of the rationalism of the Enlightenment. Robert Fine's starting point, on the other hand, is the other mainstay of German rationalist thought, Hegel. Fine examines Hegel's famous dictum that 'the rational is real and the real is rational', arguing that an understanding of the nature of Hegel's method can unlock many of the misunderstandings of his work among liberals and Marxists, and most recently the 'civil society' theorists. Fine argues that Hegel's *Philosophy of Right* should be read as offering not a prescription for what the state and law ought to be, but an analysis of what they are. His rationalism leads not to a normativism that must inevitably accentuate one side of his account against another ('civil society' versus 'statism'), but to a recognition of the 'contradiction, antagonism [and] antinomy' within modern state law.

Fine's account of Hegel can be compared with those offered by Norrie and by Tim Murphy, who examines the German Idealist tradition in order to locate the position of Max Weber as an archetypally 'modern' writer on the nature of law. Weber saw nineteenth-century projects of legal codification as part of a process of positivisation of natural law in which it lost its purity and innocence. Reason as legal reason became the site of a new form of closure and not, as it had been, a force for emancipation. This occasioned a crisis of reason and an emphasis upon irrational elements such as charisma and 'life-force'. Hence, Weber takes us on a path which leads through Freud and Heidegger to many of the problems of postmodernism which are 'compacted in Weber's notion of spirit' and its positioning in relation to rationality. Anne Barron's target is the critique of one central form of modernist rationalism: the 'rational autonomous subject as the foundation of political legitimacy' in the work of John Rawls. Through a detailed analysis and development of the work of Althusser, Freud and Lacan, she constructs an account of subjectivity which she uses as the basis for a critique of the Rawlsian conception of citizenship. She argues that the latter operates 'as a mechanism, not of inclusion, but of closure', but that it is constantly disrupted by the forces of 'the Other', forces which remain 'beyond accommodation' and haunt any attempt to close off the categories of the political realm.

While Barron draws upon post-Freudian psychoanalysis to provide a critique of the rational legal subject/citizen, Nick Land focuses upon Bataille's 'Gothic aesthetic' of Gilles de Rais, the late feudal mass-murderer, to undermine what he describes as two-and-a-half millennia of 'rationalistic desolidarisation' that begin with Socrates and end with a society dominated by the logic and morality of commodity exchange. Against this 'rational' social order, in which domination loses all dignity and the state becomes universally derided 'as the mere caretaker for retarded sectors of behavioural management', Socrates stands out as the philosopher who challenged the proclaimed wisdom of state law in the beginning, while de Rais on trial, an 'experimental Socrates' existing beyond good and evil, indicts the modern law's inability to see him as anything other than a human pathology. Peter Goodrich's target is similar to Land's. For Goodrich, the aim is to disclose the ethical failure at the heart of law as a closed system of reason, a failure to recognise 'the loss of meaning and the repression of sensibility or judgment' that such closure (the 'death of law') entails. Drawing widely upon the sources for a postmodern critique of law, from Freud and Heidegger to Lacan and Derrida, Goodrich argues for a rediscovery of fate and destiny as the basis for an ethics of law and judgment. Fate stands in opposition to reason, providing the basis for an ethics of equity applied to 'the infinite variety of changes of circumstances, of persons, places, times and their connections'.

The debate thus far has circled around the nature of reason, and the relationship of law to reason. Parallel issues arise in debates about the ability of reason to regulate legal decision-making. Neil MacCormick argues that a legal system can be understood in principle as a system of sufficiently precise rules that operate as 'instantiations of coherently grasped principles of conduct and of social organisation'. This leads to the possibility of legal science as the production of clear and systematic statements of legal doctrine. MacCormick defends a positivist commitment to the rule of law as an ethical project against those who would deny the possibility of the 'rational reconstruction' of legal doctrine. One such person would be Stanley Fish, for whom it is impossible to establish the kind of rules that MacCormick regards as necessary for the positivist task. The closure of law proclaimed by legal practitioners is impossible because the law is always 'infected by interpretation', and interpretation entails the effort of a morality or 'some group's challengeable moral vision' to inscribe its message on the law's formal surface. The law 'wishes to have a formal existence' precisely to avoid the problem of interpretations, but Fish argues that it never can. Accordingly, the positivist project cannot work in its own terms, yet Fish argues that law is able to sustain the illusion that this is how it works. It is capable of a 'creative rhetoricity' that brings about at the level of practice what is unattainable at the level of theory.

Fish's chapter can be compared with that by Roger Cotterrell, who shows the multifarious interests that are at stake in proclaiming the possibility of legal closure, and the ways in which it permits 'various forms of legal or political practice ... to enhance their own legitimacy'. But Cotterrell insists that while conceptions of legal closure may 'work' within the particular contexts in which they are developed, law is not adequately understood as a closed system. It requires recognition rather of the social conditions that make such closure appear possible for certain practical purposes. In a wide-ranging discussion, Cotterrell asserts the value of a 'self-critical, reflexive sociological perspective' which can 'transcend partial perspectives on legal experience' offered by closure theorists such as Dworkin. Cotterrell's position on the partial nature of the legal perspective can be compared with that of Norrie on the nature of law as a form of praxiology.

All the chapters in this collection are linked to questions of legal closure or critique, either about the nature of law itself or about the question of its ethical basis. Nicola Lacey draws upon many of the themes to be found in the earlier chapters from the standpoint of feminism. As regards the character of law, Lacey rejects any idea of law as an autonomous structure or a neutral force, yet she recognises that 'contingent and constructed structures' like law are nonetheless powerful and have to be reckoned and engaged with. As regards the question of philosophical closure, Lacey remains torn between a postmodern relativism that both liberates and threatens to cut the political ground from under a feminist politics. Her thoughtful discussion of the dilemmas and ambivalence involved in engaging with law at both practical and theoretical levels serves to underline the centrality of issues of closure and critique to a modern awareness of the problem(s) of law.

1

Closure and Critique:
Antinomy in Modern Legal Theory[1]

ALAN NORRIE

> Our external symbols must always express the life within us with
> absolute precision; how could they do otherwise, since that life has
> generated them? Therefore we must not blame our poor symbols if
> they take forms that seem trivial to us, or absurd, for ... the nature of
> our life alone has determined their forms.
> A critique of these symbols is a critique of our lives.
>
> Carter (1977, p. 6)

> [P]hilosophical thinking, if pursued far enough, turns into historical
> thinking, and the understanding of abstract thought ultimately re-
> solves itself back into an awareness of the content of that thought,
> which is to say, of the basic historical situation in which it took place.
>
> Jameson (1971, p. 345)

INTRODUCTION

There can rarely have been so much diversity in legal theory as there is at
the present time. The 1980s saw a blossoming of novel approaches to the
subject in a way that was quite unanticipated, and which has added much
to what has not always been a rich tapestry. But this development brings
with it a number of questions. What accounts for it? What is its nature?
What are its strengths and weaknesses? What overall assessment does it
merit with regard to its ability to explain, illuminate or contextualise the
nature of law?

In providing primarily a framework in which to locate these questions,
I shall treat this phenomenon of theoretical regeneration as both an
intellectual and a social issue, claiming that these two aspects are inseparably intertwined to provide the theoretical developments of the last ten
years. On the one hand, the movements of legal theory respond to the
inner logic of earlier positions within the field. Theory orients itself, or
rather is oriented, within an already established set of intellectual practices and paradigms, which it works to repeat or change. Theory responds
to what already exists, revealing, with the benefit of hindsight, an inherent

logic, whether of continuity or discontinuity. In one sense, the production of theory, as described, is already a social process, for it occurs within a tradition provided by a community of intellectuals (Bhaskar, 1979, ch. 1; Outhwaite, 1978, chs 1, 2; Bourdieu, 1988). But there is also a broader sense in which the intellectual is social, for the production of ideas occurs within given socioeconomic conditions, at two different but connected levels.

At the most fundamental level, the basic ideas of a tradition are historical products emerging out of a particular social period or epoch. The idea of individual freedom as the apogee of human history in eighteenth-century Europe was only possible in a world in which, as Hegel (1952; 1956, pp. 438–57) put it, the principle of human subjectivity had been realised, and this could only occur because of the breakdown of feudalism and the emergence of bourgeois civil society. Different societies – the Muslim world; the world of the state socialist societies – generate different basic ideas. At a more specific level, the ideas of a period are social and historical in that the basic intellectual structures, which are handed down from the past and engaged with in the present, are mediated and redirected according to the preoccupations of the here and now. To be a legal theorist today in the Muslim world or in eastern Europe is to engage with the available theories in a way that is quite different from even the relatively recent past.

Thus, history and society are both fundamental and conjunctural elements in the composition of legal theory, but the work of legal theory remains an intellectual practice engaged in and given life by past and present generations of theorists. History provides the structure and the colour of theory, but it is the intellectual who works on the material and produces the accomplished product. There is, then, both an internal and an external element to the historical location, comprehension and critique of current developments; and, in what follows, I approach them both as products in themselves, and as products in history.

The developments of the 1980s can be understood in a way that can genuinely be termed dialectical. On the one hand, the flourishing of theory can only be seen as a strength; on the other hand, it is the product of fundamental intellectual weakness. This theoretical efflorescence has all the appearances of vigour and vibrancy, yet it is the product of profound and long-standing intellectual crisis. The developments on view are interesting and exciting (they are our world!) yet flawed and depressing. They derive from a tradition that has grappled over and over again with what are basically the same problems, that provides us with insight and understanding, but which also obscures and occludes.

I make a division for historical and analytical purposes between two periods of intellectual development. The first, classical, period of the eighteenth and early nineteenth centuries established two sets of theories and schools which were in conflict with each other, and in which nothing was resolved other than the incommensurability of the two approaches. The second, modern, period is that of the postwar political and intellectual reconstruction which reassembled the same intellectual armies on the battlefield, in somewhat different garb, but brandishing similar weapons. In both periods, we witness processes of decline and destruction as established positions unravel before us. The difference is that the process of unravelling in the classical period is reversed in the modern period. In the former, it is classical natural law which unravels in the face of legal positivism; in the latter, it is positivism that comes under fire from natural law – *in its modern distilled and fragmented forms*. In this context, the so-called postmodern critique of law represents, in jurisprudential terms, one final throw of the natural law dice. Although it would view Enlightenment and modernity in the context of a longer philosophical tradition, and would see itself in its relation to modernity in a quite different way, its concepts are those of Enlightenment ethical jurisprudence, turned against, but remaining within, that tradition.

THE BREAKDOWN OF THE ENLIGHTENMENT TRADITION

The modern classical period of jurisprudence was the child of the Enlightenment, and died with it. It established a method for understanding law that was profoundly alien and unacceptable in the nineteenth century. Traditional accounts present this as the redefinition of the province of jurisprudence (Austin, 1861), as theorists began to separate out sets of different questions: of fact and value, of law and morality, of what the law is and ought to be, of natural and positive law. But the demise of classical natural law was essentially much more than a matter of definitional or logical refinement. It was a profound intellectual and political shift, from which there emerged the redefinition of the province of jurisprudence (cf. Halevy, 1972; Marcuse, 1941).

First, the rise of legal positivism accompanied the political securing of the well-ordered bourgeois state. Bentham sensed the need to control and contain the restless social impulses generated by the call for intellectual and political freedom (Steintrager, 1977; Rosenblum, 1978). Once the conditions for industrialisation had been achieved, it was more important to consolidate 'what is' than to dream dangerously about what might be in an ideal world of metaphysical abstractions. What 'ought to be' should be no more than a deduction based upon the actuality of what had been achieved. What was there was what there was, its positivity only requiring amelioration, not fundamental change (Cotterrell, 1989, ch. 3). Accordingly, the 'nonsense on stilts' of natural rights theory was better shut off in favour of sober evaluation of the concrete (cf. Waldron, 1987). The *source* of the evaluation had changed too. No longer was the moral standpoint that of the free individual; now it was the standpoint of the state itself through the aggregative logic of 'the greatest happiness of the greatest number'. The shift from individual egoism to general utilitarianism was a major historical development (Halevy, 1972), closely connected with the positive theory of law. It was only an organised state that could posit a coherent, rational legal system.

Second, the same development that strengthened the hand of utilitarianism also weakened that of classical natural law. The latter's raison d'être was the establishment of a synthesis of the moral and the practical, the universal and the particular, the rational and the real, the ideal and the positive. Law's importance is only seen in the light of a general metaphysical stance on the nature of the social and political order. Law is seen in terms of an ethical other, is always understood *in the first place* in terms of its *heteronomy*. This is the moving intellectual force of modern classical natural law, from Hobbes to Locke, to Kant, to Hegel: to establish an adequate methodology for the comprehension and rationalisation of law in terms that extend beyond its phenomenal appearance and self-understanding.

In the work of the British natural lawyers, moral-juridical and positive-legal concepts are promiscuously intermingled, so that one is never clear whether the argument is a direct political intervention or an abstract philosophical reflection (Strauss, 1953; Habermas, 1974, ch. 1; Neumann, 1986, chs 7, 8). The metaphysic of the social contract to establish the sovereign is also the practical basis for the powers and duties of the constitutional monarch in Locke's programme for the 'nightwatchmanstate' (Locke, 1960); in Hobbes, the philosophical constitution of sovereignty on the basis of metaphysical misanthropy is the immediate justification for contemporary political absolutism (Habermas, 1974). There is, in short, no clear method for affirming legal positivity *within* a universal moral theory of society and polity, no adequate synthesis of the two. The natural and the positive appear to be confused, so that when the master sceptic Hume (1898) pointed out the flaws in the contract philosophy, and the reducibility of political philosophy – that which concerns the 'artificial virtues' – to a consideration of the practical and the useful (Hume, 1888), he brought philosophy down to the same level as legal positivity, and the way was opened for the triumph of the utilitarian-positivist axis in British intellectual life under Bentham and Austin.

The German route was more profound. If the philosophical materialism of the contract was an inadequate method for legitimating positivity, the answer lay in the firmer establishment of metaphysics, not their discarding. For Kant (1965), law was posited as the bridge between the speculative and the practical. Law was viewed dualistically as both a rational truth embodying *a priori* concepts of right *and* as a necessary element of regulation in a world governed by empirical necessity. Law embodied rational will (*der Wille*) *and* controlled private, egoistic will (*die Willkür*). But this did not go far enough, for, as elsewhere, Kant only succeeded in establishing an unbridgeable duality between the two sides of law. Law was positive and law was rational at the same time, but the philosophical method of abstraction employed by Kant could never achieve a true synthesis (Norrie, 1991a, ch. 3). What was needed, as Hegel (1952) saw it, was a means of reconciling the two sides through a method of rational elucidation of the universal within the particular, of thus synthesising what had been posited with the universality of spirit. Law was in this view both a mechanism of civil society, and an emanation of reason within ethical life. Law was one moment in the movement of the rational within the social (Marcuse, 1941; Norrie, 1991a, ch. 4).

Thus, for both Kant and Hegel, the separation of 'is' and 'ought' was a profound mistake revealing a lack of understanding of the workings of reason in and through the natural and the social. Law was never just 'law': it was always comprehended as part of a rational 'other', and the movement of classical natural law was towards a refinement and development of what the 'other' was, reaching its final zenith in Hegel's philosophical system. However, this grand theoretical edifice turned out to be no more than a rationalisation of the status quo, with the Prussian state as the terminal point of history (Hegel, 1952, pp. 179–88; Marcuse, 1941; McLellan, 1969). Recognising the inability of the forms of individual right and self-interest (property, contract, civil society) to generate institutions entailing a genuine ethical unity of the people, Hegel was forced to stipulate the rational necessity of ever more positive statal and parastatal agencies as the basis for ethical life. The culmination of his grand dialectical method was a set of extremely 'profane', historically specific institutions. Their very historical particularity proved to be both the cause of the *Philosophy of Right*'s fall into disrepute and an important opening for positivist methodology from within the heart of its main adversary. Hegel's dialectical method increasingly embraced actually existing (posited) political and legal institutions (Marx, 1975).

Hegel had rationalised the real, but the real turned out a sore disappointment, so that, when the Prussian state began to act in authoritarian ways in order to quell the growing social crises of civil society, Hegelianism, which had predicted the end of history in a rational, liberal social order, had no means of analysing what was happening, and therefore collapsed (McLellan, 1969, ch. 1; Engels, 1968). The result in German intellectual life was a void, which was filled by positivism in social philosophy (Marcuse, 1941, pp. 360–74), and the weak abstractions of the historical school in law (cf. Therborn, 1976, pp. 178–86). The particular history of the German polity, with its relative economic under-development (Cullen, 1979), did not permit a stable and pragmatic intellectual development as occurred in Britain, but its very metaphysical sophistication nonetheless made it clear that the possibility of a grand intellectual synthesis of the ideal and the actual was impossible on the conceptual terrain provided by modern social conditions. Thus, at the very moment in which positivism was given a boost by historical develop-ments, classical natural law was fundamentally undermined, and it is a moment from which it has yet to recover.

If, under the weight of sociohistorical development, natural law was threatened by the development of a new intellectual approach, positivism too was soon to be in the position of looking over its shoulder, in its case, at the rise of sociological approaches to the study of law. Positivism flourished under the sociopolitical patronage of the consolidated bour-geois state, which affirmed the possibility of social construction according to the 'universalistic' criterion of the 'greatest happiness of the greatest number'. Positivism was formed out of the heady optimism of the early days of industrialism, and underpinned by a conviction of the eternal and natural character of contemporary developments. It relied on the support of the well-ordered economy as the counterpart to the well-ordered state and legal system, so that its intellectual partner in the elucidation of the problem of social order was the theory of the classical political economists (see e.g. Bentham, 1975, p. 265). The subsequent developments of social life in the nineteenth century revealed that the abstractions of political economy could not be a reliable basis for continuing good order, and that a more concrete sociological investigation of social ills was required (Abrams, 1968; cf. Corrigan and Sayer, 1985, ch. 6). This conclusion led to questions about the nature of law that threatened the depoliticisation and formalism, the certitude that law could be understood as an autono-mous, self-grounding regulative system, achieved under positive theory (cf. below, ch. 10).

In Britain, positivism managed to remain fairly stable because of the strength of the socioeconomic developments of the period and the result-ant growth of a legal profession that theory could feed off, legitimate, and in turn be legitimated by (Cotterrell, 1983). In the rest of Europe, where these developments were less even and successful, the problem was more stark. Whether the underlying political project was conservative, liberal or radical, it was necessary to think more historically and sociologically not only about the nature of social order but also about the nature of law itself. Thus, France could give rise to a Durkheim (1964) with his investigations of the nature of social solidarity, with legal obedience seen as a dependent factor and indicator of social health, and with his analysis of the historical evolution of modern legal form (Durkheim, 1973). Germany produced both Marx, and his diagnosis of the class basis of law (Marx and Engels, 1968) and the economic basis of legal form in generalised commodity exchange (Marx, 1973), and Weber with his historical-ideal typifications of different types of law (Weber, 1978). While modern law was attributed in neo-Kantian style a status independent of capitalist economic developments, Weber insisted upon a historical and sociological mode of investigation which both emphasised the contingency of the legal developments and threatened – in his discussion of the 'England problem' (Hunt, 1978) and his study of Islam (Turner, 1974) – to undermine his formalism.

Thus, legal positivism was itself threatened by another approach that emerged out of the social-historical developments of the nineteenth century. Law should be comprehended not in its positivity or as a metaphysical correlate, but as a social phenomenon, comprehended within sociological theory. A sociological approach shares with positivism an insistence on shearing away the metaphysical baggage of natural law, but, having done so, has this much in common with the natural lawyers: a shared belief in the impossibility of seeing law as an autonomous, self-standing institutional force. Law in this view, as with natural law, was regarded as essentially heteronomous, but now it was to be comprehended in sociological terms, in its intrinsic relationship with other social and historical forms and relations. Law's heteronomy resides in its quality as a social relation: to attempt to portray it in terms of a projected autonomy, while acceptable as a means of cutting out metaphysical speculation, may be deeply misleading as a means of understanding it.

MODERN TRENDS IN THE WAKE OF THE CLASSICAL BREAKDOWN

I have identified a historical period of development and decline which lies at the root of the modern developments in legal theory. Having established three actors on an intellectual stage, I now wish to indicate the basic scripts that they will read and the strengths and weaknesses in the characters that they will play. It will be noted that this is a genuine play, for, as we go along, we will see that the actors' lines are always part of a dialogue with each other. The play's dynamic is provided by interplay between the three characters because they exist in relational tension with each other, and in a sense need each other in order to fill out their own roles. The essence of legal theory is a grouping of intellectual ideas in a set of one-sided ways. It will also be noted that, through the process of dialogue, the different actors come to assume some of the characteristics of their opponents, for, part of the time, their competition is of a somewhat 'friendly' nature. Broadly, three connected intellectual moves can be discerned in this play.

Positivism and the Attack on Legal Closure

For the positivists, history, in the well-ordered polity, is on their side. The establishment and expansion of a legal profession in Britain provided the positivists with a set of professional practices and series of intellectual problems that were legal in a narrow sense, and on which they could feed and in their own way thrive (Cotterrell, 1983). The existence of law as a social practice in itself encouraged the development of a legal theory that would define law intellectually as an autonomous phenomenon. But, at a deeper level, the search for the autonomous essence of law proved chimerical. In the standard positivist texts, the theorist always buys certainty at the cost of limitation. Austin's sovereign is a juridical master for the purpose of legal theory, but only at the cost of hiving off all the interesting questions about power and social relations to other disciplines (cf. Fitzpatrick, 1991, on the work of Hart). The province of jurisprudence is circumscribed from the beginning, leaving for the positivist a set of technical materials that can do no more than replicate and refine an existing social practice, but which can never get beyond it. Furthermore, as American legal theorists have pointed out from the time of realism onwards, even the technical certainties of the legal positivists are hardly so certain. Law is about what judges do, not what they say they do (Llewellyn, 1951; Frank, 1963); it is about conflict and social interests, about rationalisation in the pejorative sense of covering one's political goals in a 'show' of formal impartial reasoning (Kelman, 1987). Positivist legal theory reflects the self-understanding of legal practice, and cannot move beyond it. For this reason, it can be designated as what Bhaskar (1979) calls a 'praxiology', a term to which I return below.

This battle between positivism and a sociologically-inspired realism is fought out all the time, with the argument swinging one way then the other. At the time of writing, both sides have some strong weapons in their armoury, for there has been a revival in some forms of positivism as its theorists come to terms with the onslaught of first the sociological movement in law, and then the Critical Legal Studies movement in the USA and Britain. In this context, MacCormick's work (1976; 1983; and see ch. 8) has been exemplary because of its willingness to take on, and to take on board, the criticisms of positivism's opponents, while Dworkin has sought a more forthright and dogmatic closure of the debate with critical approaches to law (see ch. 10).

This dialogue about law's heteronomy is not just between the positivists and their sociological and realist critics. It is also one that one branch of the descendants of natural law have been keen to join. To understand the nature of this further intervention, however, it is necessary first to understand the process of fragmentation that occurred after the collapse of the classical doctrine. The Hegelian system had combined deep philosophical abstraction with a close focus on the positivities of law, politics and economics. When the synthesis of these elements achieved no more than a glorification of the present, the intellectual world was sundered into a strict positivism on the one hand and a variety of one-sided theoretical abstractions on the other. Within the latter realm, theory was more or less unbounded by the 'discipline of positivity', that is, the need to explain and analyse 'what is'. Freed from this obligation, it was able to engage in radical philosophical speculations about the nature of law (cf. Land's discussion of the work of Bataille in ch. 6). In this process, law as an object of study became of secondary importance, to be pulled along on the coat tails of a master abstraction. The neoclassical world of these different writers was a world where anything went, and where fragmentation was the order of the day.[2] In this situation, intellectual stability was impossible, indeed undesirable, and the latest abstraction would reflect the political or ideological colour of its period and place. It is within this context that the current attempts by postmodern legal theory, from a diverse and varied set of perspectives, to take over the field of legal theory can be located. Postmodernism is a one-sided response to the breakdown of the classical syntheses of law and rationalism, turning the post-Enlightenment irrationalism of the declining and fragmented natural law school against the proclaimed achievement of legal positivism: a theory of law as a more or less closed and autonomous system of rules, norms or regulation.

Thus, positivism is always under attack from both sides because of its claim about the autonomy of law. These attacks are more or less well grounded, sometimes in 'realism', sometimes in sociological critique, sometimes in postmodern theory. From all sides, the claim is that law should be understood in terms of an 'other', in terms of its social or philosophical reliance upon and instantiation of practices and ideas beyond itself: in terms of its heteronomy. Positivism must always walk the line that it has chosen for itself (and that a particular historical period has generated for it) between different approaches to legal phenomena which, in their different ways, seek to ground and explain legal phenomena in relation to an 'other', whether the latter is comprehended in terms that are predominantly ethical or social.

Natural Law Distillations and Filtrations

For the natural lawyer, a variety of responses has emerged to the break-down of the classical mode. First, there is the neo-Kantian response, which replaces the transcendental basis of the categorical imperative with a scaled-down, prosaic *sollen* (cf. Rose, 1984; Lukacs, 1971, pp. 108–9). This is then attached directly to the categories of law, producing an 'ethicalised' legal positivism, as in the work of Kelsen and, in quite different ways, in that of Weber (cf. Schluchter, 1981; and see ch. 4), Fuller (1969; cf. Summers, 1984) and even, through Weber, the Marxist Lukacs (1971, pp. 83–110). The problem with this approach is that, in its purest, Kelsenian form, it gets the worst of both worlds. On the one hand, the diminution of the 'ought' required by the theory's non-transcendental quality provides an unconvincing account of law as a series of logically linked but empirically unspecified oughts, which suffer for their 'purity' in a parallel way to the original Kantian metaphysic: that is, they remain barren. The unbridgeable gap between Kant's moral law (the noumenal) and the world of nature (the phaenomenal) (MacIntyre, 1967, pp. 197–8; Wolff, 1973, ch. 2) is replicated in the gulf in Kelsen's work between the form of law and its content (cf. Pashukanis, 1978, p. 52). On the other hand, where Kelsen does say something about law, it appears as little more than a mystified doppelganger for its positivist counterpart – for example, in the employment of the *Grundnorm* in place of the sovereign's command. More broadly, the problem with neo-Kantianism, even in its sociological form, is that it fails to get 'behind', or to penetrate into the nature of law. It takes law on its own terms, as in Weber's embrace of the legal paradigm as a rational practical form (Albrow, 1975), or in Teubner's affirmation of the self-closing character of the juridical sphere in an autopoietic system (Teubner, 1987; and cf. ch. 10). Neo-Kantianism is no more than a scaled-down version of Kantianism itself in which the antinomies of the noumenal and the phaenomenal are replicated in a narrower ambit.

A second response, one that has been partially described already, is to break away from the rationalism of the classical and neo-Kantian discourses, and to replace them with one of the many varieties of irrationalism which stem from the radical conclusions drawn by Nietzsche and others about the value of classicism. From this viewpoint, the pretensions of law are swept away as its discourse is hitched to a 'will to power' (Foucault, 1977, 1980), or the vagaries of a historical text (Foucault, 1972), or its suppression or denial of 'the Other', however that might be conceived (Derrida, 1990; and see, variously, chs 5, 6, 7 and 11). One danger with this response to the demise of classicism is that the object of study (law) remains secondary to the motivating theoretical impulse, and underdeveloped in its specificity. This may be claimed to be no more than a function of the newness of the disciplines that have only recently sprung up, and which require time to attain a synthesis, but there is also an inherent methodological tendency for such approaches not to engage thoroughly with law, for two reasons. One is that the perspectives that are developed in this mode are necessarily fragmentary, and therefore lack the concepts necessary to engage in a full critique of law. Where they do make the effort of engagement with law, they are likely indeed to replicate its self-image, like the neo-Kantian. Thus, in Goodrich's work (Goodrich, 1986), it is not clear whether bringing a hermeneutic critique to bear on legal discourse does more than affirm the recognised practice of lawyers (Norrie, 1989), while a positivist appropriation of hermeneutics is possible (MacCormick, 1983). Similarly, the representation of law as a system of technical and bureaucratic rules (see chs 6 and 7), albeit one that is closed off against authenticity or wholeness, is not that far from the positivist's own stance. The second is that in these approaches, the 'critical' is out of balance with the 'analytical', so that the theorist is motivated by the kind of thoroughgoing negativity that makes 'trashing' a satisfactory and sufficient response to law (cf. Kelman, 1984). Instead of seeking the intrinsic specificity and modalities of the legal enterprise (which is not thereby to accord them the positivist's claimed autonomy), the tendency may be to dismiss these elements as epiphenomenal, and to reduce the critical enterprise to one of full-blown negation. To make these criticisms is not, however, to deny the value of postmodern critical tools such as deconstruction to our understanding of law, or the possibility of using them to investigate the nature of law as a social phenomenon (cf. Spivak, 1988; Guha and Spivak, 1988); my concern is that, pursued to their full extent, such approaches may miss as many legal targets as they hit.

Is so ambivalent a reaction to postmodernism possible? Only a brief answer to that question can be made here. If we take Derrida's work as exemplary, he would deny the charge of nihilism, yet his account of deconstruction is hitched to the affirmation of a justice so 'mystical' that it beggars description. Justice 'would be the experience that we are not able to experience ... an experience of the impossible' (Derrida, 1990, p. 947). Justice is at best a negative moment defined against all that positively is, an outside, a beyond, that cannot be expressed, only felt as an 'impulse', an 'unsatisfied appeal' (ibid., p. 957). Yet this irrationality, this 'madness' (ibid., p. 965), this 'anxiety-ridden moment of suspense' (ibid., p. 955), this upturning of the moral rationalism of the Enlightenment,[3] is allied to the prior, more valuable, deconstructive tasks of seeking out the contradictions within discourse and tracing the 'historical and interpretative memory' of the concepts. One must 'do justice' to the historical and political concept of justice, interrogating its 'origin, grounds and limits', attending to 'the theoretical or normative apparatus surrounding' it (ibid., p. 955). This genealogical investigation into justice can then go two ways. Either it can go back into the moral-philosophical tradition that it is deconstructing, in the process seeking some precarious foothold on the classical terrain it has already deconstructed; or it can probe more deeply the historical and social relations within which the concept has flourished. Either it can go back to natural law, or it can go forward to a sociological understanding of the nature of the concepts at play. Derrida's deconstructionism does the former, but his deconstructive project strikes important chords with anyone who, as I will indicate below, wishes to follow the latter course.[4]

A third response is to attempt some kind of return to the classical tradition, and this is in many ways still the most popular approach. From Hart's 'minimum content of natural law' (Hart, 1961), to Dworkin's view of the animating values of the western polity (Dworkin, 1977; cf. MacCormick, 1978), to MacCormick's 'ethical positivism' (MacCormick, 1989), to Habermas's discourse ethics (Habermas, 1984, 1989; see also Alexy, 1989), to Rawls's original position and contractarianism (Rawls, 1972; cf. Rawls, 1985), to Nozick's Lockean natural rights theory (Nozick, 1975), to Rose's reading of Hegel (Rose, 1981), to Beyleveld and Brownsword's Gewirthian, and Kantian, rationalism (Beyleveld and Brownsword, 1986, and see ch. 2), a host of different 'back to the Enlightenment' approaches have been adopted. The difficulty for all these approaches, which exhibit a wide variety,[5] is to know whether they have been able to achieve what their classical predecessors could not, i.e. the resolution of the difficulties of combining the ethical and the positive. It has been said that 'positivists are not so positivist as they were', but the question is whether any of these approaches achieves a synthesis between their positivism and classicism. Positivism has been under attack for many years from many directions, and this return to natural law premises is part of a response. But in reversing the historical process that saw positivism triumph on the back of a natural law in decline, it is doubtful just how much mileage there is in these late and neo-classical syntheses.

Locating Legal Specificity Sociologically

It will already be clear that in separating off three approaches to the study of law, it is only possible to construct models for analytical purposes since our three main characters are so frequently the product of intellectual crossover. Thus, in considering a sociological approach, it must be noted that one of the main theoretical traditions, the Weberian, has already come under scrutiny for its neo-Kantianism. However, for those who believe that the study of law is a matter of building theoretical concepts out of the observation of a social phenomenon, in its relatedness to other such phenomena, a sociological approach does offer the possibility of breaking out from the one-sidedness that leads either to the over-reduction of law within analyses stressing heteronomy, or to its secular deification through the stress on autonomy. In recent times, there have been attempts to view law in this synthesised way through a legal form analysis that combines an insistence on the historicity of all social forms with a regard for their particularity in different historical periods. In this way, form and content are merged on the basis that law is a specific social form emerging within certain sets of social relations, and mediating them. To name two such attempts, there has been the earlier work of Unger (1976) in the USA, and the rediscovery and use of the legal form analysis of Pashukanis in western Europe (Pashukanis, 1978; cf. Neumann, 1986; Neumann and Kircheimer, 1987).

These approaches have been important for their ability to re-establish broad historical-conceptual frameworks for the study of law both in its juridical specificity and as a social phenomenon; however, both remain somewhat isolated within the intellectual traditions of which they are a part, and exhibit certain weaknesses. This may be for a variety of reasons that are extrinsic to the theories themselves, but there are serious internal problems with them that should be explored.

The major problem of the Ungerian analysis is that it rests on an idealised conception of the economic and political processes underlying the western legal polity. Resting on a theoretical basis of sociological pluralism and evolutionism, the dynamics of liberal society are founded upon abstractions that are themselves liberal in their conception (group pluralism, the impartial state), with the result that the predicted future of 'post-liberal society' (based on welfarism and corporatism) can only recapitulate the developments on the surface of western social life, which the last fifteen years have shown to be highly contingent, reversible, and by no means necessary. Unger's account is shown by the current historical period of conservativism and authoritarianism to be unable to grasp the real underlying trends within which the development of legal forms must be located, and within which they perform their sociopolitical roles. Nonetheless, his work is an important attempt, utilising an impressively broad comparative and historical analysis, to comprehend different legal forms in particular historical periods (cf. the important but now dated essay by Kamenka and Tay, 1975).

The problem with the latter approach is that legal form analysis in the Marxian tradition has been hamstrung by certain assumptions, the most important of which is the indefensible claim that law and capitalism are coextensive on the basis of the commodity form. This view has been promulgated by those who are particularly critical of Pashukanis's work (Collins, 1981, pp. 108–11; Warrington, 1981). I do not think that so crude a view can be attributed to him (Norrie, 1982), but the charge appears largely to have stuck, discouraging further work. It is necessary to discard this view through a deeper awareness of the nature of the theoretical premises which underlie form analysis (Sayer, 1987). A more flexible approach to legal forms is required which can locate different kinds of law in different kinds of societies, starting from a deeper analysis of the social relations which constitute particular social formations (see e.g. Fitzpatrick, 1982; Norrie, 1990b, 1993a).

There remains much strength and potential in such an approach, both in terms of its comparative and historical dimensions, and in terms of its ability to understand the nature of modern western law. The focus of a sociological approach should be the specificity of law, but to explain it as a particular historical form of discursive practice. The aim should be to steer a path between the autonomisation of law sought by positivist and neo-Kantian approaches on the one hand, and reductivist accounts, such as those suggested by postmodern analysis on the other. Law is to be understood neither as the fruit of a regulative system which can achieve, by its own efforts, a measure of closure and autonomy (cf. Teubner, 1987), nor as the pale reflection or negation of forces beyond it that it can never embrace. Law must be seen in its specificity as a historical practice which operates on the basis of particular forms and mechanisms which are real, effective and differentiated, and which are related but irreducible to broader social relations. A useful way to capture this duality of law is through Bhaskar's already mentioned concept of 'praxiology', by which he refers to any theoretical account of some form of action that is tied to, and limited by, a set of possible practices and outcomes. The range of concepts available within a praxiology is governed by the set of social practices that they represent, inform and legitimate. The extent to which the social practice represents a partial or particular mode of intervention in social affairs is the extent to which the knowledge forms that it generates are also limited. A praxiology 'may best be regarded as a normative theory of efficient action, generating a set of techniques for achieving given ends, rather than as an explanatory theory capable of casting light on actual empirical episodes' (Bhaskar, 1979, p. 37). A primary example of a praxiology would be neoclassical economic theory, but also other theoretical accounts such as that provided by different kinds of 'games', and rational and public-choice, theories in the social sciences, by utilitarianism, and by political liberalism. All such accounts seek to explain and guide action individualistically while remaining rooted in particular, historically given, social relations which they seek to bracket off or deny. Orthodox, positivistic theories of law which attempt both to explain the nature of law and to provide normative guidance for legal practice share many characteristics with these praxiologies. The essence of a praxiology is that it takes the part represented by the practice to be the whole, and in so doing both obscures the whole and misrepresents the practice. By ignoring the relationship between the practice and its broader social context, the need for a radical reinterpretation of the nature of the practice in the light of its social context is hidden. Praxiologies both describe real social practices and obscure and mystify their deeper foundations, where recognition of those foundations would force a reappraisal of the practices themselves.

I will illustrate this position with a brief discussion of the descriptive and normative concept of the legal subject as a responsible agent which lies at the heart of the 'general principles' of the criminal law (for a general critique, see Norrie, 1993b). Such a concept is instantiated through the doctrines of *mens rea*, *actus reus* and the general defences which go to make up the 'General Part' of the law. The concept of a 'responsible legal subject' is constructed through ideas of intention, recklessness, voluntariness and rationality which refer to real characteristics of human agency as it has evolved in modern western societies (Harré, 1983). Modern western agents are constructed as, and understand themselves as, agents in terms that correspond to those of the law. Nonetheless, the law's conception of these terms remains partial and mystificatory because it seeks to abstract the actor from the context of social conflict and deprivation which generates crime, and to exclude that context from the judicial gaze. Modern agency is intentional, but intention is always linked to motives which are socially constituted and normatively determinative for agents. In order to exclude this broader social context of agency, legal responsibility abstracts the issue of 'intention' from its twin concept of 'motive'. Were these to be seen as genetically unified in the creation of agency, the responsibility of the individual would dissolve into, or at least require a very different articulation with (Norrie, 1990a, discussing Lacey, 1988), the society's own responsibility for criminal actions. Similarly, legal praxiology abstracts the 'factual' question of awareness of risk in the law of recklessness from the sociopolitical and normative question of the justifiability of risk in order to locate criminal responsibility individualistically in the law of recklessness (Norrie, 1992); while in the law of causation, it attributes causal responsibility individualistically by sociopolitical fiat in order to separate off the consequences of individual agency from the broad flux and structure of social causation (Norrie, 1991a).

Thus, the praxiological explanation of juridical subjectivity takes the modern social fact of individually constituted mentality as the basis for a descriptive and normative account of criminal responsibility, but takes it in an entirely one-sided way: individually instantiated social agency is translated into individual*istically* constituted, desocialised responsibility. Recognition of the social dimension of individual agency transforms our knowledge and understanding of the implications of such agency. Legal knowledge, tied to the criminal law practice of punishing individuals, is founded upon the denial of a recognition which would radically challenge its legitimacy. It is this tying of knowledge to a particular, partial, mystificatory view of agency that justifies the designation of legal knowledge as praxiological.

One starting point for the sociology of law would thus be the investigation of the various ways in which legal praxiologies operate to govern

social conduct and mediate social relations, informing practices that are
in the same moment real and unreal, i.e. which represent practical but
distorted or non-necessary interventions within the social world. Such an
approach can recognise the specificity and particularity of legal forms at
the same time as it relates them to, and explains them by, the broader
social processes of which they are a part. Law must be understood
methodologically, at the same time, in itself and in its otherness, and this
is only possible by regarding it as a specific, historical, sociopolitical
practice.

CONCLUSION

My brief conclusions, or perhaps alternatives to a conclusion, on the basis
of this largely inadequate account of the development of legal theory, are
presented in the light of the two contexts within which I have sought to
understand it.

First, the problems of legal theory are to be located in a historical-
intellectual development that established a framework for future positions
which contained important defects. Legal theory came out of a period of
intellectual crisis, in which theoretical unities were sundered, leaving a
mixture of approaches which, for all that they are in dispute, have one
thing in common: a one-sided approach to the phenomenon of law.
Those theories that emphasise law's heteronomy fail to account for its
specificity, and those theories that emphasise its autonomy fail to account
for its relatedness. Thus, no one theory is adequate, but to combine
different theories will not produce a synthesis, only eclecticism. In approaching theory today, it is paradoxical that the exciting diversity of the
modern scene is a product of this process of fragmentation and decline
occurring in the nineteenth century, so that the variation of the present
comes out of and is caught up in the problems of the past. The tendency
is usually to one-sided understandings of the nature of law.

This is the first context within which I seek to understand modern
developments in legal theory. At the same time, I would stress as a more
specific context the nature of the current conjuncture within which
particular theories are constituted. We live at the end of the period of
post-Second World War reconstruction, and it is this which provides the
present with its more specific colouration. What we have witnessed in this
period is the construction, and then crisis, of a theoretically hegemonic
project. That project was largely positivist, but with a minimum of ideas
strained from the natural law tradition, and buttressed by the normative
argumentative approach of modern Anglo-American political philosophy. The iconic works in this tradition, which reached its head in the mid-
to late 1960s, were those of Hart (1961) and Rawls (1972). But no sooner
had this modern liberal project been consolidated than events in the form

of the social strife of the late 1960s and early 1970s overtook it. The response to this was a critical approach which began in legal sociology and the sociology of deviance, and reverberated in different narrower forms through Critical Legal Studies and postmodernist approaches to law. It is this countertradition that has opened up the theoretical debate in the present period, albeit within the broader historical confines which we have identified. The interest in legal theory today stems not just from the vibrancy of the countertradition but also from the responses to it that have been elicited from those whose ideas have developed out of legal positivism. There has on occasion been a willingness to defend and renew the older tradition in much more intellectually interesting ways, so that, on all sides, the level of theoretical engagement has been raised.

In this dual context, it is notable that the current period replicates the classical period – in reverse. Whereas then, positivism emerged from the downfall of natural law, today the postmodern residues of natural law have begun to take their revenge. Meanwhile, lurking somewhere in the wings, temporarily eclipsed by the bright lights of postmodernism, and not, perhaps, clear as to its future agenda, sociological approaches rooted in classical sociology await their return to centre stage. The result of all this theoretical endeavour may or may not be more satisfactory answers, but certainly it has produced a more stimulating set of questions in an area of the social sciences that has for too long been marked by a certain 'leather-tongued' dryness. I have sought to uncover the foundational and conjunctural historical elements behind this repetition in reverse of classical jurisprudence, and to suggest, in a necessarily limited manner, a way forward that can move beyond the different reductionisms perpetrated by attempts to autonomise (positivism, neo-Kantianism) or heteronomise (natural law, postmodernism) law. What is required is a historical and sociological approach which can grasp the duality of law as a specific form of historically constituted sociality.

NOTES

1. Earlier versions of this chapter appear, less developed, in de Lange and Raes (1991) and the Indian Socio-Legal Journal (1992).
2. For a helpful account of the intellectual development from romanticism to Nietzsche, and beyond to Heidegger and Bataille, see Habermas, 1987.
3. Derrida's self-expressed orientation to classical thought is that, while he might not be 'in the race' (*dans la course*), in an inside lane, deconstruction 'keeps him running' (*fait courir*) 'faster and stronger' (ibid., p. 966).
4. According to Habermas (1987, p. 97), this division within deconstruction is already present in Nietzsche as the two paths of (1)

sceptical unmasking of 'the perversion of the will to power, the revolt of the reactionary forces, and the emergence of a subject-centred reason by using anthropological, psychological, and historical methods', and (2) the initiate's critique 'of metaphysics [which] pretends to a unique kind of knowledge and pursues the rise of the philosophy of the subject back to its pre-Socratic beginnings'.

5. To briefly clarify my position in the light of Beyleveld and Brownsword's comments (see ch. 2), I agree that there is a substantial distance separating their return to the Enlightenment tradition, which is essentially Kantian, from that of, for example, Hart, which is essentially Humean. The Hartian approach returns to natural law on the basis of an already achieved separation of the legal and the moral, whereas for Beyleveld and Brownsword, as I understand them, the legal can only be understood as informed by the moral. For Hart, the legal can be identified according to non-moral criteria, so that the moral is combined with the legal after the latter has already been constituted, and it makes perfect sense to talk of an immoral law. For Beyleveld and Brownsword, an 'immoral law' is not a law properly so-called, because the moral is intrinsically combined with the legal in such a way that an immoral law requires another designation – for example, an immoral rule, or the use of inverted commas: 'law' (Beyleveld and Brownsword, 1986, pp. 163, 452). It is in the sense of a theory that combines a morality with the ability to distinguish between law and 'law' that I understand their account as synthetic.

REFERENCES

Abrahams, P. (1968), *The Origins of British Sociology: 1834–1914*, Chicago: University of Chicago Press.

Albrow, M. (1975), 'Legal positivism and bourgeois materialism: Max Weber's view of the sociology of law', *British Journal of Sociology of Law* 2, 14.

Alexy, R. (1989), *A Theory of Legal Argumentation*, Oxford: Oxford University Press.

Austin, J. (1861), *The Province of Jurisprudence Determined*, London: John Murray.

Bentham, J. (1975), *Theory of Legislation*, New York: Oceana.

Beyleveld, D. and Brownsword, R. (1986), *Law as a Moral Judgment*, London: Sweet and Maxwell.

Bhaskar, R. (1979), *The Possibility of Naturalism*, Brighton: Harvester.

Bourdieu, P. (1988), *Homo Academicus*, Cambridge: Polity.

Carter, A. (1977), *The Passion of New Eve*, London, Gollancz.

Collins, H. (1981), *Marxism and Law*, Oxford: Oxford University Press.

Corrigan, P. and Sayer, D. (1985), *The Great Arch*, Oxford: Basil Blackwell.

Cotterrell, R. (1983), 'English conceptions of the role of theory in legal analysis', *Modern Law Review* 46, 481.

—— (1989), *The Politics of Jurisprudence*, London: Butterworths.

Cullen, B. (1979), *Hegel's Social and Political Thought*, Dublin: Gill and MacMillan.

Derrida, J. (1990), 'Force of the law: the "mystical foundation of authority"', *Cardozo Law Review* 11, 919.

Durkheim, E. (1964), *The Division of Labour in Society*, New York: Free Press.

—— (1973), 'Two Laws of Penal Evolution', *Economy and Society*, 307.

Dworkin, R. (1977), *Taking Rights Seriously*, London: Duckworth.

Engels, F. (1968), 'Ludwig Feuerbach and the end of classical German philosophy', in K. Marx and F. Engels, *Selected Works in One Volume*, London: Lawrence and Wishart.

Fitzpatrick, P. (1982), 'The political economy of dispute settlement in Papua New Guinea', in C. Sumner (ed.), *Crime, Justice and Underdevelopment*, London: Heinemann.

—— (1991), 'The abstracts and brief chronicles of the time: supplementing jurisprudence', in P. Fitzpatrick (ed.), *Resistance and Renewal in Jurisprudence*, London: Pluto.

Foucault, M. (1972), *The Archaeology of Knowledge*, London: Tavistock.

—— (1977), *Discipline and Punish*, London: Peregrine.

—— (1980), *Power/Knowledge*, Brighton: Harvester.

Frank, J. (1963), *Law and the Modern Mind*, New York: Anchor.

Fuller, L. (1969), *The Morality of Law*, New Haven: Yale University Press.

Goodrich, P. (1986), *Reading the Law*, Oxford: Basil Blackwell.

Guha, R. and Spivak, G. (1988), *Selected Subaltern Studies*, Oxford, Oxford University Press.

Habermas, J. (1974), *Theory and Practice*, London: Heinemann.

—— (1984), *A Theory of Communicative Action*, London: Heinemann.

—— (1987), 'The entry into modernity: Nietzsche as a turning point', in *The Philosophical Discourse of Modernity*, Cambridge, Ma: MIT.

—— (1989), *Moral Consciousness and Communicative Action*, Cambridge: Polity.

Halevy, E. (1972), *The Growth of Philosophic Radicalism*, London: Faber.

Harré, R. (1983), *Personal Being*, Oxford: Basil Blackwell.

Hart, H. L. A. (1961), *The Concept of Law*, Oxford: Clarendon.

Hegel, G. (1952), *The Philosophy of Right* Oxford: Oxford University Press.

—— (1956), *The Philosophy of History*, New York: Dover.

Hume, D. (1888), *A Treatise on Human Nature*, Oxford: Clarendon.

—— (1898), 'Of the original contract', in *Essays, Literary, Moral and Political*, London: Longman.

Hunt, A. (1978), *The Sociological Movement in Law*, London: Macmillan.

Jameson, F. (1971), *Marxism and Form*, Princeton: University Press.

Kamenka, E. and Erh-Soon Tay, A. (1975), 'Beyond bourgeois individualism: the contemporary crisis in law and legal ideology', in E. Kamenka and R. S. Neale, *Feudalism, Capitalism and Beyond*, London: Edward Arnold.

Kant, I. (1965), *The Metaphysical Elements of Justice* (trans. J. Ladd), Indianopolis: Bobbs-Merrill.

Kelman, M. (1984), 'Trashing', *Stanford Law Review* 36, 293.

—— (1987), *A Guide to Critical Legal Studies*, Cambridge, Ma: Harvard University Press.

Lacey, N. (1988), *State Punishment*, London: Routledge and Kegan Paul.

Lange, R. de and Raes, K. (1991), 'Plural Legalities', *Recht en Kritiek*, 17, 113.

Llewellyn, K. (1951), *The Bramble Bush*, New York: Oceana.

Locke, J. (1960), *Two Treatises on Government*, Cambridge: Cambridge University Press.

Lukacs, G. (1971), *History and Class Consciousness*, London: Merlin.

MacCormick, D. N. (1976), 'Challenging sociological definitions', *British Journal of Law and Society* 3, 88.

—— (1978a), *Legal Reasoning and Legal Theory*, Oxford: Clarendon.

—— (1978b), 'Dworkin as pre-Benthamite', *Philosophical Review* 87, 585.

—— (1983), 'Contemporary legal philosophy: the rediscovery of practical reason', *Journal of Law and Society* 10.

—— (1989), 'The ethics of legalism', *Ratio Iuris*, 2, 184.

MacIntyre, A. (1967), *A Short History of Ethics*, London: Routledge and Kegan Paul.

McLellan, D. (1969), *The Young Hegelians and Karl Marx*, London: Macmillan.

Marcuse, H. (1941), *Reason and Revolution*, London: Routledge and Kegan Paul.

Marx, K. (1954), *Capital*, Vol. 1, London: Lawrence and Wishart.

—— (1973), *Grundrisse*, Harmondsworth: Pelican.

—— (1975), 'Critique of Hegel's Doctrine of the State', in *Early Writings*, Harmondsworth: Pelican.

Marx, K. and Engels, F. (1968), 'The Communist Manifesto', in K. Marx and F. Engels, *Selected Works in One Volume*, London: Lawrence and Wishart.

Newmann, F. (1986), *The Rule of Law*, Leamington Spa: Berg.

Neumann, F. and Kircheimer, D. (1987), *Social Democracy and the Rule of Law*, London: Allen and Unwin.

Norrie, A. (1982), 'Pashukanis and the commodity form theory: a reply to Warrington', *International Journal of the Sociology of Law* 10, 49.

—— (1989), 'Review of Goodrich, *Reading the Law*', *Juridical Review* 222.

—— (1990a), 'Review of Lacey, *State Punishment*', *International Journal of the Sociology of Law*, 18, 112.

—— (1990b), 'Locating the socialist *Rechtsstaat*: underdevelopment and criminal justice in the Soviet Union', *International Journal of the Sociology of Law*, 18, 343.

—— (1991a), *Law, Ideology and Punishment*, Dordrecht: Kluwer.

—— (1991b), 'A critique of criminal causation, *Modern Law Review*, 54, 685.

—— (1992), 'Subjectivism, objectivism and the limits of criminal recklessness', *Oxford Journal of Legal Studies* 12, 45.

—— (1993a), 'Criminal justice, the rule of law and human emancipation: an historical and comparative study', in S. Adelman and A. Paliwala, *Law, Underdevelopment and Crisis in the Third World*, London: Hans Zell.

—— (1993b), *Crime, Reason and History*, London: Weidenfeld and Nicholson.

Nozick, R. (1975), *Anarchy, State and Utopia*, Oxford: Basil Blackwell.

Outhwaite, W. (1978), *New Philosophies of Social Science*, London: Macmillan.

Pashukanis, E. B. (1978), *Law and Marxism*, London: Ink Links.

Rawls, J. (1972), *A Theory of Justice*, Oxford University Press.

—— (1985), 'Justice as fairness: political not metaphysical', *Philosophy and Public Affairs*, 14, 219.

Rose, G. (1981), *Hegel Contra Sociology*, London: Athlone.

—— (1984), *Dialectic of Nihilism*, Oxford: Basil Blackwell.

Rosenblum, N. (1978), *Bentham's Theory of the Modern State*, Cambridge, Ma: Harvard University Press.

Sayer, D. (1987), *The Violence of Abstraction*, Oxford: Basil Blackwell.

Schluchter, W. (1981), *The Rise of Western Rationalism*, Berkeley: University of California Press.

Spivak, G. (1988), 'Subaltern studies: deconstructing historiography', in R. Guha and G. Spivak, *Selected Subaltern Studies*, Oxford: Oxford University Press.

Steintrager, J. (1977), *Bentham*, London: Allen and Unwin.

Strauss, L. (1953), *Natural Right and History*, Chicago: University of Chicago Press.

Summers, R. (1984), *Lon Fuller*, London: Edward Arnold.
Teubner, G. (1987), '"Juridification": concepts, aspects, limits, solutions', in G. Teubner (ed.), *Juridification of Social Spheres*, Berlin: Walter De Gruyter.
Therborn, G. (1976), *Science, Class and Society*, London: New Left Books.
Turner, B. (1974), *Weber and Islam*, London: Routledge and Kegan Paul.
Unger, R. M. (1976), *Law in Modern Society*, New York: Monthly Review Press.
Waldron, J. (1987), *Nonsense Upon Stilts: Bentham, Burke and Marx on the Rights of Man*, London: Methuen.
Warrington, R. (1981), 'Pashukanis and the commodity form theory', *International Journal of the Sociology of Law* 9, 1.
Weber, M. (1978), *Economy and Society*, Berkeley: University of California Press.
Wolff, R. P. (1973), *The Autonomy of Reason*, New York: Harper.

2

The Dialectically Necessary Foundation of Natural Law

DERYCK BEYLEVELD AND ROGER BROWNSWORD

In *Law as a Moral Judgment* (Beyleveld and Brownsword, 1986), we argued that all agents must, if they are not to contradict that they are agents, view legal validity as the morally legitimate exercise of social control. More specifically, we argued that it is logically necessary for agents to view the rule of law as observed only when social control obeys a supreme moral principle, the Principle of Generic Consistency (PGC).[1] Since the PGC has a determinate content, agents must hold legal validity to be limited by substantive moral requirements.

We begin by indicating how this position is derived from Alan Gewirth's argument for the dialectical necessity of the PGC (Gewirth, 1978) and we explain why we hold that any adequate argument for a concept of law must provide it with a logically necessary justification. We then present a defence of Gewirth's argument to the PGC[2] and we conclude with some general comments about the location of our position in legal theory.

THE DIALECTICAL NECESSITY OF VIEWING LAW AS A MORAL JUDGMENT

Gewirth argues that agents and prospective purposive agents (PPAS)[3] *contradict* that they are PPAS if they do not accept the PGC, or if they violate its precepts in practice. He contends that it is no less than *incoherent* to suppose that it is rational for PPAS to guide their conduct by principles prescribing in opposition to the PGC. The statement 'PPAS ought to guide their conduct by the PGC' is a necessary truth,[4] the predicate 'ought to guide their conduct by the PGC' attaching to PPAS with logical necessity: to suppose that some being is not categorically bound by the PGC is to deny that it is a PPA.

In effect, the argument presents a 'real definition' or 'transcendental conception' of voluntary purposive subjectivity. Since such subjectivity is the presupposed address of all practical directives,[5] the argument entails that the requirement to obey the PGC is presupposed by all who engage in any form of practical reasoning. On pain of self-contradiction, PPAS must treat the PGC as the supreme regulative principle of all practical discourse, as the absolute determinant of what constitutes 'practically reasonable' action.

Gewirth's argument is dialectical, not assertoric: that is, its premises are claims that PPAS make about their agency, not statements presumed to have free-standing validity. However, it purports to be dialectically *necessary* (rather then *contingent*), in that its material premises are held to be claims *necessarily* made by PPAS. Its premises are not the purposes that PPAS are contingently willing to pursue, nor the principles that they might employ to rationalise them, but are claims implicit in the abstract relation between subjectivity and voluntary purposiveness per se, which Gewirth holds to characterise PPAS *as PPAS*. Hence, the argument purports to establish the PGC as categorically binding on PPAS, as binding on PPAS *regardless* of their contingent purposive preferences or characteristics.

Given its dialectical nature, the argument is relative to PPAS, and does not purport to establish the PGC itself as a necessary truth. Thus, Gewirth does not contend that moral relativism, amoralism and other positions opposed to the PGC, are themselves self-contradictory. However, if Gewirth's argument succeeds in showing the PGC to be dialectically *necessary*, then it provides the PGC with the same degree of justification inherent in a proof that the PGC is itself a necessary truth. If the PGC itself were a necessary truth, then to guide one's conduct by opposed principles would be to guide one's conduct by self-contradictory prescriptions. As a dialectically necessary prescription, to guide one's conduct by opposed principles is to assert simultaneously, and in the same respects, that one both is and is not a PPA. In both cases, the justification provided is the avoidance of logical contradiction.[6]

Directly, Gewirth's argument entails that it is logically necessary for PPAS to refer the practical reasonableness of all activities and rules constituting the legal enterprise to the PGC. However, since these activities and rules are themselves purposive activities (or products of purposive activities) of PPAS, and can be altered by purposive activites of PPAS, there are also consequences for how PPAS may *conceptualise* the nature of the legal enterprise.

The argument entails that, on pain of self-contradiction, PPAS must attach a determinate normative goal to the legal enterprise *as part of its description*. Just as PPAS must accept the PGC and act in accordance with it, PPAS must hold that the legal enterprise – related as it is to the purposive activities of PPAS – ought (in all its facets) to conform to the PGC. But, just as the statement that PPAS ought to obey the PGC is *both* a dialectically necessary prescription directed at PPAS and a dialectically necessary characterisation of what PPAS are, the statement that the legal enterprise ought to follow the PGC is a dialectically necessary statement *both* about what the legal enterprise ought to be *and about what it is*. All PPAS must conceive of the requirement to obey the PGC as *internal* (necessarily related) to the legal enterprise (i.e., as *defining it*) – not as *external* (only contingently related) to it (if at all) – as *the* categorical imperative rooted *in its very nature*.

Now, if we must conceive of the requirement to obey the PGC as internal to the legal enterprise, and the PGC must be taken to be the supreme principle of practical reasoning, overriding the prescriptive force of all opposed principles, then it follows (against various forms of non-normative positivism)[7] that the legal enterprise must be conceived of normatively, and, additionally (against normative forms of legal positivism),[8] that a *moral* principle, the PGC, must be taken to be the supreme principle of normative validity *within* the legal enterprise, and thus as the supreme principle of *legal* validity (which vindicates the traditional natural law slogan, '*Lex injustia non est lex*').[9]

Clearly, the validity of Gewirth's argument is *sufficient* to justify moralisation of the concept of law. However, given the enormously stringent conditions for justification imposed by a 'transcendental essentialist'[10] or dialectically necessary strategy, it might be queried whether it is *necessary* to impose such conditions. For example, although Mark Ockleton (1988) praises our critiques of other positions (especially that of Kelsen, 1967) as well as our application of the PGC in handling questions concerning a moral obligation to obey state powers, he thinks that Gewirth's argument is unsound.[11] More than this, he implies that the sort of 'strong' (necessitarian) justificatory programme to which we are committed *cannot* succeed. Because this is not an uncommon reaction to Gewirth's argument, he wonders why we did not offer supplementary 'weaker' (contingent) types of considerations for our position, which, though lacking the capacity to 'prove' our concept of law, might be more efficacious in securing its adoption.

We concede that, in principle, 'weaker' arguments for *morality* are, indeed, possible.[12] It is necessary, however, to be clear about their efficacy for foundational ethics and legal concept formation.

It is true that to give justificatory reasons for being moral, or even for the espousal of specific substantive moral principles, it is not necessary to show that morality is dialectically necessary. It is only necessary to show that morality is required by considerations that the addressees of these arguments are willing to employ. However, only by employing criteria of rationality that PPAS categorically must accept,[13] operating on premises that PPAS cannot coherently deny,[14] can *categorically binding* reasons be given for morality. There are at least two reasons why we should not rest content with anything less.

First, although morality may be binding *from the viewpoint of those* whose contingent commitments justify morality, a central point of seeking a justification for morality is to justify its precepts *to those who do not accept* them. This simply cannot be done on considerations that 'deviants' do not categorically have to accept. A non-authoritarian (and non-question-begging) imposition of practical precepts on those who dissent from them demands that foundations for morality be apodictic.

Second, moral principles *themselves* are frequently characterised as setting categorical requirements for the actions of their addressees. This categorical quality comprises two components: the requirements set by moral principles are conatively independent ('exclusionary reasons')[15] and override non-moral requirements in cases of conflict. However, *if* moral principles are characterised in this way, then justificatory programmes that operate with contingent criteria of rationality are attempting to demonstrate that there are non-categorically binding reasons for treating the requirements set by specific principles as categorically binding. But, there is a contradiction here. If the reasons for espousing a particular principle are not categorically binding, then the principle, thereby justified, can hardy be said to set requirements for conduct that are justified as categorically binding. Thus, justificatory programmes that operate with contingent considerations (no matter how widely assented to) need to conceive of morality differently, as not setting requirements that purport to be categorically binding. There is, of course, no absolute prohibition on designating precepts with different characteristics as 'moral' precepts. The point, however, is that use of a dialectically necessary method is dictated by what is needed to prove the requirements of specific principles as *categorically binding*.

Now, whereas Gewirth attempts to establish that the requirements set by the PGC must be taken as categorically binding by PPAs, our concern is (additionally) to resolve the dispute over whether or not there is a *conceptually necessary* connection between law and morality. Deploying Gewirth's argument for the dialectical necessity of the PGC (whatever it might mean to say that there is 'assertorically' a conceptual connection between law and morality) enables us to argue that it is *logically necessary* for PPAs to conceive of law as regulated by the PGC *by its very nature* (given that it comprises some subset of the activities of PPAs, or the products thereof).

The suggestion that dialectically contingent reasons for being moral can be taken as reasons to treat law as morally regulated *by its very nature* runs into problems parallel to those incurred by the suggestion that we may rest content with dialectically contingent justifications for morality.

First, supposing (for the moment) that dialectically contingent reasons for being moral are dialectically contingent reasons for treating law as morally regulated by its very nature, it is question-begging against those who do not operate with these dialectically contingent considerations to suggest that they rationally ought to take law as moral.

Second, and here more importantly, it is not, as we have just supposed, tenable to hold that dialectically contingent reasons for being moral are reasons (at all) for treating law as morally regulated *by its very nature*. Suppose that we were to show that reasons of type X require PPAs to be moral (to adopt the PGC, specifically); but suppose also that there is no categorically binding reason why X criteria should be used as criteria for practical reasonableness. What we would have shown is that those who happen to be willing to espouse X criteria for practical reasonableness ought (if they are not to contradict their espousal of X criteria) to bind themselves by the PGC. Should they, however, decide to abandon their commitment to X criteria, or should there be other PPAs who are not willing to espouse X criteria, then we will not have shown that there is any irrationality in their not espousing the PGC. But, this means that we will not have shown that the legal enterprise must be taken to be regulated by the PGC *by its very nature, even by those who espouse X criteria*. Because it will not have been shown that PPAs, *regardless of their contingent characteristics and commitments*, categorically must (logically ought to) accept the PGC, it will not have been shown that the components of the legal enterprise (as activities of PPAs, or products thereof) categorically ought to be regulated by the PGC. The requirement to obey the PGC will not have been shown to be dialectically *internal* to the legal enterprise itself. It will remain external to the legal enterprise, deriving from contingent commitments of PPAs. It will no longer be true that 'The legal enterprise ought to conform to the PGC' is *both* a prescription *and a definition* of the legal enterprise. In short, justificatory arguments for morality lack force for the concept of law, *unless* they are dialectically *necessary*. In no sense would we have got beyond what legal positivists are willing to accept, viz., that the legal enterprise *might* be guided by moral considerations (and even that this is morally desirable), but the criteria of legal validity are autonomous from (external to) those of moral validity. Because what is at issue is a conceptually necessary connection between law and morality, dialectically *contingent* arguments for being moral have no efficacy against the conceptual thesis of legal positivism.

Thus, our response to Ockleton's suggestion that we supplement Gewirth's argument with 'weaker' considerations is that if dialectically necessary arguments for being moral *cannot* be valid, and all we are left with is dialectically contingent ones, then we are not left with 'second-best' arguments for the conceptual thesis of natural law theory; we are left with no arguments at all. We must stick with a dialectically necessary strategy, or abandon the field altogether.[16]

This is not, however, a counsel of despair, for the objections that have been raised against Gewirth's argument, though numerous and persistent, are not sound, and it is to this that we now turn our attention.

GEWIRTH'S ARGUMENT TO THE PGC

Introduction

Gewirth's argument for the dialectical necessity of the PGC has three stages. (Dialectically necessary statements are presented in curly brackets, and the appended subscript specifies who is required to assent to the statements. Abbreviations are not Gewirth's, but follow Beyleveld 1991.)

I

I^{17} am a PPA → {My F&WB are necessary goods}$_I$

II

→ {PPAO ought (at least)[18] not to interfere with my F&WB against my will}$_I$ ≡ {I have a right to F&WB}$_I$

III

→ {PPAO has a right to its F&WB}$_I$ (thus {PGC}$_I$; and thus {PGC}$_{PPA}$).[19]

In the present context, we can neither present Gewirth's reasoning in full, nor try to refute *all* the objections that have been raised against his argument.[20] However, although all three stages have been queried, most commentators are willing to accept Stage I. We shall, therefore, concentrate on the more controversial Stages II and III. However, even with this limited focus, selection is needed. We attend only to a sample of objections, including the most common.

We begin by being more expansive about the three stages. We then look in some detail at Stage III. We concentrate on Stage III, initially, because we believe that a proper understanding of Gewirth's treatment of logical universalisation clarifies not only Stage III, but Stage II as well.

In more detail, the argument looks like this.

I

1. I am a PPA (≡ I have at least some freely chosen[21] purpose/purposes that I pursue/intend to pursue) →
2. {IP}$_I$[22] ({My freely chosen purposes have value that is sufficient to motivate me to pursue them}$_I$ ≡ {My freely chosen purposes are good relative to the criteria I choose to follow in choosing to pursue them}$_I$).
3. IC[23] (I categorically need F&WB in order to pursue/achieve any purpose by my agency). (2&3) →
4. {My F&WB are necessary goods}$_I$ ≡ {I value my F&WB proactively as

instrumental to whatever my purposes$\}_I \to$ (*since I would deny that I was a PPA by not so valuing my F&WB*)[24]

II

$\{SRO\}_I$ ($\{I$ categorically instrumentally ought to pursue/defend my F&WB$\}_I$) $\to$ (*by 'Ought implies can' – since 'I ought to do X'* $\to$ *'I ought to be able to do X/I ought to have the necessary means to do X'*)

5. $(ORO\}_I$[25] ($\{PPAO$ categorically ought [has a duty/obligation] (at least) not to interfere with my having F&WB against my will$\}_I$) $\to$

6. $\{MyR\}_I$[26] ($\{I$ have a right to F&WB$\}_I$) $\to$ (*by the LPU* [logical principle of universalisability])

III

7. $\{PPAOR\}_I$[27] ($\{PPAO$ has a right to F&WB$\}_I$) $\to$ (*by the union of 6 and 7*)

8. $\{PGC\}_I$ ($\{Every$ PPA has a right to F&WB$\}_I$) $\to$ (*by the LPU*)

9. $\{PGC\}_{PPAO}$ ($\{Every$ PPA has a right to F&WB$\}_{PPAO}$) $\to$ (*by the union of 8 and 9*)

10. $\{PGC\}_{PPA}$ ($\{Every$ PPA has a right to F&WB$\}_{PPA}$).

Is Stage III valid?

Assuming, for the sake of argument, that Stages I and II are both valid, what we have is

I am a PPA $\to \{MyR\}_I$.

There is no doubt that, by the LPU, this entails

PPAO is a PPA $\to \{PPAOR\}_{PPAO}$.

What the argument requires, however, is

I am a PPA $\to \{PPAOR\}_I$.

or

PPAO is a PPA $\to \{MyR\}_{PPAO}$;

and many critics contend that the LPU will not license these inferences without question-begging assumptions. (For example, 'I take favourable account of PPAO's F&WB/PPAO takes favourable account of my F&WB'.)

Suppose, however, that it were shown, prior to universalisation, not merely that [I am a PPA $\to \{MyR\}_I$], but that

I am a PPA $\to \{I$ am a PPA $\to MyR\}_I$.

From this, as we shall shortly explain,

I am a PPA $\to \{PPAO$ is a PPA $\to PPAOR\}_I \to \{PPAOR\}_I$

can be derived by the LPU without making any additional assumptions. Since this is so, critics must say that (even if Stage II is valid) it is not logically necessary for a PPA to make its *being a PPA* the sufficient condition for its possession of the rights to F&WB that it must consider it has.[28] It is, therefore, significant that critics have almost completely ignored Gewirth's argument to demonstrate that [I am a PPA $\to \{MyR\}_I$] *logically* entails [I am a PPA $\to \{I$ am a PPA $\to MyR\}_I$].

Gewirth calls this argument 'the argument from the sufficiency of agency' ('ASA'; see Gewirth, 1978, pp. 109–10).[29] This takes the form of a reductio ad absurdum.

To deny {I am a PPA $\rightarrow$ MyR}$_I$ (i.e. to deny that it is logically necessary for me to take my being a PPA as the *sufficient* condition for my having MyR) is to claim that I do not contradict {MyR}$_I$ (and thus 'I am a PPA' – since [I am a PPA $\rightarrow$ {MyR}$_I$] if Stage II is valid) if I hold (MyR $\rightarrow$ I am X) (i.e., that my having X is a *necessary* condition of my having MyR), where X is a property that is not necessarily possessed by me as a PPA.[30]

So, suppose I maintain (as I must if Stage II is valid) that MyR, but insist that it is a necessary condition of my possession of MyR that I have X. This qualification, however, requires me to hold that if I did not have X then I would not have MyR, *even if I were a* PPA! and this is a denial that I *must* hold that I have MyR if I am a PPA. Thus, by holding (MyR $\rightarrow$ X) I contradict [I am a PPA $\rightarrow$ {MyR}$_I$] (and, hence, that I am a PPA). Thus, having granted [I am a PPA $\rightarrow$ {MyR}$_I$], I must deny (MyR $\rightarrow$ X). Since it is in the nature of a rights-claim that I must adduce *some* feature as that by virtue of which I possess this right, by having to deny that a necessary condition of this feature is one not necessarily connected with being a PPA, I must adduce as this feature only such properties as I necessarily possess by virtue of being a PPA. Thus, I must hold (I am a PPA $\rightarrow$ MyR). Thus

[I am a PPA $\rightarrow$ {MyR}$_I$] $\rightarrow$ [I am a PPA $\rightarrow$ {I am a PPA $\rightarrow$ MyR}$_I$].[31]

By applying the LPU to the *inference* [I am a PPA $\rightarrow$ MyR], which is the content of my dialectically necessary internal viewpoint as a PPA, it follows that I must grant the same right to PPAO, without making any further assumptions.

It should be noted that Gewirth applies the LPU in *two different ways*:

(a) to [I am a PPA $\rightarrow$ {Every PPA has a right to F&WB}$_I$] to infer [PPAO is a PPA $\rightarrow$ {Every PPA has a right to F&WB}$_{PPAO}$] (the inference from 8 to 9); and the same application is employed to infer that from [I, because I am a PPA, must hold that I have MyR] (i.e., [I am a PPA $\rightarrow$ {MyR}$_I$]) it follows that [PPAO, because it is a PPA, must hold that it has PPAOR] (i.e. [PPAO is a PPA $\rightarrow$ {PPAOR}$_{PPAO}$]), which critics accept. This application permits inferences about *one PPA's dialectically necessary internal viewpoint from another's*. It specifies that whatever is logically necessary for any one PPA to hold *relative to its own position* in a transaction is logically necessary for any PPA to hold *relative to that specific PPA's position* in a transaction.

(b) to [I (a PPA) must hold (I have MyR because I am a PPA)] (i.e., {I am a PPA $\rightarrow$ I have MyR}$_I$) to yield [I must hold (PPAO has PPAOR because it is a PPA)] (i.e., {PPAO is a PPA $\rightarrow$ PPAOR}$_I$). This application operates *within the same PPA's internal viewpoint*. It specifies that if it is logically necessary for a PPA to grant itself a position in a transaction (here, having a right to F&WB) on a given ground (property) (here, being a PPA), then it is logically necessary for it to grant this position to everything that shares this property.

In (a) and (b), the *same logical principle* is involved: viz:

If for any x, x has $\pi \rightarrow$ x has μ, then for all x, x has $\pi \rightarrow$ x has μ, which may also be expressed as

For all x and for all y, (x has $\pi \rightarrow$ x has μ) $\rightarrow$ (y has $\pi \rightarrow$ y has μ).[32]

The difference between (a) and (b) is that, in (a), the LPU is applied to the logical relation between being a PPA and *having to make a judgment/ inference*, whereas in (b), it is applied to *the inference that a PPA has to make within its internal viewpoint*, viz., that being a PPA is a sufficient condition for having a right to F&WB. The difference between the application (a) to 6 (which critics accept) and Gewirth's application (b) in inferring 7 is simply in what μ stands for (π standing for the property of being a PPA in both applications). In the uncontested application, μ stands for the property of *having to hold* that one has a right to F&WB. In Gewirth's application to infer 7, μ stands for the property of *having* a right to F&WB. Application (a) operates on the proposition 'I, because I am a PPA, *must hold* that I have a right to F&WB'. (Gewirth calls this 'judgmental univer-salisation' (see Gewirth, 1988, p. 253), because it operates on the necessity for making a claim; but it may also be called 'external applica-tion of the LPU', because it operates on a relation external to the content of a PPA's dialectically necessary claim.) Application (b) operates on the dialectically necessary inference (given the ASA) – 'I *have* a right to F&WB because I am a PPA'. (Gewirth calls this 'possessive universalisation' (see ibid.), because it operates on an inference to having a right; but it may also be called 'internal application of the LPU', because it operates on the inference internal to a PPA's dialectically necessary viewpoint.) There can be no doubt that the LPU itself is valid, and that both applications are logically sound. So, if the ASA is valid, Stage III must be valid, and questioning it must be attributed to failure to attend to the internal application of the LPU/the ASA that makes this application possible.[33]

Is Stage II Valid?

Objection I

Although 5 is correlative to 6, 5 does not follow from 4, because, for X to have a duty to do y, it is necessary that X have a categorically binding reason to do y. The fact that I categorically need my F&WB provides *me* with a categorically binding reason to act in various ways, and provides *me* with a reason why PPAO categorically ought not to interfere with my F&WB; but it provides PPAO with no reason not to interfere with my F&WB – *unless* it is assumed that PPAO adopts a moral point of view (takes favourable account of my interests),[34] or that PPAO categorically needs my F&WB for *its* agency (which is false).[35]

Reply

It is certainly correct that we cannot, by *'Ought implies can'* (without making false or question-begging assumptions), infer from 4 that PPAO *must accept* that it ought not to interfere with my F&WB. Gewirth, however, does not think that we can. What he maintains is that, *relative to a criterion* (SRO), the prescription 'PPAO categorically ought not to interfere with my F&WB (against my will)' is valid. So, since *I* must accept SRO, *I* must accept that PPAO categorically ought not to interfere with my F&WB (against my will). From my dialectically necessary viewpoint, the state of affairs 'PPAO's interfering with my F&WB' categorically ought not to be (i.e., PPAO's not interfering categorically ought to be brought about by those who can).

Critics who press this objection may be divided into two groups. First there are those (almost all) who are prepared to concede that, thus interpreted, 5 can be derived from 4,[36] and those who are even prepared to accept that, so interpreted, 5 is correlative to a rights-claim in *some* sense.[37] However, these critics claim that, so interpreted, neither 5 nor 6 yields the dialectical necessity of the PGC by purely logical universalisation. They claim that 5/6 only do so if they are not merely other-*directed* claims, but other-*directing* ones as well.[38]

Our analysis of Stage III provides a direct response to these critics. Applying the ASA to $[1 \rightarrow \{5/6\}_I]$ yields [I am a PPA $\rightarrow$ {I am a PPA $\rightarrow$ PPAO's not interfering with my F&WB categorically ought to be/I have a 'right' to my F&WB$\}_I$], and this may be universalised by the internal application of the LPU to {PPAO is a PPA $\rightarrow$ My interfering with PPAO's F&WB categorically ought not to be$\}_I$, without any question-begging or false assumptions.[39]

Second, there are those (few) who hold that it is literally unintelligible to claim that PPAO has a duty not to interfere with my F&WB if this prescription is not other-*directing* – for example, Bond (1980, pp. 49–50), Lomasky (1981, p. 250), MacCormick (1984) and Arrington (1989, p. 108).

Now, while it makes no sense to say that PPAO has a duty not to interfere with my F&WB if no criterion formally validates this prescription that PPAO *could* accept or choose to follow, it is an extremely dubious analysis of 'PPAO's having a duty/obligation' (or of 'my having a right against PPAO') that requires PPAO to accept (or have to accept) a criterion that validates these prescriptions. Such an analysis implies that it is *unintelligible* for me to consider that someone has an obligation/duty to do y if this someone does not accept that he/she has this duty. This, in turn, implies that what a criterion formally validates is affected by acceptance of the criterion. It implies that 'Greece is in Europe' and 'Napoleon was a Greek' jointly entail 'Napoleon was a European' only for those who accept that Napoleon was a Greek (or if Napoleon was a Greek). This is untenable. Instead, we submit that for a PPA to say (formally) that PPAO has a D duty not to interfere with PPA's F&WB is for PPA to say that, relative to D criteria, there is a reason why PPAO's not interfering with PPA's F&WB is the state of affairs that categorically ought to be; that PPAO *could* espouse D criteria as action-guiding for its conduct; and that PPAO *could* interfere/not interfere with PPA's F&WB. From this it follows that whoever espouses (or must espouse) D criteria – that is, takes (or must take) D criteria as specifying what state of affairs ought to/may be – must consider (prescriptively)[40] that PPAO has a duty not to interfere with PPA's F&WB, provided only that PPAO fulfils the two 'could' subconditions.

Objection 2

Alasdair MacIntyre (1981, p. 65) points out that if Stage II is valid, then 5/6 (duty/rights-claims) are derived from a statement of necessary good. However, duty/rights-claims cannot be derived from claims about good, not even from those about necessary good, because, whereas deontic claims are necessarily universalisable, claims about good, even necessary good, are not.

Reply

This objection is pertinent because, if the argument is a *logically* necessary sequence, then (by the principle of the transitivity of logical entailment) it must be possible to alter the order of the logical operations that generate the dialectical necessity of the PGC. In particular, it must be possible to universalise from SRO and only then apply 'Ought implies can' to generate the final result.

However, to begin with, this objection ignores the fact that, because the judgments of value that a PPA must make about its purposes are proactive, 4 is equivalent to SRO, the *deontic* judgment that I categorically (albeit only instrumentally) *ought* to pursue/defend my F&WB. From my perspective in agency, at least, 4 ($\equiv$ SRO) is not a statement of mere desirability devoid of action-guiding implications. Second, we submit that the formal principle involved in the ASA ('If X *must*, because it has z, claim that it has y, then X must claim "I have y because I have z"') may be applied to [I am a PPA $\rightarrow$ {SRO}$_I$] to yield [I am a PPA $\rightarrow$ {I am a PPA $\rightarrow$ SRO}$_I$], and that this is universalisable by the internal application of the LPU to {PPAO is a PPA $\rightarrow$ PPAO's pursuit/defence of its F&WB categorically ought to be}$_I$; from which {I categorically ought not to interfere with PPAO's F&WB}$_I$ can be uncontentiously derived, as the proximate premise requires me to take favourable account of PPAO's F&WB, being a prescription of what I require PPAO to do.

Furthermore, the contention that rights-claims, etc., are necessarily universalisable (that rights claimed *must* be extended to others) is false; as is the assertion (which the objection really requires)[41] that statements of good, etc., are necessarily not. Universalisation operates on predicative inferences of the form 'If A has B, then A has C'. What determines whether C must be attributed to others than A is whether others than A have B. There is nothing about the nature of rights-claims that prohibits them from being particularistic. If I (A) claim that I have a right (C) if and only if I am some unique person, myself (have B), then I am not required to extend this right to anyone else. Conversely, claims about good *can* (and must) be universalised, *provided only* that these claims can be construed in inferential predicative terms. [I am a PPA → {My F&WB are necessary goods}$_I$] → (by the formal principle involved in the ASA) {I am a PPA → My F&WB are necessary goods}$_I$. By the internal application of the LPU, it follows that {PPAO is a PPA → PPAO's F&WB are necessary goods}$_I$, *provided only that* 'My F&WB are necessary goods' may be construed, at least in part, as 'My having F&WB is a state of affairs that has the property of being good'. We can see no reason why this should not be the case.

Objection 3

It is possible that PPAs might, for example, desire a life of competition (see Held (1979, pp. 246–8), White (1982, p. 288), Williams (1985, pp. 62–3) and Gamwell (1984, pp. 61–2; 64–5). As such, they will not claim rights to F&WB; at most, they will claim rights to try to have F&WB (see Held ibid.), unless (which Gewirth denies – as he must – because the judgments of value in Stage I are (categorically) instrumental, not intrinsic) it is dialectically inconsistent for PPAs to desire such a life. Thus, 5/6 is not dialectically necessary (or, to the extent that it is, it is merely a claim about attempt, which, by universalisation, does not prohibit attempts to interfere with PPAO's F&WB).

Reply

It is true that it is not dialectically inconsistent for a PPA to desire a life of competition of a sort that would threaten its possession of F&WB, any more than it is dialectically inconsistent for a PPA to wish to commit suicide – and this is because a PPA must value its F&WB as categorically necessary *means* to its purposes, not as ends in themselves. However, this means that a PPA must pursue its F&WB *as means* even if its end is to forfeit its F&WB or to achieve something that endangers it. And it means that a PPA must pursue its F&WB as an end in itself subject only to *its not choosing* to forfeit or risk it. But this means that what 4 entails (by 'Ought implies can') is that a PPA must judge that PPAO categorically ought not to interfere with PPA's F&WB against PPA's will. This, in turn, means that the right that a PPA must claim is 'waivable', in the sense that PPA may permit PPAO to interfere with PPA's F&WB (may release PPAO from its duty of non-interference). However, the right is not waivable if described as a right to non-interference *against PPA's will*. The right to non-interference is only waivable as the exercise of the right to non-interference *against PPA's will*. Thus, the dialectical consistency of choosing a 'competitive' lifestyle does not constitute a concession of the dialectical consistency of denying that one has a right to F&WB.[42]

On the claim that a PPA need only claim a right *to try to have* F&WB, two points need to be made. First, even if so, this still entails that a PPA must claim a right to *have basic* F&WB, since these are conditions of its *attempting* to have F&WB. Second, the whole point of trying to do x is to succeed *in achieving* x. From this, it follows that rights to non-subtractive and additive goods (necessary conditions for succeeding in one's attempts) must also be claimed. This latter point is, perhaps, more clearly made by pointing out that the reason why I must pursue my F&WB is that (given the proactive evaluational relation that I have to my purposes) the needs of my agency require me to accept that I ought to *have* F&WB. Granted, it is true that SRO is subject to 'Ought implies can', in the sense that I will be released from SRO if I am prevented from fulfilling it, and that I can do no more than try to defend my F&WB, there being no guarantee of my success. In a sense, SRO says that I ought to secure my F&WB *if I can*. But the way in which this condition operates does not entail that there is no implied prescription that PPAO ought not to prevent me having F&WB. For it to do so, we would need to say that I am not required to hold that my having F&WB is a state of affairs that ought to be if PPAO happens to prevent that state of affairs from coming about (even when, without PPAO's interference, such a state of affairs could be brought about, and PPAO could refrain from interference). (For a detailed discussion of the untenability of holding this, see the discussion of Davies's (1975) objection to Gewirth's argument in Beyleveld, 1991.)

Objection 4

In specifying that I ought to pursue/defend my F&WB, SRO entails that I ought to have the necessary means to pursue/secure my F&WB. According to Paske (1989, p. 55), however, it does not follow from this that PPAO ought not to interfere with my having F&WB. This is because it is not true that I categorically need non-interference by PPAO in order to pursue/defend my F&WB. I might be able to overcome interference, in some circumstances at least.

Reply

This objection trades on an ambiguity in 'PPAO ought not to interfere'.

This can mean 'PPAO ought not *to prevent*', or it can mean 'PPAO ought not to try to prevent'. Where it carries the former meaning, non- interference is a necessary condition of my pursuit/securing of my F&WB, and the inference from 4 to 5 is clearly valid. Where it carries the latter meaning, non-interference is, indeed, not a necessary condition of my pursuing/ securing my F&WB. But, if PPAO tries to prevent my having F&WB, there is no guarantee that I will be able to overcome this attempt. Since there can be no such guarantee, it follows that I must hold that PPAO ought not to try to prevent me having F&WB, *unless I choose* to take this risk for other gains. And this is still equivalent to my having to claim that I have a right to non-interference (in either meaning) *against my will*.

An Overview of Objections to Stage II

It should be apparent that our analysis of Stage III enables us to short-circuit objections to Stage II. On this analysis, the ASA (or arguments of the same form), together with the internal application of the LPU, permits us to universalise from 4/5/6 to prescriptions *within my dialectically neces-sary viewpoint* that require me to take favourable account of the F&WB of PPAO. No critics question that the logical operations of Stage II are valid if the prescriptions that we begin with are other-regarding/directing and not merely self-directing/other-directed, so they will not question the genera-tion of the PGC from other-regarding universalised conclusions of 4, 5 or 6. Furthermore, we have shown that if we begin with 5/6, then there is no problem with such universalisation. Thus, the problem, to circumvent objections to Stage II, is to make good the claim that 4/SRO can be universalised by the same procedures to other-regarding prescriptions. As we have already indicated, 4 and SRO can be universalised in the required manner if, in being required to make these judgments, I am required to judge that my having F&WB is the state of affairs that is good (regardless of my purposes)/the state of affairs of my having F&WB ought to be – my having to accept 4/SRO being a function of the fact that the requirements of my pursuit/achievement of any purposes (and I am necessarily commit-ted to some purposes as a PPA) specify these evaluations (validate them). What is required is that *on (relative to)* my dialectically necessary criterion ({IP}), my having F&WB is good/ought to be *in the sense that, relative to this criterion*, it is the case that *anyone* ought to accept 4/SRO. (That only I categorically have to accept 4/SRO at the pertinent stage is a function of the fact that only I am shown to have to operate with IP. Thus, although PPAO is not yet shown to have to accept IP, one could say that *if* PPAO accepted IP, then PPAO would have to prescribe 4/SRO with action-guiding implica-tions not only for its own actions, but also for any PPA's actions.) In brief, our defence of the argument rests, we believe, only on the claim that criteria validate their conclusions impersonally (that they are, in principle, *directed to* – though not *directing for* – all who can fulfil them), independent of anyone's acceptance of the criteria. This is not an issue that has surfaced clearly and unambiguously in discussions of Gewirth's argument, and we must confess that we have been unable, thus far, to construct what we consider to be a tenable alternative viewpoint. (Various alternative suggestions are made and considered in Beyleveld, 1991. The discussions of objections made by Kalin (1984) and McMahon (1986) are most significant in this regard.) Be this as it may, we are confident that *if* the view that we have put forward is correct, then the PGC is, as Gewirth insists, dialectically necessary.

THE POSITION OF *LAW AS A MORAL JUDGMENT* IN LEGAL THEORY

Like Kant, Gewirth maintains that a supreme moral principle can be established a priori, as necessarily binding on all agents. Although the precise relations between Kant's *justificatory* argument for his supreme moral principle and Gewirth's argument to the PGC are by no means clear, there can be no doubt that the aims of the two arguments are identical (viz., to prove the apodictic status of a supreme moral principle), and the relationship between *Law as a Moral Judgment* and the foundational argument of *Reason and Morality* is not unlike the relationship between *The Metaphysical Elements of Justice* (Kant, 1965) and Kant's justification of a categorical imperative.[43]

In the previous chapter, Alan Norrie classifies our position as an attempt to return to 'the classicism of the Enlightenment'. With this we can have no quarrel. But we are perplexed by some of his other comments. For example:

1. that classicism attempts to understand law in terms of something other than law (in our case, presumably morality);
2. that our position is one of a number of attempted syntheses of positivism and classicism, by which he seems to mean moralised understandings of a category 'law' that is not inherently moral;
3. that our position is opposed to a 'sociological approach'.

The first of these propositions is odd, because we hold that law has an identity only *within* the sphere of morality.[44] Law does not exist apart from morality; hence to comprehend it morally is not to analyse it in terms external to its nature. Another way of putting this is that we hold (as does Kant), that rules and activities, insofar as they are properly classified as legally valid, have autonomy; but this autonomy is *the autonomy of morality itself*.

This dovetails with our unease about Norrie's second proposition. Norrie appears to locate our view along a *continuum* of positions, with Hart at one end and ourselves at the other, that press for a moral understanding of law (our position putting the most emphasis on morality,

Hart's the least). This is misleading if the continuum is viewed as a *quantitative* one. We do not merely attach *more* significance to morality in understanding law than Hart does. The significance that we attach is of a wholly different kind; it is *conceptual* as well as moral significance. Where we maintain a conceptually necessary connection between law and morality, Hart insists on a contingent connection. Given this, Norrie's classification of the new 'classicism' as an attempt to *synthesise* the ethical and the positive confuses matters. For *positivists* (like Hart and MacCormick), there is no philosophical problem in such a combination, because none of the emphasis that they place on morality affects their view of the nature of law as law. Their ethical concerns notwithstanding, they portray law as a phenomenon to be identified independently of their moral judgments.[45] The philosophical problem that they confront is to justify that law and morality are distinct; no philosophical problem is presented by asserting contingent connections between law and morality *on the assumption* that they are autonomous spheres. For us, on the other hand, there is a philosophical problem in the conjunction of morality and legality; but it is not the problem of identifying 'law' *precharacterised* as a 'positive' category (i.e., a morally neutral 'what is'), with 'the moral' ('what ought to be'). It is the question of whether a moral viewpoint on action is dialectically necessary, of whether PPAS rationally *must* view phenomena related to social action (which include the subject matter of law) as having moral goals. Ergo, since we give opposite answers to this from Hart (and positivists generally), if both we and Hart are 'classicists', then we are not so in the same sense.

Finally, it must be said that we do not view our position as *opposed* to sociological approaches per se. At issue is how one conceives of the relationship between the conceptual and empirical components of sociological inquiry. And this, in turn, is a function of the epistemological stance that one adopts. We hold that there is an irreducible (synthetic) a priori element in all empirical knowledge: metaphysics (*transcendental* metaphysics) is an irreducible part of empirical inquiry, neither replacing it nor competing with it, but foundational for it. Insofar as we find ourselves at odds with sociological approaches, it is with the epistemological positions that sometimes underlie what is done in the name of doing sociology, not with an interest per se to differentiate, display and explain the contingencies that are and might be manifested in the legal enterprise *even as we view it.* For there is nothing in our concern with the necessary and universal that precludes objects classified in these terms from evincing contingent variation. Our thesis (in opposition to *some* sociological approaches), that components of the legal enterprise that do not instantiate its ideal (which hence are, in our terms, legally invalid) have to be described and understood from the viewpoint of the legal ideal (the legally valid), does not obliterate sociological questions. It merely specifies how sociology must characterise law in and for its explanations. Our natural-law view is underpinned by a Kantian epistemological stance that is equally at odds with the main streams of current philosophical thinking. However, all we can say about this, here, is that our rationalistic intentions need to be recognised, no matter how unfashionable, anachronistic or contentious they might seem, if our position is to be properly understood and classified.[46]

NOTES

1. This principle prescribes that all agents (and prospective purposive agents) have claim rights (which are correlative to duties on the part of others) to their freedom and well-being (F&WB). 'An agent' is someone who pursues a purpose that he or she has voluntarily chosen. Prospective purposive agents are beings with the capacity to be agents, who are disposed to exercise it. We use the abbreviation 'PPA' to stand for 'agent' as well as for 'prospective purposive agent'.

   More specifically, the PGC prescribes that a PPA (any PPA) categorically ought not to interfere with the F&WB of PPAO (other PPA/s) against its (his/her/its) will (and, indeed, ought to aid PPAO in securing its F&WB, when PPAO cannot do so by its own unaided efforts, and doing so does not involve comparable costs to the F&WB of PPA), provided only that such interference is not required to resist interference with PPA's F&WB by PPAO.

   'Freedom' and 'well-being' refer to capacities (related, respectively, to the voluntariness and purposiveness conditions of agency) that Alan Gewirth (1978, pp. 52–63), maintains are 'generic features of agency' (capacities that are necessary for the voluntary pursuit/achievement of any purposes whatsoever – ('categorical agency needs')). The components of F&WB are hierarchically ordered according to their importance for agency (assessed by a criterion of 'degrees of necessity'). Most important are 'basic' needs (necessary for the pursuit of purposes). 'Non-subtractive' needs are necessary for the maintenance of agency capacities; and 'additive' needs are necessary for improving them. Needs within these three levels are also hierarchically ordered. To the extent that there are any problems with specifying the precise content of these features, the content of the PGC is controversial. However, it is possible to specify at least some generic features of agency unambivalently (e.g., life), and the criterion for being a generic feature of agency (being a categorical agency need) makes the content of the PGC, at least in principle, objectively determinate.

2. This is Gewirth's foundational argument for the PGC as against his applications of the PGC to resolve particular moral problems.

3. See note 1.

4. The 'ought' here is logical, generated by the need to avoid contradicting that one is a PPA. The 'ought' prescribed by the PGC is not logical, but moral. (See Beyleveld, 1991, p. 104).

5. This is because it is pointless to prescribe to X that X ought to do y/may do y, unless X can choose to do y or refrain from doing so (i.e., unless X is a PPA.)

6. Contrary to the claim of Bond (1980, pp. 36–7), the *dialectical* necessity of the PGC does not reduce morality to logic. (See Beyleveld, 1991, pp. 102–5).

7. We include under this heading not only John Austin's Imperativism and what Hans Kelsen calls 'realism', but also any position (whether or not it belongs to the 'analytical' tradition of jurisprudence) that does not characterise legal validity as a matter of authorisation by norms, but in terms of enforcement.

8. For example, Hart (1961), Kelsen (1967) and MacCormick (1978). Normative positivists make legal validity a matter of authorisation by norms. But these norms *need not* be moral as a matter of *conceptual* necessity. (Hart's thesis of 'the minimum content of natural law', his view that *stable* societies (causally) require a specific content of rules, is not a thesis about the concept of legal validity, and involves no concession to the *conceptual* thesis of natural law theory.)

9. This means that the objects of an interest in law may not be taken to be legally valid if they are immoral. 'Law' does not bear the same meaning in both of its occurrences in this slogan; so the slogan is not self-contradictory.

10. See Beyleveld and Brownsword, 1986, ch. 3.

11. On two specific grounds: against Stage I (see below), that PPAs need not hold their F&WB to be necessary goods, because some have not done so; against Stage II, that it is not necessary for 'law makers', by *logical* universalisation, to grant rights to F&WB to all other PPAs (only, in principle, to other 'law-makers' – but, in practice, to no-one else, because, in 'non-revolutionary societies', the 'law-maker is unique' (Ockleton, 1988, p. 236)).

    The first observation is irrelevant, unless Gewirth were arguing that it is logically *impossible* for PPAs to violate or eschew the PGC (whereas he is arguing that it is logically *impermissible* for them to do so). The second claim is false *if Stage II is valid,* for then (as we argue in our consideration of the validity of Stage II below) it is dialectically necessary for PPAs (regardless of their contingent characteristics) to consider that the sufficient reason why they have rights to F&WB is that they are PPAs, under which claim they must grant these rights to all other PPAs by logical universalisation. And it is worth noting that Ockleton is also wrong to suggest that 'law-makers' must grant these rights to other law-makers because they are 'law-makers'. They would only be required to do so by logical universalisation if it were dialectically necessary for them to consider that the sufficient reason why they have the rights is because they are 'law-makers' (which is not the case).

12. Indeed, quite popular, including the 'contractarianism' of Rawls (1971) and of Gauthier (1986), and 'moral point of view' theories such as that of Hare (1981), and all forms of utilitarianism.

13. In particular, the principle of non-contradiction, the law of identity, *modus ponens, modus tollens,* and the predicative principle of sufficient reason (or logical principle of universalisability).

14. The features of voluntariness and proactive purposive intent that define a PPA as the addressee of practical precepts.
15. That is to say, bind their addressees irrespective of what they might or might not wish to do.
16. Not to legal positivism, we hasten to add, but to 'conventionalism' (the view that, in the final analysis, concepts of law are stipulations that cannot be rationally adjudicated), *unless* legal positivists can establish that it is logically necessary for PPAs to hold that there is no conceptually necessary connection between law and morality. But, if a dialectically necessary vindication of natural law theory is impossible, why should it be thought that a dialectically necessary vindication of legal positivism is possible?
17. The argument is conducted from a PPA's (any PPA's) first-person perspective on its agency. The reader may imagine that he or she is the 'I' to whom we refer in our discussion.
18. This qualification corresponds to presentation of the argument as one to at least negative rights (rights to non-interference). However, like Gewirth (see Gewirth, 1978, p. 218; Gewirth, 1984, pp. 228–9), we hold that the argument is valid as an argument to positive rights (rights to aid) as well. (See Beyleveld, 1991, ch. 10.)
19. 'PPA' in subscript standing for 'any (or every) PPA'.
20. This has been done in Beyleveld (1991), in which Gewirth's argument is reconstructed with some emendations, and (by intent) all published objections (in English, minimally by June 1989) are considered under 66 headings with numerous variants. Our presentation of the argument follows Beyleveld (1991).
21. The voluntariness that characterises a PPA is not present where a PPA merely does what it wants to do, for desires may be compulsive or the products of forced choices over which the PPA has no control, and thus not objects that practical precepts directed at the PPA can affect through its agency.
22. 'IP' = 'I proactively value'.
23. 'IC' = 'I categorically need'.
24. The judgments of value in Stage I are not necessarily moral. The value that I attach to a particular occurrent purpose is in terms of whatever criteria I follow in choosing to pursue a purpose (see Gewirth, 1978, pp. 49–50). This evaluation need not involve conscious reflective appraisal – it might be dispositional only (see ibid., p. 50); and it also need not be definitive. I could choose to be motivated by a criterion that I consider I ought not to be motivated by (see ibid.). The value that I must attach to my F&WB, however, is definitive, because my F&WB must be at least instrumentally good in terms of *whatever* criteria I might follow in choosing to pursue purposes. The value that I must attach to my F&WB is not value relative to some particular occurrent criteria but not others. It is value *relative only to my being a PPA (*to my possessing a voluntary motivation to pursue some purpose/s). Failure to appreciate one or more of these things is responsible for many criticisms of Stage I (which are considered in Beyleveld, 1991, ch. 4).
25. 'ORO' = 'other-referring/directed "ought"'.
26. 'MyR' = 'My right'.

27. 'PPAOR' = 'PPAO's right'.
28. With one proviso. 'I am a PPA' must be interpreted as 'I am a member of the class of beings who necessarily value their own purposes'. Scheuermann (1987, p. 304), who (we think) accepts that [I am a PPA → {I am a PPA → MyR}$_I$], claims (as we interpret him) that 'I am a PPA' must be taken to stand for 'I am a member of the class of beings who necessarily value *my own* purposes', and cannot, without begging the question, be taken to stand for 'I am a member of the class of beings who necessarily value *their own* purposes'. (See Beyleveld, 1991, pp. 288–300 for a refutation of this claim.)
29. We think that this is better called 'the argument *for* the sufficiency of agency', because it is an argument for having to claim agency as the sufficient condition for having a right to F&WB from the premise that agency is the sufficient condition for having to consider that one has this right. Calling it an argument *from* the sufficiency of agency concentrates attention on the premise when it is the conclusion that needs to be highlighted.
30. IP (my having the property of a proactive evaluational relation to my purposes) or IC (my having the property of a categorical need for F&WB) could, rather than my being a PPA, be cited as the sufficient reason for my having MyR, because both of these properties are *necessarily* possessed by me as a PPA.
31. Friedman (1981, p. 153), for example, implicitly denies the validity of the ASA. O'Meara (1982, p. 375) is the *only* critic who explicitly does so. (For replies, see Beyleveld, 1991, pp. 244–6, 251–2.)
32. Gewirth himself expresses the LPU as follows: '[I]f some predicate P belongs to some subject S because S has the property Q (where the 'because' is that of sufficient reason or condition), then P must also belong to all other subjects $S_1, S_2 ..., S_n$ that have Q' (Gewirth, 1978, p. 105).
33. It is important to appreciate that Gewirth's criteria of rationality are restricted to canons of deductive and inductive logic. Dialectically necessary claims are ones that a PPA must make on pain of *logically* contradicting that it is a PPA. Thus, despite Gewirth's insistence that the claims of Stages I and II are 'prudential' (see note 34), the universalisation that effects Stage III is intended to be purely logical. Gewirth does not argue that a PPA must grant PPAOR because the PPA needs PPAO to have a right to PPAO's F&WB. And, if the logical universalisation is valid, then it is irrelevant that, in terms of its particular occurrent purposes, it might not be 'prudent' for a PPA to grant PPAOR – a claim that is (correctly) made by Narveson (1979, pp. 429–30). Gewirth's argument is not a form of utilitarian cost-benefit analysis.
34. Because it is part of Gewirth's definition of a moral (as against a non-moral) position that it be *other-regarding* (i.e., that favourable account be taken by it of the interests, especially the most important interests, of PPAs other than or in addition to the PPA who adopts the position), Gewirth calls the claims prior to Stage II 'prudential', because they are validated by *my* interests (hence, *self-regarding*), without the assumption that I am altruistically motivated (though I

am not, thereby, *prohibited* from having altruistic motivations; see Gewirth, 1978, p. 71). Some philosophers would define 'a moral position' differently, and some would consider the claims of Stage II to be 'moral' simply because they are deontic. However, Gewirth's definition of 'morality' has no more than a terminological effect on his argument. Gewirth is concerned to demonstrate that PPAs must accept an other-regarding criterion of practical reasonableness with a determinate content (the PGC), not with labelling this principle 'moral'. Stage I purports to show that PPAs must accept (determinate) self-directing deontic claims. Stage II purports to show that they must accept other-directed deontic claims on self-regarding criteria at least; and Stage III purports to show that they must accept other-regarding deontic claims as well.

35. For example, Bond (1980, pp. 49–50), Lomasky (1981, pp. 249–50), MacCormick (1984, p. 347), Hare (1984), Harman (1983, pp. 117–18), McMahon (1986, p. 269) and Kalin (1984, pp. 142–4).
36. For example, all the critics mentioned in footnote 35.
37. Most clearly, Harman (1983, p. 118) and Hare (1984, p. 56).
38. This is, in terms of frequency, the single most important objection to Gewirth's argument. An other-*directed* claim is one that prescribes requirements for PPAO's actions (prescribes *to* PPAO). An other-*directing* claim is one that PPAO takes as offering good reasons for it to act (prescribes *for* PPAO). As Gewirth intends 5, it must be prescribed *by me* to PPAO, because justified on grounds (my categorical interests) that *I* must accept; but no assumption is permitted that *PPAO* will or must take these grounds as offering *it* good reasons to act.
39. It should be noted that, although MyR is not taken to be other-directing in Stage II, once it is established that $\{PPAOR\}_I$ (by the internal application of the LPU), and hence that $\{MyR\}_{PPAO}$ (by the external application of the LPU), it is *ultimately* established that I must think that I have a right to F&WB ($\equiv$I must think that PPAO categorically ought not to interfere with my F&WB) in the other-*directing* sense that some critics wish to reserve for the expression 'a right'. (For, it follows from $[(I \text{ am a PPA} \rightarrow \{PPAO\}_I) \rightarrow \{MyR\}_{PPAO}]$ that $\{\{MyR\}_{PPAO}\}_I$).
40. A 'formal' statement of obligation merely asserts what is required by a criterion, and is independent of endorsement of the criterion. A 'prescriptive' statement endorses a criterion that validates the requirement. This corresponds, somewhat, to Kelsen's distinction between 'objective' and 'subjective' 'oughts' (see Kelsen, 1967, pp. 17–23).
41. It is not enough to say that statements of (necessary) good are not *necessarily* universalisable. This leaves it open for certain sorts of statements of (necessary) good to be *necessarily* universalisable; and the argument only requires that *its kind* of necessary good be necessarily universalisable.
42. Incidentally, this analysis entails that a PPA, even if it chooses to permit interference with its F&WB, must, by universalisation, still grant PPAO a right to non-interference with PPAO's F&WB against PPAO's will.

43. We hope to clarify these relations at a later date.
44. We distinguish the realm of law (that of legal-*moral* rights and duties) from that of *non-legal* moral rights and duties under the aspect of the question of a right to *enforce* rules and activities, rather than under the aspect of the question of what activities must/may be performed (see Beyleveld and Brownsword, 1986, pp. 168–9).
45. We may have misunderstood Norrie here. He might be pointing to difficulties inherent in the notion of normative positivism, difficulties that we ourselves hold to be insuperable (see Beyleveld and Brownsword, 1989). But, if so, then there is no difficulty for us; for in no sense do we wish to secure a normative *positivism*.
46. Complete clarification of our position requires a comprehensive critique of philosophical developments since Kant. However, the validity of Gewirth's argument can be appreciated without attending to such matters, and is sufficient to indicate that there is something seriously awry with the main paths taken by post-Kantian philosophy.

REFERENCES

Arrington, R. (1989), *Rationalism, Realism, and Relativism: Perspectives in Contemporary Moral Epistemology*, New York: Cornell University Press.

Beyleveld, D. (1991), *The Dialectical Necessity of Morality: An Analysis and Defense of Alan Gewirth's Argument to the Principle of Generic Consistency*, Chicago: University of Chicago Press.

Beyleveld, D. and Brownsword, R. (1986), *Law as a Moral Judgment*, London: Sweet and Maxwell.

———— (1989), 'Normative Positivism: the mirage of the middle-way,' *Oxford Journal of Legal Studies* 9/4: 463–512.

Bond, E. J. (1980), 'Gewirth on reason and morality', *Metaphilosophy* 11: 36–53.

Davies, C. (1975), 'Egoism and consistency', *Australasian Journal of Philosophy* 53/1: 19–27.

Friedman, R.B. (1981), 'The basis and content of human rights: a criticism of Gewirth's theory', in J. R. Pennock and J. W. Chapman (eds), *Nomos XXIII: Human Rights*, New York: New York University Press, pp. 148–57.

Gamwell, F. I. (1984), *Beyond Preference: Liberal Theories of Independent Associations*, Chicago: University of Chicago Press.

Gauthier, D. (1986), *Morals By Agreement*, Oxford: Clarendon Press.

Gewirth, A. (1978), *Reason and Morality*, Chicago: University of Chicago Press.

———— (1984), 'Replies to my critics', in Edward Regis Jr (ed.), *Gewirth's Ethical Rationalism*, Chicago, University of Chicago Press, pp. 192–255.

———— (1988), 'The justification of morality', *Philosophical Studies*, 53: 245–62.

Hare, R. M. (1981), *Moral Thinking*, Oxford: Clarendon Press.

———— (1984), 'Do agents have to be moralists?', in Edward Regis Jr (ed.), *Gewirth's Ethical Rationalism*, Chicago: University of Chicago Press, pp. 52–8.

Harman, G. (1983), 'Justice and moral bargaining', *Social Philosophy and Policy* 1/1: 114–31.

Hart, H. L. A. (1961), *The Concept of Law*, Oxford: Clarendon Press.

Held, V. (1979), 'Review of *Reason and Morality*, by Alan Gewirth', *Social Theory and Practice* 5: 243–50.

Kalin, J. (1984) 'Public pursuit and private escape: the persistence of Egoism', in

Edward Regis Jr (ed.), *Gewirth's Ethical Rationalism,* Chicago: University of Chicago Press, pp. 128–46.

Kant, I. (1965), *The Metaphysical Elements of Justice* (Part I of *The Metaphysics of Morals,* originally published in 1797) (transl. J. Ladd), Indianapolis: Bobbs-Merrill.

Kelsen, H. (1967), *Pure Theory of Law* (transl. M. Knight from the 2nd revised, enlarged edition, 1960), Berkeley: University of California Press.

Lomasky, L. E. (1981), 'Gewirth's generation of rights', *Philosophical Quarterly* 31: 248–53.

MacCormick, N. (1978), *Legal Reasoning and Legal Theory,* Oxford: Clarendon Press.

—— (1984), 'Gewirth's fallacy', *Queen's Law Journal* 9/2: 345–51.

MacIntyre, A. (1981), *After Virtue: A Study in Moral Theory,* Notre Dame, Indiana: University of Notre Dame Press.

McMahon, C. (1986), 'Gewirth's justification of morality', *Philosophical Studies* 50: 261–81.

Narveson, J. (1979), 'Review of *Reason and Morality,* by Alan Gewirth', *Political Theory* 7: 428–31.

Ockleton, M. (1988), 'Review of *Law as a Moral Judgment,* by Deryck Beyleveld and Roger Brownsword', *Legal Studies* 8/2: 234–8.

O'Meara, W. M. (1982), 'Gewirth and Adams on the foundation of morality', *Philosophy Research Archives,* 8: 367–81.

Paske, G. H. (1989), 'Magic and morality: remarks on Gewirth and Hare', *Journal of Value Inquiry* 23: 51–8.

Rawls, J. (1971), *A Theory of Justice,* Cambridge, MA: Harvard University Press.

Scheuermann, J. (1987), 'Gewirth's concept of prudential rights', *Philosophical Quarterly* 37: 291–304.

White S. K. (1982), 'On the normative structure of action: Gewirth and Habermas', *Review of Politics* 44: 282–301.

Williams, B. (1985), *Ethics and the Limits of Philosophy,* Cambridge, MA: Harvard University Press.

3

'The Rose in the Cross of the Present': Closure and Critique in Hegel's Philosophy of Right

ROBERT FINE

> To recognise reason as the rose in the cross of the present and thereby to enjoy the present, this rational insight is the *reconciliation* with reality which philosophy grants to those who have received the inner call to *comprehend*, to preserve their subjective freedom and at the same time to stand with their subjective freedom ... in what exists absolutely.
>
> (Hegel, 1991, p. 22)[1]

INTRODUCTION

Hegel's *The Philosophy of Right* has rarely been a popular text: attacked by liberals as a recipe for state authoritarianism or even totalitarianism, by Marxists as an uncritical justification of undemocratic aspects of the modern capitalist state, and by postmodernists as a form of 'foundationalism' whose commitment to the 'absolute' is at best a relic of classicism, at worst a token of totalitarian intent. If there is one thing which liberalism, Marxism and postmodernism have in common, it is their shared hostility to Hegel's philosophy of right.

In my view, the unpopularity of *The Philosophy of Right* is closely related to the challenge that it poses to modern political theory. Hegel polemicised against the 'shallow thinking' and 'sophistries' of his contemporaries, including both the reactionary Von Haller and the radical Fries. His assessments of the Enlightenment, though more respectful, were no less critical. Kant's constitutional doctrine of representative government, Rousseau's radical doctrine of popular sovereignty, Montesquieu's theory of 'division of powers', Fichte's theory of the 'ephorate', Adam Smith's 'laisser-faire' theory of the state, indeed modern natural law theories in their entirety were confronted. It is the nature of Hegel's challenge and the (in)capacity of modern social theory to meet it that is my subject.

The 'traditional' liberal critique of *The Philosophy of Right* is that it was an ode to authoritarian statism. The more productive and faithful way in which modern scholarship has recovered the text, however, is to read it as an effort to reconcile 'subjective freedom' and 'what exists absolutely', the principle of Christianity and that of the ancient *polis*. Within this general interpretive framework, however, there have been marked differences of emphasis.

The radical liberal reading is that Hegel's synthesis was successful as a harbinger of the modern social democratic state, or at least as easily corrected to expel from the text Hegel's personal compromises with Prussian authoritarianism. Marxists have read *The Philosophy of Right* as a failed synthesis which nonetheless pointed the way to a higher form of freedom beyond bourgeois private property. Civil society theorists have read *The Philosophy of Right* as prescribing the transformation of civil society into a 'public sphere' that is the locus of sovereignty.

Though these approaches capture in different ways the limitations of the traditional polemics against *The Philosophy of Right*, it is my contention that they fail to grasp the positive contribution of the text to the critique of law. The result is a repetition of the same defects which Hegel had already identified and surpassed. The key point is that *The Philosophy of Right* is a foundational text for critical legal theory, not because it offers a prescription for what the ideal forms of right *ought to be*, but rather because it offers a scientific treatment of what they *actually are*. To miss the 'objective' rather than 'normative' character of *The Philosophy of Right* is not only to misread the text, it is also to lose sight of the scientific advance made by Hegel's critique.

THE LIBERAL DEFENCE OF RIGHTS AND HEGEL'S CRITIQUE OF LIBERALISM

The outrage expressed by liberal critics towards *The Philosophy of Right* focused on Hegel's claim that the existence of individuals is 'a matter of indifference to the objective ethical order which alone is steadfast' (§145 A) or that subjective rights are merely 'abstract, unreal moments' while the state is the 'actuality of the ethical idea' (§257). The crime for which *The Philosophy of Right* was indicted was to legitimise authoritarian statism under the philosophical sophistry that 'what is, is reason' (1991, p. 21).

When a degenerate form of 'Hegelianism' became the official doctrine of the nineteenth-century Prussian state, liberals such as Rudolf Haym complained bitterly that the Preface to *The Philosophy of Right* – with its assertion that 'the rational is real and the real is rational' and that the 'rational insight' of philosophy is 'the reconciliation with actuality' – was 'nothing other than a scholarly justification of the Karlsbad police state and its political persecution' (Haym, 1857, cited in Hyland, 1990, p. 1774).

A century later, *The Philosophy of Right* was charged by liberalism with responsibility for (or at least complicity in) the rise of fascist ideologies. Hobhouse (1918) described it as a 'false and wicked doctrine' which inverted the freedom of the individual into the freedom of the state against the individual. Karl Popper wrote that, in Hegel's theory, 'the power and expansion of the state must overrule all other considerations in the private life of the citizens', and characterised Hegel as an enemy of the 'open society' (Popper, 1966, p. 2). Ernst Cassirer wrote that 'no other philosophical system has done so much for the preparation of fascism and imperialism as Hegel's doctrine of the state' (Cassirer, 1946, p. 273). Bertrand Russell was convinced that Hegel's doctrine of the date 'justifies every internal tyranny and every external aggression that can possibly be imagined' (Russell, 1948, pp. 768–9). John Plamenatz commented on the 'unpleasant tone' of 'colossal arrogance' which ran through *The Philosophy of Right*, warning the reader to 'mistrust the arrogant, especially when they speak of freedom' (Plamenatz, 1963, p. 268). The list of indictments is long and ongoing.

In the introduction to the new Cambridge University Press edition of *The Philosophy of Right*, Allen Wood writes that this image of Hegel as philosopher of the reactionary Prussian restoration and forerunner of modern totalitarianism is 'simply wrong' (Hegel, 1991, p. ix). His argument is that, in relation to the institutions of his own time, Hegel's political theory of the state – supporting a written constitution, a professional civil service, public criminal trials, trials by jury, representative institutions, etc. – firmly sided with the Prussian reform movement against the old state establishment.

This is true, but I think that the problem goes deeper, for the liberal indictment of *The Philosophy of Right* as the emblem of authoritarian statism was based on liberalism's own guilty conscience. Hegel's 'ideal' state was an abstract representation of the modern liberal state, stripped of its illusions, its anatomy laid bare to the public eye, its inner relations freed from the mask of 'popular sovereignty' which surrounds it. It was not Hegel's ideal, but the ideal of the modern state that *The Philosophy of Right* was designed to portray. When liberalism attacked Hegel for *his* authoritarianism, it projected its anxieties about the message onto the messenger; the bearer of ill tidings was crucified as its author. In *The Philosophy of Right*, Hegel exposed the hidden authoritarianism of the modern state, the state of liberalism itself. Rather than meet the challenge posed by Hegel, liberalism ducked it.

Look 'objectively' at the '*thing itself*', Hegel insisted, not at the aura of sanctity which surrounds it. There is perhaps no aura more sanctified in modern society – more difficult to penetrate scientifically – than that which surrounds the hallowed ground of liberal institutions. Behind the furious indignation of liberalism lay the trauma of seeing its own most *'hardened prejudices'* (Hegel, 1989, p. 121) in favour of private property, bourgeois civil society, constitutionalism, representative government, etc. brought to the light of day, laid out on a table and dispassionately dissected.

Hegel reminded liberalism of its own degeneration from a vision of 'absolute freedom' to its subordination to the demands of capitalist private property. What we might call 'vulgar' liberalism grasped one side of modern freedom, which Hegel called 'the right of subjective freedom' and especially private property, identifying liberty in general with 'negative liberty' of doing what you please without interference. Declaring that the sole function of the state was to be the 'nightwatchman', impartially protecting the property rights of all, it dissipated the riches of its classical origins.

Hegel had a better understanding of classical liberalism than liberal critics who simply rose to the defence of the right of private property against the claims of the state. He saw that the framework of classical liberal thought was *triadic* rather than *dyadic* – not devoted to affirming private right against public authority, property against the state, but to theorising the form of state appropriate to a market society, which could on the one hand serve as a guarantee of private property and on the other resolve the contradictions deriving from private property (Tully, 1982; Winch, 1978, Fine, 1985; Fine, 1991).

Hegel recognised that classical liberalism operated within a formal dialectic of thesis, antithesis and synthesis. The *thesis* was the idealisation of private property as the natural or rational foundation of ethical life and social organisation. Private property appeared as the foundation of free individuality, the breakdown of artificial hierarchies and dependencies, the wealth of nations, the evolution of morality and culture, all the individualistic virtues of reflection, romantic love, conscience, etc.

The *antithesis* consisted of the contradictions which beset modern civil society based on the free movement of private property and the generalisation of exchange relations. These contradictions took off from the disintegrative effects of universal egoism, the 'war of all against all', in which life becomes 'nasty, brutish and short' (Hobbes); proceeded to the growth of social inequalities between rich and poor (Rousseau) and of class antagonisms between owners of labour, land and capital (Smith); and culminated in the loss of public spirit among all classes, with the consequent growth of state despotism.

The *synthesis* was provided by the emergence of the modern state (though not usually by the state alone). On the one hand, the ideal state would reconcile the antagonisms of civil society – tempering self-interest through a framework of law, guaranteeing mutual respect, alleviating poverty, reducing inequality, fostering public spirit, educating those culturally impoverished by the division of labour, performing public works left undone by private property, etc. On the other hand, the ideal state would embody in its own form and institutions the general will or public interest of the people as a whole, allowing for a state of natural liberty in which the self-regulation of society by society would replace the blind forces of nature.

Within the framework of classical jurisprudence, some were more optimistic than others about the possibility of effecting this synthesis, but this did not affect their basic way of seeing. Hegel recognised that it was within this architectonic that the classical liberalism fought out its differences: not on the basis of simply affirming property right against state authority, but on the basis of their reconciliation. In *The Philosophy of Right*, Hegel characterised classical liberalism through a formal dialectical structure which enriched and explained the triadic relations not yet explicit in the former.

THE RADICAL NEGATION OF RIGHTS AND HEGEL'S CRITIQUE OF RADICALISM

Recognition of the relation of *The Philosophy of Right* to classical liberalism led new generations of Hegel-readers to draw the conclusion that the text was located firmly *within* the classical liberal tradition and made them blind to the extent of his disagreement. Such a rendering emerged with particular sharpness in the anti-Nazi period among scholars seeking to rescue Hegel from the totalitarian image projected upon his work.

Karl Lowith argued in this mode that the task of the modern European state set by *The Philosophy of Right* 'is to reconcile the principle of the *polis* – substantive generality – with the principle of Christian religion – subjective individuality' (Lowith, 1967, pp. 240–1). Lowith read with sceptical astonishment, however, Hegel's apparent belief that reconciliation was not only possible in the modern state but also achieved in the Prussian state! This theory, he insisted, took little account of the problems which were to

> determine the future development of bourgeois society: how to control the poverty brought about by wealth ... the progressive division of labour ... the necessity of organising for the masses forcing their way upward ... and the collision with liberalism ... the increasing claims of the will of the many ... which now seeks to rule by force of numbers. (Lowith, 1967, pp. 240–1)

Take these problems into account, Lowith concluded, and they explain why Hegel's search for 'the mean' was soon to be overtaken by the Young Hegelians who 'demanded decisions in place of mediations' and became 'radical and extreme'.

Herbert Marcuse pushed this line of thought further when he summarised Hegel's doctrine thus:

The anarchy of self-seeking property owners could not produce from its mechanism an integrated, rational and universal social scheme. At the same time, a proper social order ... could not be imposed with private property rights [denied,] for the free individual would be annulled ... The task of making the necessary integration devolved, therefore, upon an institution that would stand above the individual interests ... and yet would preserve their holdings. (Marcuse, 1968, p. 201)

By contrast, Marcuse argued, National Socialism represented the seizure of the state by the most powerful interests of civil society – the corporations, trusts and cartels – which used it to mould the economy to the needs of monopoly production, destroy working-class opposition and wage expansionary war. The Nazi 'state' had become exactly what Hegel warned against, an instrument used by one element of civil society to terrorise the rest: 'Civil society under Fascism rules the state; Hegel's state rules civil society' (Marcuse, 1968, p. 216). Fascism expressed the violence of modern civil society when its subordination to the state broke down.

Carl Schmitt was not wrong when he wrote that, on the day of Hitler's rise to power, 'Hegel so to speak died' (Schmitt, 1933, p. 32). From the opposite standpoint, Franz Neumann appreciated that Hegelianism was incompatible with the German racial myth because Hegel's state stood for the realisation of reason, which meant individual rights, the rule of law and an impartial bureaucracy acting on the basis of rational and calculable norms (Neumann, 1942, pp. 69–73). There could be no greater contrast with the *Führerprinzip* than Hegel's doctrine of the rational state, based on the reconciliation of individual rights and constitutional authority.

Marcuse argued, however, that authoritarian tendencies were present in Hegel's *concept* of the 'rational state' and that these were derived from the antagonistic structure of bourgeois civil society which necessitated *in actuality* the tendency to state authoritarianism. Hegel's irrational embodiment of the 'rational state' appeared as but a mirror of the actual bourgeois state, the betrayal of its liberal ideals seemingly determined by the chasm between the concentration of modern capital and living labour.

Hegel was guilty, in Marcuse's view, 'of betraying his highest philosophical ideals' by reflecting 'the destiny of the social order that falls, while in pursuit of its freedom, into a state of nature far below reason' (Marcuse, 1968, p. 218). But Hegel was right to be less deterministic about the death of liberalism than Marcuse. The same class relations between capital and labour which produced the demise of classical liberalism also ushered in the rise of new forms of radical liberalism in the shape of labourism and social democracy. The development of the modern proletariat did not only threaten the legal order from below, it also buttressed the legal order through the weight of its own demands.

According to Marcuse, Hegel's authoritarianism could not be undone as long as he conceived totality as a 'closed ontological system' based on natural presuppositions and identical with the end of history. It seemed that Hegel's 'deduction of private property from the essence of the free will' was the presupposition which deprived his concept of critical content, spawned his defence of the modern state and turned his philosophy of freedom into one of necessity. Marcuse criticised Hegel for conceiving totality as 'the totality of reason, a closed ontological system, finally identical with the rational system of history' (Marcuse, 1968, p. 314). Marcuse's solution was to 'detach dialectic from this ontological base' and move beyond what Marx called 'the abstract, logical, speculative expression of the movement of history' (Marcuse, 1968, p. 315). Marcuse sought to surpass 'the prevailing negativity' of bourgeois forms of right and to aim towards the establishment of 'a new order of things'.

Breaking from Lowith's reading of Marx as 'radical and extreme' in favour of a communistic community, Marcuse read Marx as the true heir to Hegel's search for the 'mean'. Did not Marx from his earliest writings dismiss as 'primitive' that form of communism which 'negates man's personality' and has not yet 'reached the level of private property' (Marx, 1975, p. 346)? True communism is the full development of individuals in all their faculties alongside the full development of the community, the reconciliation of 'subjectivism and objectivism, spiritualism and materialism, activity and passivity' (Marx, 1975, p. 348). As Marcuse put it, 'communism, with its *positive* abolition of private property, is of its very nature a new form of individualism' (Marcuse, 1968, p. 286). In the association of free individuals, 'the particular and the common interest have been merged' (ibid., p. 283).

Rereading Marx's relation to Hegel in this fashion allowed Marcuse to free Marxism from the primitive grip of Stalinist 'collectivism', but at the expense of 'ontologising' Hegel's *The Philosophy of Right*. Not only did Marcuse misread Hegel – by turning the object of his critique into the ideal subject of his commitments – but as a consequence he repeated the defect which Hegel had endeavoured to forestall: an abstract notion of freedom ('the negation of the negation') which exists only 'in the philosopher's opinions' and 'overleaps its own age' (Preface, p. 11). The relation of Marcuse to Hegel was the inverse of what Marcuse thought it to be: Hegel rooted philosophy in historical reality when he affirmed that 'philosophy is its own time apprehended in thoughts'; it was Marcuse who wished to 'jump over Rhodes' (Preface, p. 11).

The substantive issue was the relation of freedom to 'right'. Hegel wrote in respect of the reactionary, von Haller, that 'hatred of law, of

legally determined *right*, is the shibboleth whereby fanaticism, imbecility
and hypocritical good intentions manifestly and infallibly reveal themselves for what they are, no matter what disguise they adopt' (§258 R).
Against the radical Fries, Hegel wrote in similar vein that hatred of the law
is 'the chief shibboleth by which the false brethren and friends of the so-
called "people" give themselves away' (Preface, p. 7). If the possibility
and truth immanent in bourgeois right is the self-conscious activity of free
individuals and in the modern state is humankind becoming 'the conscious subject of its own development' (Marcuse, 1968, p. 316), Marcuse
argued that the realisation of the idea of freedom requires liberation from
the forms of right themselves, the transcendence of the given historical
reality.

Marcuse of course cannot be compared with von Haller or Fries, but
his abstract opposition of freedom to right, justice to law, universality to
the state, reproduces the same shibboleth. His conviction that the prevailing state of affairs is one of 'universal negativity' (p. 288) and that Hegel's
philosophy of right 'preserved and in the last analysis condoned the
negativity of the existing system' (p. 294) was based on an 'affirmative
materialism' which affirms 'the idea of happiness' and 'material satisfaction' over that of right. However narrow the horizon of bourgeois right
might be, Marx, by contrast, appreciated that it must necessarily be
preserved in socialist society, albeit with 'form and content changed'
(Marx, 1970, pp. 319–20). Though the principle of communism was
affirmed as 'to each according to his or her needs, from each according to
his or her abilities', the *positive* supersession of right is necessarily the
endpoint of its fullest extension and development. Certainly, Marx had
his own ambivalences, but the dialectic of 'right' and 'need' derived from
Hegel's philosophy transcended Marcuse's abstract negations. In spite of
his profound understanding of the totalitarian suppression of rational law,
whether in the form of National Socialism or Soviet Marxism, Marcuse's
negation of right could not escape the trap of legal nihilism.

CIVIL SOCIETY THEORY AND HEGEL'S CRITIQUE OF CIVIL SOCIETY

The trajectory taken by the scholarly interpretation of Hegel's political
philosophy in the postwar period mirrored the new-found self-confidence
of liberalism. Its fundamental proposition was that the integration of civil
and political freedom could be achieved *within the forms of bourgeois right*.
For example, Shlomo Avineri portrayed *The Philosophy of Right* as a prescription for 'a modern state, free from the shackles of the old absolutism,
based on representation, served by a rationally ordered bureaucracy,
allowing ample space for voluntary associations and trying to strike a
balance ... between *homo economicus* and *zoom politikon*' (Avineri, 1972,
p. 240). K. H. Ilting conceded that there was an authoritarian thread

running through *The Philosophy of Right*, but that it represented no more than Hegel's own concession to Prussian reaction in violation of his basic philosophy. Purified of the old man's compromises, *The Philosophy of Right* could easily be revised as an integrative philosophy of civil and political freedom (Ilting, 1984, p. 105; Ilting, 1971).

The idea of 'two Hegels' fighting an internal battle became a dominant theme within the interpretive literature. One side of Hegel, it seemed, treated the state as a secular deity whose claims upon its citizens are always 'unquestionable and irresistible'; the other side identified universality with a free body of citizens. It was the latter idea which modern democratic thought embraced. For this reason, contemporary criticism has had a particularly ambivalent relation to *The Philosophy of Right*.

Jürgen Habermas placed his emphasis on *The Philosophy of Right*'s statist conception of absolute ethical life, reading it as a move away from the young Hegel's earlier recognition of intersubjectivity – that is, from a search for second-order norms which recognise the heterogeneity and plurality of modern society and which regulate social difference without imposing any absolute conceptions of social morality – toward the old man's implicitly totalitarian conception of the 'absolute' as embodied in the modern state. In this reading, the intersubjective dimension of Hegel's early thinking appears to have been defeated by his regression into absolute *Sittlichkeit*.

Habermas employed the concept of 'emphatic institutionalism' to support the claim that, in *The Philosophy of Right*, 'the individual will ... is totally bound to the institutional order and only justified at all to the extent that the institutions are one with it' (Habermas, 1990, p. 40). Contrasting Hegel's monarchical view of the state, elevated in *The Philosophy of Right* to 'something rational in and for itself', with the democratic self-organisation of society, Habermas argued that when the demand of democratic self-determination reached the older Hegel's ears, he could only hear it as a 'note of discord', since political movements which press beyond the boundaries set by philosophy 'offend against reason itself'. According to Habermas, Hegel's equation of the real and the rational absolved philosophy 'of the task of confronting with its concept the decadent existence of social and political life' (Habermas, 1990, p. 43). The result was 'the blunting of critique'.

From a similar standpoint, the opposite interpretation of Hegel has been developed within modern civil society theory. Andrew Arato declares the Hegel of *The Philosophy of Right* to be 'the representative theorist of civil society' (Arato, 1991, p. 301), though he too finds a conflict within the text. The *civil society* Hegel posits 'the autonomous generation of solidarity and identity' by means of the associations of civil society (estates and corporations), their representatives in parliament (the estates assembly) and public opinion. The *étatiste* Hegel imposes order on civil society by means of police, executive, crown and other organs of the state. Both the civil society and *étatiste* Hegels are present, but it is the former which appears to Arato as the true Hegel and foundation for 'the generation of a modern rational collective identity' (Arato, 1991, p. 316).

According to Arato, Hegel's concept of 'bourgeois civil society' is neither wholly civil nor wholly bourgeois but a dynamic whole, vulnerable to its own disintegrative tendencies, yet capable of performing the tasks of social integration with only peripheral help from the state. Hegel is said to have recognised that, in modern society, citizens have only a restricted part in the general business of the state, but regarded it as essential to provide people with activity of a general character over and above their private business. Hegel's innovation was that he expanded the liberties of civil society into rights of participation through mediating institutions such as corporations and estates. The corporations were to involve high levels of participation in a particularistic mode; the estates were to be universalistic but less participatory. The result was a proper balance of direct and representative democracy.

Arato's argument is that Hegel derived the category of a 'public sphere' from classical republican thought, but, instead of restricting it to a single social level, that of political society, 'a series of levels have key roles to play, including the public rights of private persons, the publicity of legal processes, the public life of the corporation, and finally the interaction between public opinion and the public deliberation of the legislature' (Arato, 1991, p. 318). *The Philosophy of Right* is turned into a normative theory of social integration based on the intermediate institutions of civil society operating within a public framework of legal regulation. The universal and particular (state and private property) are both recognised as 'rightful' but also as the two great disruptive forces of freedom: the one sweeping away all differentiation in the name of the 'general will', the other sweeping away all community in the name of private interest. Hegel's philosophy is reformulated as a normative sociology (prefiguring Durkheim and Parsons) which seeks to reconcile egoism and community, private property and the state, through the associational forms of modern civil society.

A similar argument is found in Fred Dallmayr's (1991) reading of *The Philosophy of Right*, when he argues for a new institutional format of the state which takes cognisance of the instrumentalisation of existing state structures in the hands of bureaucratic and economic elites. He locates the ideal state in the associations of civil society, in particular the new social movements which are attached to one another through 'rainbow coalitions', constitute an 'open-ended public space' and become the emblem of a 'democratic social bond'. How an aggregate of passing particular interests in civil society could be transformed into the institutional embodiment of the universal, and how this is consonant with Hegel's political philosophy, is unclear.

Habermas was right to read *The Philosophy of Right* as antithetical to civil society theory, since Hegel saw this resolution as entirely spurious. It was a sign of Habermas's own prejudices that he treated Hegel's opposition to civil society theory as proof of his 'absolutism'. Association, intersubjectivity and presence – the holy trinity invoked by Habermas, Arato, Dallmayr and others to turn civil society into the public sphere like water into wine – cannot possess the sacred qualities attributed to them.

Hegel characterised the creation of civil society as the 'achievement of the modern age which for the first time has given all the facets of the "idea" their due' (§182 A), but at the same time he identified the diremption of bourgeois civil society: because 'particularity and universality have become separated in civil society', he wrote, 'civil society affords a spectacle of (boundless) extravagance and misery as well as of the physical and ethical corruption common to both' (§185). If the state is confused with civil society, 'the interest of individuals *as such* becomes the ultimate end for which they are united' (§258 R). We are back to Marcuse's insight: Nazism was the triumph of the most powerful interests of civil society over the state. Modern civil society theory, however, seems unable to confront the violence of civil society; it cannot break from the assumption of its benevolence. The normative prescription that social integration *ought* to take place through the self-generated resources of civil society says nothing about what civil society is.

Through the lens of civil society theory, *The Philosophy of Right* becomes little more than a 'middle way' between individualism and collectivism, libertarianism and communitarianism. It is argued that Hegel's analysis of the legal sphere – as *necessary* to the development of 'relationships of mutual recognition and respect among autonomous social actors' – was superior to Marx's 'instrumentalist' rejection of law; and that Hegel's analysis of individual rights of property as *insufficient* – since they 'cannot alone bring about the common good' – was superior to liberalism's idealisation of the legal state as the 'impartial enforcer of generally applicable legal rules'. *The Philosophy of Right* is read as confirming that rights of private property are essential to intersubjective relationships based on mutual respect, but at the same time that individuals must be educated in the ethical life of the community as a whole (Cornell et al., 1991, pp. viii–ix). This simple compromise was then identified with Hegel's contribution to political thought.

SCIENCE AS CRITIQUE

It was pointed out that Hegel affirmed 'the right of subjective freedom' as the 'pivot and centre of the difference between antiquity and modern times' (§124 R). It was also recognised that the task of the modern state, as Hegel saw it, was to *reconcile* this principle of subjective right with that of universal will. Hegel's most affirmative statement of this position runs as follows:

> The principle of modern states has enormous strength and depth because it allows the principle of subjectivity to attain fulfilment in the self-sufficient extreme of personal particularity, while at the same time bringing it back to substantive unity (the state) and so preserving this unity in the principle of the subjectivity itself. ... The essence of the modern state is that the universal should be linked with the complete freedom of particularity and the well-being of individuals ... the universality of the end cannot make further progress without the personal knowledge and volition of the particular individuals who must retain their rights ... The universal must be activated but subjectivity must be developed as a living whole. Only when both moments are present in full measure can the state be regarded as articulated and truly organised. (§260 A)

When Hegel acknowledged the 'strength and depth' of this *principle of the modern state*, it did not mean that he uncritically adopted it as his own. On the contrary, Hegel went on to break decisively from the framework of classical liberalism and explore the hidden sphere of power relations.

In *The Philosophy of Right*, Hegel did not offer a *prescription* for what the ideal state ought to be; this conventional assimilation of *The Philosophy of Right* to modern natural law theory misses the whole point of his theory. It was not a philosophical blueprint for an ideal state – giving instruction on how it ought to be structured, what functions it ought to perform, where it ought to draw its limits – but a *scientific analysis* of the forms and functions of the *actual state*. It should therefore be assessed on these grounds.

That the purpose of *The Philosophy of Right* was not prescriptive but analytical was very clearly stated by Hegel in the Preface:

> As a work of philosophy, it must be poles apart from an attempt to construct a state *as it ought to be*. The instruction which it may contain cannot consist in teaching the state what it ought to be; it can only show how the state ... is to be understood. (Preface, p. 11)

Hegel rejected an approach which 'goes beyond the world as it is and builds an ideal one as it ought to be', for that world exists 'only in the philosopher's opinions, an unsubstantial element where anything you please may in fancy be built' (Preface, p. 11). When Hegel defines the task of philosophy as 'to comprehend *what is* ... for what is is reason', this is not to award either the existing state or some imagined state the philosophical prize of 'rationality', but to shift the ground of philosophy from the construction of the ideal to the science of the real. It was not a call for political quietism but for philosophy to discover reason in 'the actual'. Put simply, if we do not understand the rationality of the existing state, then we shall be unable to move beyond it. It certainly tells us not one jot about the nature of the state that it is or is not in accord with the idea of reason.

The modern state was the object of Hegel's 'scientific treatment', in the knowledge that the actual state 'is *no ideal art-work* but stands on earth and so in the sphere of caprice, accident and error' (§258 A). Hegel's own political opinions would 'count only as a personal epilogue and as capricious assertion' and should be treated 'with indifference'. What is important philosophically is the 'scientific discussion of the thing itself' (Preface, p. 13).

In *The Philosophy of Right*, Hegel traces the forms of 'right' from its simplest juridic category to its most complex. He begins with abstract right because this is the simplest expression of right as it is found in modern society. Step by step, we are taken through the increasingly complex forms of right present in modern society: private property, contract, wrong, punishment, morality, family, law, police, associations, state, constitution, monarchy, legislature, bureaucracy and relations between sovereign states. *The Philosophy of Right* is a an exploration of the juridic forms of right characteristic of modern society, analogous in many respects to the exploration of the economic forms of value carried out by Karl Marx in his critique of political economy. The movement from private property through law to the state is the juridic equivalent of the movement from value through money to capital. Indeed, *The Philosophy of Right* paved the way for Marx's *Grundrisse* and *Capital*, all of which were indebted to Hegel's *Logic* (Uchida, 1988).

Private property is not a 'natural presupposition' of *The Philosophy of Right* but only the simplest, most abstract expression of right. It is the starting point because it is the elementary atom out of which all more complex and concrete forms of right are constructed. It is not Hegel who derives private property from the idea of free will, but rather modern bourgeois society that turns private property into 'the first embodiment of freedom and therefore a substantial end in itself' (§40). What is at issue here is not Hegel's logical deduction of the particular from the universal but the materialisation of freedom in contemporary society.[2]

The purpose of *The Philosophy of Right* is to explore the relation between concept and experience of right. What we find at every point is contradiction, antagonism, antinomy. Thus, what first appears as the embodiment of freedom, private property, pays no heed to what and how much a person possesses. When Hegel declares that 'right is unconcerned about differences in individuals' (§49 A), it is Right that is unconcerned, not Hegel. It is Right that transforms all relations between people into property relations, so that the Law of Persons should be read as a derivation from the Law of Property and turns everything into an object for purchase and sale: 'mental endowments, science, art, even such matters of religion as sermons, masses, prayers, blessings' (§43). 'Persons' turn their own selves – including their capacity to labour – into property for sale. The idea of freedom which begins as the supremacy of persons over things is inverted by its own logic into the supremacy of things over persons.

The rule of reason turns into the rule of 'blind necessity' once we enter civil society; even the law reflects the abstractness of its origins in private property. Hegel concludes this section with the comment that 'by means of its own dialectic, civil society is driven beyond its own limits as a definite and complete society' (§246), and envisages a time when 'the labour of all will be subject to administrative regulation' (§236). The state whose concept is that of 'concrete freedom' and which starts life as the 'mind on earth consciously realising itself there' becomes the 'independent and autonomous power' in which 'individuals are mere moments'.

The state justifies monarchy on the ground that 'there must always be individuals at the head' (§279 R), raises the constitution to divine status as if it had no historical origins (§273 R), legitimates a House of Lords as a 'guarantee of surer ripeness of decision', treats the executive as having 'a deeper and more comprehensive insight into the nature of the state' than elected representatives (§301 R) and repudiates 'the democratic element … coming into the organism of the state without any rational form'. Finally, we are confronted with the state of nature in which sovereign states relate to one another through war as the inevitable test of sovereignty and means by which is 'strengthened the internal power of the state' (§324 A).

The different forms of right – property, law, state, etc. – are revealed as *intrinsically* related to one another by virtue of being more or less developed forms of right. The critical force of the concept of 'sublation' is lost when it is interpreted simply as a transition to a higher stage of freedom which preserves the lower stage as one of its moments. When civil society is revealed as a developed form of right and the state as a developed form of civil society, this means that the contradictions present in the lower form are preserved in the higher. Relations between property, law and the state are *not extrinsic*, as if for instance law is merely an instrument of private property or the state merely functions for the reproduction of civil society; rather, the form of law contains within itself all the *contradictions* immanent in private property, and the form of state contains within itself the contradictions immanent in civil society.

There was no reconciliation at the end of this road! Rather than offering a 'closed ontological system', it is the framework of classical liberalism that is finally undone in *The Philosophy of Right*. Well in advance of its materialisation, Hegel uncovered the authoritarian tendencies inherent in the modern state. It makes no sense either to turn the authoritarianism against which Hegel directed his critique into his own commitment or to will away this authoritarianism as something insignificant.

The Philosophy of Right represented the dialectic of freedom and necessity in modern society. It laid the *foundation* for the critique of juridic forms based on contradiction between form and content, concept and experience. Hegel does not tell us where resolution lies, but how could he? He wrote at the *dawn* of the modern state, whereas such knowledge arises like the owl of Minerva 'at the falling of the dusk' (Preface, p. 13).

NOTES

1. Henceforth, all unaccredited reference will refer to *The Philosophy of Right*. The sign '§' will refer to the paragraph in question; the letter 'A' to Hegel's Addition to that paragraph and the letter 'R' to Hegel's Remark on that paragraph. I have sometimes used Knox's translation and sometimes Nisbet's.
2. In his critique of Hegel's alleged logical derivation of the institution of private property from the ideas of free will, Waldron (1990) concludes that Hegel's 'central mistake was his failure to see that private property can be justified as a right of personality only if it can be made available to every person on whose behalf that argument can be made out' (p. 389). Waldron here obfuscates the nature of private property, according to which 'what and how much I possess is a matter of indifference' (§49). Smith (1991) argues that 'Hegel presents the emergence of rights as originating in the desire of two individuals, each seeking some sign of recognition from the other' (p. 115). Hegel recognised of course that the desire of individuals for mutual recognition long preceded the historical development of abstract rights (see Hegel, 1956, §3).

REFERENCES

Arato, A. (1991), 'A reconstruction of Hegel's theory of civil society', in Cornell et al. (eds), *Hegel and Legal Theory*, London: Routledge.

Avineri, S. (1972), *Hegel's Theory of the Modern State*, Cambridge: Cambridge University Press.

Cassirer, E. (1946), *The Myth of the State*, New Haven: Yale University Press.

Cornell, D., Rosenfeld, M. and Carlson, D. (eds) (1991), *Hegel and Legal Theory*, London: Routledge.

Dallmayr, F. (1991), 'Rethinking the Hegelian state', in Cornell et al. (eds), *Hegel and Legal Theory*, London: Routledge.

Fine, R. (1985), *Democracy and the Rule of Law: Liberal Ideals and Marxist Critiques*, London: Pluto Press.

────── (1991), 'Hegel's Critique of Law: a reappraisal', in R. de Lange and K. Raes, *Plural Legalities: Critical Legal Studies in Europe*, Nijmegen: Recht en Kritiek.

Habermas, J. (1990), *The Philosophical Discourse of Modernity*, Cambridge: Polity.

Haym, R. (1867), *Hegel und Seine Zeit*, Berlin.

Hegel, G. W. F. (1956), *The Philosophy of History*, New York: Dover.

────── (1973), *The Philosophy of Right*, London: Oxford University Press.

────── (1989), *Lectures on the Philosophy of World History. Introduction: Reason in History*, Cambridge: Cambridge University Press.

────── (1991), *Elements of the Philosophy of Right* (ed. A. W. Wood), Cambridge: Cambridge University Press.

Hobhouse, L. T. (1918), *The Metaphysical Theory of the State*, London: Allen and Unwin.

Hyland, R. (1990), 'Hegel's *Philosophy of Right*: a user's manual', *Cardozo Law Review* 11, 5–6, July–August.

Ilting, K. -H. (1971), 'The structure of Hegel's *Philosophy of Right*', in Z. A. Pelczynski, *Hegel's Political Philosophy*, Cambridge: Cambridge University Press.

────── (1984), 'Hegel's concept of the state and Marx's early critique', in Z. A. Pelczynski, *The State and Civil Society: Studies in Hegel's Political Philosophy*, Cambridge: Cambridge University Press.

Lowith, K. (1967), *From Hegel to Nietzsche*, New York: Anchor.

Marcuse, H. (1968), *Reason and Revolution*, London: RKP.

Marx, K. (1970), 'Critique of the Gotha Programme', in K. Marx and F. Engels, *Selected Works in One Volume*, London: Lawrence and Wishart.

────── (1975), 'Economic and philosophical manuscripts', in L. Colletti (ed.), *Marx's Early Writings*, London: Penguin.

Neumann, F. (1942), *Behemoth*, London: Gollancz.

Plamenatz, J. (1963), *Man and Society*, vol. 2, London: Longman.

Popper, K. (1966), *The Open Society and Its Enemies*, London: Routledge.

Rose, G. (1981), *Hegel Contra Sociology*, London: Athlone.

Russell, B. (1984), *A History of Western Philosophy*, London: Unwin.

Schmitt, C. (1933), *Staat, Bewegung, Volk*, Hamberg: Hanseatischer Verlaganstalt.

Smith, S. (1991), *Hegel's Critique of Liberalism*, Chicago: University of Chicago Press.

Tully, J. (1982), *A Discourse on Property: John Locke and his Adversaries*, Cambridge: Cambridge University Press.

Uchida, H. (1988), *Marx's Grundrisse and Hegel's Logic*, London: Routledge.

Waldron, J. (1990), *The Right to Private Property*, Oxford: Clarendon Press.

Winch, D. (1978), *Adam Smith's Politics*, Cambridge: Cambridge University Press.

ACKNOWLEDGEMENTS

My special thanks go to Gillian Rose, Alan Norrie, George Iannareas, Mick O'Sullivan and Glyn Cousin for their excellent advice.

4

The Bondage of Freedom:
Max Weber in the Present Tense

W. T. MURPHY

> ... the author, in the face of the magnitude of the task, has had to
> content himself with what it was possible to achieve in circumstances
> of external necessity, of the inevitable distractions caused by the
> magnitude and many-sidedness of contemporary affair, even under
> the *doubt* whether the noisy clamour of current affairs and the
> deafening chatter of a conceit which prides itself on confining itself to
> such matters leave any room for participation in the *passionless calm* of
> a knowledge which is in the element of pure thought alone.
>
> (Hegel, 1969, p. 42)

The efforts of Habermas, Luhmann and Foucault notwithstanding,
Weber is still with us and continues to afford an essential vehicle for
approaching some of the central questions which arise in relation to late
modern law, government and society. But to read Weber requires, I think,
a detour, a non-philosophical retrieval of the lineaments of German
Idealism. This is necessary for the simple reason that to read Weber,
rather than 'merely' to 'apply' him in a mechanical fashion, requires some
attempt at understanding what he meant. And this, in turn, requires a
certain 'archaeology' of his writings, an attempt to make explicit what
Weber took for granted, an attempt to describe the flavour of the air that
he breathed.

Weber was not a philosopher. But he inhabited an intellectual universe
enframed by a particular set of philosophical categories. His sociology was
a play with – but, equally, within – these categories. So, any contemporary
invocation of the Weberian apparatus today might draw at least some
benefit from a momentary pause in which these categories themselves –
and the oppositions that they take for granted – are subjected to some kind
of critical – or distanced – appraisal. What, in brief, underpinned a
scheme which still seems to enclose the way we understand those bits of
the world which we designate as 'law' and 'politics'?

LAW, POLITICS AND WHAT IS CALLED PHILOSOPHY

The Real and the Rational

'True thoughts and scientific insight', wrote Hegel, 'are only to be won through the labour of the Notion.' The cultivation of self-consciousness is at the heart of the enterprise of philosophy. 'Though the embryo is indeed in itself a human being, it is not so for itself; this it only is as cultivated Reason, which has made itself into what it is in itself' (Hegel, 1977, p. 12). All this is rooted in some assumptions about the nature of man and the appropriate regimen for its realisation. As Gadamer writes, 'Man is characterised by the break with the immediate and the natural that the intellectual, rational side of his nature demands of him' (Gadamer, 1979, p. 13).

But the regimen could be Weber's, and this is because it is a Protestant regimen (see especially Dickey, 1987). '"Cultivation" requires the sacrifice of particularity for the sake of the universal ... sacrifice of particularity means, in negative terms, the restraint of desire and hence freedom from the object of desire and freedom for its objectivity' (Gadamer, 1979, p. 13).

'Work is restrained desire.' Working consciousness, 'by forming the thing ... forms itself'. In other words, freedom is realised only in work, in acting. And, further, to know yourself is to produce yourself. There is not something simply given – 'you' – with which to come to terms: knowledge and the production of self are one; only a worked-up self is capable of self-knowledge, and the process of working-up, of *Bildung*, is of necessity a process of transformation. And a process of transformation is of necessity a process of absorption of what is always-already given in a life, in a culture, in a society. For the most part, the name of the game is clear. *Bildung* 'has no goals outside of itself' (ibid.). One can see here, of course, the thrust of Marx's criticism: that 'the only labour which Hegel knows and recognises is mental labour' (quoted in Hawthorn, 1976, p. 56). But, equally, we should note that Weber's Protestant Ethic, or, perhaps more exactly, his Spirit of Capitalism, is here, *avant la lettre*, heralded, duly transmuted, as the task of Philosophy.

Thinking and Freedom

Cultivation and freedom are intimately linked

> To think is in fact *ipso facto* to be free, for thought as the action of the universal is an abstract relating of self to self, where, being at home with ourselves, and as regards our subjectivity utterly blank, our consciousness is, in the matter of its contents, only in the fact and its characteristics. (Hegel, 1975, p. 36, and cf. pp. 22–3).

True science is not transcendent, but it transcends individuals. There is thought, and there is the person who engages in it. The two are not the same. As Kant, Hegel's 'subjective idealist', expresses the sentiment, 'Sapere aude! "Have courage to use your own understanding!" – that is the motto of enlightenment' (Kant, 1983, p. 41). But this is not a call for individual opinion to prevail: reason is rather what is common, poten-tially, to humanity. It is free in the sense that it entails something other than the 'blind obedience' to higher authority which is appropriate to the conduct of one's activity in one's private – particular, non-universal – position in society as soldier, priest and, possibly, professor.

> The public use of one's reason must always be free, and it alone can bring about enlightenment among men ... by the public use of one's own reason I understand the use that anyone as a scholar makes of reason before the entire literate world. I call the private use of reason that which a person may make in a civic post or office that has been entrusted to him. (Kant, 1983, p. 42).

Kant here reworks the classical opposition between the public and the private into a contrast between the universal and the particular which is structured according to a quite distinctive rationale. It is by now perhaps tiresome to continue to argue over whether such reworking is better seen in terms of continuity or rupture with what had gone before. It is sufficient to note that, in concrete terms, the public sphere which, for Aristotle, was the realm of human freedom, to be understood in terms of a non-utilitarian attention to matters which pertained to the *polis*, becomes here the (primarily) non-utilitarian realm of human thought free from the distractions of the routines of ordinary life. In still more concrete terms, the German university was, *par excellence*, in those times, the site of the public sphere.[1] In the university, what had in ancient Athens belonged to the *agora* found a new home. Just as, in the *agora*, man had been free and (the two are not distinct) realised his freedom, so in the university, in the life of the mind, this new form of freedom, the universal citizenship of the mind, would be realised. With this difference perhaps: in ancient Athens, the freedom which was *logos* was the freedom to speak in a public place; in Kant and Hegel's time, this can be seen as being transformed (some would say diminished) into the freedom to lecture. This change is itself of some significance: in the lecture-room, by contrast with the *agora*, speak-ing is formally privileged. *Isonomia* – the equal right of all to speak – is lacking. Fundamentally, then, this new freedom of *logos* is the freedom to think, the freedom of reason, not the freedom to speak and the freedom which resides in speaking well.[2] By Hegel's time, immersion in the art of rhetoric is no longer intimately tied to one's ability to realise oneself as a human being in the world.

The freedom which is thinking is free because it is entirely autono-mous:

in logic a thought is understood to include nothing else but what depends on thinking and what thinking has brought into existence. It is in these circumstances that thoughts are *pure* thoughts. The mind is then in its own home element and therefore free: for freedom means that the other thing with which you deal is a second self – so that you never leave your own ground but give the law to yourself. In the impulses or appetites the beginning is from something else, from something which we feel to be external. In this case, we speak of dependence. For freedom it is necessary that we should feel no pressure of something else which is not ourselves. (Hegel, 1975, p. 39)

Self-consciousness is desire certain of the sublatedness of the other.[3] 'Thought which is free starts out from itself and thereupon claims to know itself as united in its innermost being with the truth' (Hegel, 1967, p. 3). Such extensions of the idea of human autonomy need to be kept in mind when what seems to be the same theme of autonomy is reread in the light of the writings of Weber and Marx. Here again, I suggest, we see, as we already see in Kant and Hegel, but only intensified, a certain overdetermination of the available conceptual apparatus and its organising structure by the accumulations of inheritances from the past. One further such set of accumulations is essential for this: this is the quite explicit attack on dogmatism which we find in Fichte.

The Critique of Dogmatism

Fichte, too, insists upon the labour of the life of the mind:

What sort of philosophy one chooses depends ... on what sort of man one is; for a philosophical system is not a dead piece of furniture that we can reject or accept as we wish; it is rather a thing animated by the soul of the person who holds it. A person indolent by nature or dulled and distorted by mental servitude, learned luxury, and vanity will never raise himself to the level of idealism. (Fichte, 1982, p. 16)

At the core of Fichte's system, as of Hegel's, is the fact that man can abstract from experience: 'A finite rational being has nothing beyond experience ... the philosopher is necessarily in the same position ... But he is able to abstract; that is, he can separate what is conjoined in experience through the freedom of thought' (Fichte, 1982, pp 8–9). Fichte opposes idealism to 'dogmatism':

According to [the dogmatist], everything that appears in our consciousness, along with our presumed determinations through freedom and the very belief that we are free, is the product of a thing-in-itself. This latter belief is evoked in us by the operation of the thing, and the determinations which we deduce from our freedom are brought about by the same cause: but this we do not know and hence we attribute them to no cause, and thus to freedom. Every consistent dogmatist is necessarily a fatalist; he does not deny the fact of consciousness that we consider ourselves free ... but he demonstrates, on the basis of his principle, the falsity of this belief. He completely denies the independence of the self upon which the idealist relies, and construes the self merely as a product of things, an accident of the world; the consistent dogmatist is necessarily also a materialist. (Fichte, 1982, p. 13)

For Fichte, one must simply choose between idealism and dogmatism. ('Neither of these systems can directly refute its opposite, for their quarrel is about the first principle, which admits of no derivation from anything beyond it ... Even if they appear to agree about the words in a sentence, each takes them in a different sense' (Fichte, 1982, p. 12).) That is, Fichte grounds the problem in the motivation of (or in the a priori decisions made by) the thinking subject, and this decisionism must be stressed. 'Reason provides no principle of choice. ... the choice is governed by caprice, and since even a capricious decision must have some source, it is governed by *inclination* and *interest*. The ultimate basis of the difference between idealists and dogmatists is thus the difference of their interests' (Fichte, 1982, pp. 14–15).[4] In philosophy as in life – for the idealist, of course, *vera philosophia* is in any case life, just an arduous form of it – 'the highest interest and the ground of all others is self-interest' (Fichte, 1982, p. 15). The interest which 'invisibly governs' the philosopher's every thought is the 'desire not to lose, but to maintain and assert himself in the rational process' (ibid.).

There are, Fichte suggests, two types of man, two levels of humanity; before 'the second level is reached by everyone in the progress of our species' (Fichte, 1982, p. 15), there persists the first type which is rooted to the world, to the realm of necessity, and is therefore unfree.[5] The idealist, by contrast, is free because he is self-sufficient:

The man who becomes conscious of his self-sufficiency and independence of everything that is outside himself, however – and this can be achieved only by making oneself into something independently of everything else – does not need things for the support of himself, and cannot use them, because they destroy that self-sufficiency, and convert it into mere appearance. The self which he possesses, and which is the subject of his interest, annuls this belief in things; he believes in his independence out of inclination, he embraces it with feeling. (Fichte, 1982, p. 15)

Perhaps this comes close to arguing that I am free because I believe I am free, with why I believe this to be so remaining opaque. But Fichte tries to push his argument down rather different channels. For his version of idealism, the intellect 'is only active and absolute, never passive' (Fichte, 1982, p. 21).

> The intellect, for idealism, in an *act*, and absolutely nothing more; we should not even call it an *active* something, for this expression refers to something subsistent in which activity inheres ... out of the activity of this intellect we must deduce *specific* presentations: of a world, of a material, spatially located world existing without our aid etc., which notoriously occur in consciousness. (ibid.)

As we shall see, in this insistent combination of reason, will, anti-dogmatism and decision, Weber is in large measure Fichte's 'spiritual' heir. But the thematic linkage of these elements with freedom, with the project of human emancipation, becomes, in Weber's writings, tragically obscure. And this is not because the project of emancipation is somehow deflected; it is, rather, because the project is realised in the rational organisation of society.

THE DISPLACEMENT OF HOPE

These different philosophical systems – and we have here made casual reference only to two or three of a much larger number – had one thing in common, for all the internal differences between them (which are not my concern here). This is best described as hope. The world is in the process of improving itself, and humanity – through reason – is the decisive medium in this process. In this matrix of thought, reason, improvement and human emancipation are inextricably linked. Marx and Weber put hope into question, though in varying degrees. In a contrapuntal sort of way, Marx helps us to place Weber on the plane of modernity. In Marx, hope was deferred but still present; in Weber, it was abandoned.

Marx: Homo Faber

Throughout the writings of Marx, it is the ability of human beings to transform the material world through their ability to labour which re-places the Aristotelian *logos* as that which separates mankind from the rest of creation.[6] This metaphysical assumption, in the end, is why labour-power (the ability to labour) is at the core of his critique of political economy. Labour is more than a factor of production (though in so postulating it, political economy registered the fact that, under capitalism, labour-power had become a commodity); labour-power as the only source of value was a unique commodity such that its exchange in the market-place, while superficially governed by the logic of equivalent exchange (otherwise it could not be a commodity), in fact concealed the transfer of surplus labour to capital which was realised as surplus value beneath the surface of relations of exchange. This also concealed the fact that capital was not an autonomous factor of production, as it appeared on the surface and as was again registered in the (ideological) discourse of political economy. Phenomenal form and essence were thus contrasted, and *homo faber* stood at the heart of Marx's conceptualisation of the essence of things, or, rather, of the difference between persons and things.

In so emphasising the role of material labour, Marx operated within the organising framework of the Idealist tradition in a number of central respects. First, he simply reversed the relationship between the mental and the material[7] while retaining the emphasis upon work – *homo faber* – as such. Second, he retained the conceptualisation of the relationship between humans and their environment in terms of an antagonism – the world as other – and a transformation of the other by the one, of the world by humans. Marx substituted one idea of the human for another, thereby reversing 2,000 years of political thought: freedom was equated with labour, not thought; the ability to labour was what made humans unique.[8]

Whether these moves should be characterised as an escape from or a mere reversal within the Idealist tradition is more a matter of labels than anything else. What is clear is that the ability to labour is a theoretical abstraction from the plurality of what there is to say about human beings. And the problem with this is not theoretical abstraction as such, but the privileging of one aspect of man above others. What results is an impossibly naive sociology and anthropology.[9] Two examples suffice: the catastrophic error made by Lenin in deriving from this image of man the possibility of the spontaneous mass organisation of society; the subtle *pointillisme* of a fine historian sitting in strange juxtaposition to the leaden and abstract cadences of a dedicated member of the *nomenklatura*. If de Ste Croix's *The Class Struggle in the Ancient Greek World* (1981) demonstrates anything, it is that a 'classical' Marxist account of that world is an intellectual impossibility, and this for a simple reason: it entirely bypasses the problem of whether 'class' is what we would call an emic or an etic category. For Marx, it was both at one and the same time; but, for Lenin, where did the peasants fit in? History gave us the answer in the project of collectivisation.[10] This was just the first main example with genuine significance of the new scholasticism and the new dogmatism which Marxism inaugurated as a 'practical philosophy'.

It is appropriate to invoke the Idealist usage of dogmatism here for another reason. Marxism is most awkwardly positioned in relation to that tradition insofar as it seeks to subject the realm of natural consciousness, of the dogmatic slumber, now retermed 'ideology', to the critique of reason, while at the same time seeking to valorise man's natural characteristics – the ability through human labour to transform nature – over his rational, ideological ones. Or, at least, thought only participated in the production of reality rather than in the perpetuation of illusion when it was directed towards the conceptualising of the end – the *telos* – of the exercise of human labour-power.

In retrospect – but, of course, everything is much easier in retrospect – it should be clear that Marxist-Leninism has little to say about law and state not because this was an always-deferred research project, but because of the way in which this theoretical tradition was fundamentally positioned in regard to its own project of enclosing the world.[11] Both law and state were merely derivative and ephemeral, derivative because they were epiphenomenal in relation to what was real – the mode of organisation of human labour; ephemeral because of what was to be grasped from the philosophy of history – the history of human labour now phrased as the history of class struggles.

Weber: Homo Rationalis

Even Marx, who unlike his apparatchik successors was more idealist than dogmatist, wavered in the face of ancient Greek art.[12] Weber, by contrast, wavered in the face of the whole enterprise of the rational organisation of life. In one sense, Weber returned explicitly, if non-philosophically, to the terrain of the Idealists sketched above. But he did not re-enter the Idealist project as such. Rather, relying on its central organising principles – most particularly, its fundamental opposition between the natural and the rational – he embarked on an interminable historical sociology of rationalities, a sociology in which law and religion were absolutely central. In so doing, Weber problematised rationality as such. His entire endeavour is best grasped as an attempt at a dispassionate appraisal (here, the *sine ira et studio* continuity with the passionless calm of Idealism is evident) of the improbability of western rationality. But two points must be emphasised about this enterprise. First, Weber regarded the achievement of rationality as improbable or exceptional, in the light of comparative history and sociology; second, the essential notion of rationality with which he was working was one carried over from the tradition of German Idealism – a philosophical rationality instantiated in certain social institutions.[13]

Weber departs from Marx in two crucial respects. First, in place of a monolithic transformative force running through history – class struggle, premissed upon human labour – he substitutes a plurality of rationalisations occurring in increasingly differentiated spheres of life. The common thread is little more than that already present in the grounding antinomies of Idealist philosophy. Second, there is no one essential thing to be said about human beings or their abilities. What can be asked of humans is the character and existence of the animating spirit which drives them to do what they do. But humans have ceased to organise history. In place of this is put the fundamental irrationality of the world, the simple idea that the road to hell is paved with good intentions (see especially Weber, 1978b). Everything Weber says about rationality must be read in the light of this governing assumption, which in the end coheres with Veyne's somewhat melancholy pronouncement that 'the world has promised us nothing, and we cannot read our truths in it ... Eternal realities – government, domination, Power, the State – cannot explain the haze of detailed events. Such noble draperies are nothing but rationalist abstractions laid over program[me]s whose diversity is secretly enormous' (Veyne, 1988, p. 125, p. 120).

Weber never went this far, and yet he has rarely since been rivalled in his scepticism and irony towards the pretensions which have accompanied the products of modernity, in whose number I would think we could include much of modern jurisprudence.

THE RATIONAL CHARACTER OF WEBERIAN MODERN LAW

The Categories

Insofar as Weber's categories still dominate the agenda of the comparative sociology of law – and, indeed, other somewhat less ambitious critical enterprises – it remains important to reflect upon the 'substructure' of Weber's thought about law, in order to elucidate what motivated the formation of his ideal-types of law. It is not Weber's 'bias' or 'values' which are principally of interest here. Of course, as Weber himself wrote, 'without the investigator's evaluative ideas, there would be no principle of selection of subject-matter and no meaningful knowledge of the concrete reality' (quoted in McLemore, 1984, p. 287). But it is Weber's assumptions about the need for and intrinsic logic of government, and its connection with 'rationality', which require examination, because they are not just Weber's assumptions. At the risk of some exaggeration, they might be described as foundational self-images of post-Enlightenment legal culture in the West.

The outline of Weber's ideal-typical scheme of law is well known and rehearsed here only so far as is necessary to get at his underlying assumptions, which have received much less scrutiny. Law-making and law-finding can be irrational or rational. It is formally irrational when it applies means which cannot be controlled by the intellect. It is substantively irrational to the extent that a legal decision is influenced by 'concrete' factors such as immediate ethical, emotional or political considerations. As guides to decisions, such concrete factors stand opposed to general norms. 'Rational' law is formal to the extent that only unambiguous general characteristics of the facts are taken into account (Weber 1978a, p. 637). There are two types of formality. In the first, the legally relevant characteristics are of a 'tangible' nature, that is, are perceptible as sense

data. Here, Weber has in mind the utterance of words, the execution of a
signature, the performance of a symbolic act with a fixed (legal) meaning.
This is the most rigorous type of legal formalism, but Weber himself is not
much caught by its general significance. (Had he been, his treatment of
the common law tradition might have been less one-sided.) The second
type of legal formalism is of much greater moment for Weber. This is
where the legally relevant characteristics of a set of facts are disclosed
through the logical analysis of meaning, where definitely fixed legal
concepts in the form of highly abstract rules are formulated and applied.
Such logical rationality, for Weber, diminishes the significance of extrinsic elements in the legal decision-making process and softens the rigidity
of concrete formalism.

Most modern discussion by legal commentators centre around the
contrast between formal legal rationality, so sketched, and substantive
legal rationality, and Weber is commonly attacked for apparently prefer-
ring the first to the second. Substantive rationality in decision-making
means that decisions are influenced by norms – ethical imperatives,
utilitarian and other expediential rules, political maxims – which are
different from those obtained through the logical generalisation of abstract interpretations of meaning. For Weber, such substantive rationality
was an impediment to 'legal unification and consistency' and was a
'natural consequence ... wherever the validity of sacred law or immutable
tradition has been taken seriously, in China and India just as in the
territories of Islam' (Weber, 1978a, p. 822).

Thus, for Weber, the rationality of ecclesiastical hierarchies and of
patrimonial rulers is substantive in character, since, in such regimes, the
self-contained and specialised juridical treatment of legal questions is an
alien idea, and law and ethics are not separated (Weber, 1978a, p. 810).
The most obvious difficulty here is that Weber is unable to state with
much clarity what distinguishes, within the typology, substantive rationality from substantive irrationality. The core of the distinction seems to
regard substantive rationality as grounded in the purposive, deliberate
exercise of the human will, and, to that extent, in the supersession of the
supernatural and the conquest of the ties that bind man to the life world
of tradition.[14] The persistence of sacred law meant that man had not taken
charge of his own destiny, and to that extent, irrationality endured. Thus
he draws attention to the factors which meant that, in Islamic law,
'systematic lawmaking, aimed at legal uniformity and consistency', was
impossible, in the following terms:

> The sacred law could not be disregarded, nor could it, despite many
> adaptations, be really carried out in practice. As in the Roman
> system, officially licensed jurists ... can be called on for opinions by
> the khadis or the parties as the occasion arises. Their opinions are

authoritative, but they also vary from person to person; like the opinions of oracles, they are given without any statement of rational reasons. Thus they actually increase the irrationality of the sacred law rather than contribute, however slightly, to its rationalisation. (Weber, 1978a, p. 821)

But this link to his disenchantment thesis is only one, certainly important, element in Weber's interpretation of the relationship between law and modernisation. The second element is what might be called his anti-particularism, his insistence upon rationality as a matter of transcending, purposefully, artificially, the immediate conditions of life: rationality in other words, as a matter of universality and consistency, where mind and its products override the contingent pressures of the environment in the process of decision-making. Hence his association of 'special law' with irrational law:

As a status group law, the sacred law applies only to the Muslim but not to the subject population of unbelievers. As a consequence, legal particularism continued to exist not only for the several tolerated denominations ... but also as local or vocational custom. The scope of the maxim that 'special law prevails over the general law of the land', although it claimed an absolute validity, was of doubtful application whenever particular laws happened to conflict with sacred norms, which, themselves, were subject to thoroughly unstable interpretations. (Weber, 1978a, p. 821)

In other words, rational law is to be found where man is consciously in charge of his own destiny – disenchanted – and where his mode of being in charge transcends the particularities of day-to-day existence, that is, where he proceeds generally. Rational law, for Weber, envisages an autonomous ruler laying down general, situation-transcending, universal rules. This, of course, is precisely the Prussian experience in idealised, or stylised, form. In Weber's Germany, particularism was precisely the antithesis of unification and nationhood. Only by transcending what distinguished Swabia from Prussia, or Bavaria from Schleswig-Holstein, could Germany become, in law as in ideology, one.

The Positivisation of Natural Law

Whatever their internal differences, the German Idealists all inhabited a world in which natural law was primarily a matter of Thought, of critical reflection upon what we would now call traditional legal practices (whether the thinking in question was at the level of the understanding or of Hegelian speculative philosophy). Weber was so positioned as to be able to recognise unequivocally that the various European projects of codification amounted to no less than the positivisation of natural law, and therefore, though he did not put it in precisely this way, the rendering empirical – and therefore contingent, changeable and manipulable – of what had previously been understood to belong to another order of reality and of human experience. Weber called this the loss of the 'metaphysical dignity' of the law, so that in 'the great majority of its most important provisions, it has been unmasked all too visibly ... as the product or the technical means of a compromise between conflicting interests' (Weber, 1978a, p. 875).

So long as natural law was only merely thought, i.e. had not been posited, which is to say reduced to a text which was endorsed by sovereign power, it could remain amenable to, or approachable by, philosophy because it was, to that extent, the product of reason as such, uncontaminated by empirical reality or the natural attitude, a contrast, as we have seen, so central to German Idealism. Rendered operational in the world – of government, of sovereign power – it lost this purity and this innocence. Once set to work, nothing could be the same again in the world of law. All that remained was the unwritten law, or the law which was written, if at all, upon the hearts of men, the law of morality which was not law in the codified sense of the word.

Once, reason had stood opposed to power; it provided the resources for the critique of domination. Now, in codifications of the law, reason and sovereign power were conjoined, And what this meant is that a problem long discernible in philosophy and theology – the relationship between reason and will – came to affect law too, in a new, and significant, way. Weber's rational law was transparent law – law as a perfect medium through which the commands of the ruler could be transmitted. Law became pure, merely a medium, an instrument of command unaffected by dogmatic slumber, and the problem of why the law should be obeyed – or, more exactly, of why law should bind, should *attract* obedience – was made quite explicit. Such pure law was tragic law.

The Tragedy of Legal Autonomy

Wrenched from its roots by New Deal enthusiasts, Weber's problem-set, suitably recoded, became emblematic of a certain kind of self-understanding of late, western, modernity.[15] The Weberian influence was particularly marked in Parsons's still influential sociology, and, in part through that, has seeped into the way in which both Luhmann and Habermas have constructed alternative sociologies for 'new times'. Yet the theory of autopoiesis in particular, whether this is taken to exemplify contemporary closure or critique, registers a continuity with Weberian preoccupations. It involves a sophisticated reworking of law as closure, as a self-referring and self-reproducing system turned in upon itself; but to the extent that it analyses law's closure from outside, it simultaneously serves as a form of critique.[16] Luhmann provides a framework through which modernity can be viewed with an extreme cynicism; man is no longer available to himself, except through the medium of a range of heterogeneous rubrics, of which the 'man' of the law – the legal subject – is merely one. In this sense, nothing remains of 'spirit'; but Weber's specialists without spirit had anticipated this already.

Equally, Weber's notion of legal rationality had already anticipated this autopoietic phenomenon. Idealism is turned against itself to the extent that Weber asks, with a certain resignation and even despair, how it could be desirable to be rational. The legitimacy of rational law was sociologically improbable, because, for it to have any 'pull' or 'attraction', it needed to presuppose a man who was inwardly dead, a 'Man Without Qualities', without *Innerlichkeit*.

Yet the autonomy which results may – must? – dissipate into an iron cage. Within this view of things, law is central. Even if, for Marx, law held out a false promise, the future could be glimpsed in the very things that went to make the promise false. Abstract, general, rational law represented precisely the mastery by human thought of the world, of the natural, of tradition, a mastery which Idealism had previously supposed to be attainable only, or principally, in the uncontaminated region of philosophy. In different terms, what began in the 'public sphere' of reason as the critique of tradition and the 'dogmatic slumber' became a new form of closure, especially in law, in which human rationality, pure thought thinking only of itself, now codified, loomed large over its subjects in a manner no less all-encompassing and no less remote than the stern Protestant God of Donne, of Locke, of Kant or of Weber ever did.

Here we reach the core of the so-called dialectic of Enlightenment – the bifurcated critique of rationalism under the sign, on the one hand, of an authentic romanticism[17] and, on the other, of an ersatz traditionalism[18] (and sometimes in the name of a mixture of both).[19] Weber attests to and anticipates many of the tensions and antinomies inherent in seeking to articulate the space and direction of such a critique very well. And here he is very hard-headed on the impossibility of a return to traditional society and government (as he defines it: the problems with these definitions are elaborated elsewhere)[20].

But as Weber initially characterises the dialectic of Enlightenment, few tools are left at his disposal to articulate the position from which, or the criteria through which, the critique of rationality can be undertaken. As is well known, his resolution of these problems congealed around the notion of charisma. Only this, whatever it was ever intended to represent, promised a way out from the iron cage of rationality. But charismatic leadership could not, exactly, provide many materials for an articulate critique. Charisma could serve as an alternative to the closure effected by rationality; it could not provide a stable basis for the development of critique. And the modern world was to provide, through the new mass technologies of film and music recording, a range of vehicles through which charisma could operate. At the heart of this development is the loss of *logos*. Compare the film of the novel with the novel itself – aphasia sets in.

Weber, of course, developed his concept of charisma in the specific context of *Herrschaft*; and if we were to render Weber even more parochially, we could suggest that his fundamental tripartite ideal-typical scheme of legitimate domination closely mirrored that of the structure of the German polity of his mature years – the traditional Junkers, the rational, anti-traditional bourgeoisie, and the quasi-charismatic authoritarian rulers – Bismarck and Wilhelm II. But for present purposes, we need to widen rather than narrow the route of enquiry. The charismatic mode of legitimating commands rested upon a particular orientation to social action – affectual action. The love of the leader in effect presupposed the possibility of humans being oriented to their worlds in terms of such passion rather than in terms of sober, rationalistic calculation.

Weber thus presupposes, in one sense, the success of the triumph of rationalism over traditionalism (as he rephrases the natural attitude), and marshals in opposition to it the play of the affects. The undeveloped part of his analysis concerns the character of this play. Its critical character resides in the fact that it is 'free' play, and thus stands in contrast with the iron cage of rationality. But, perhaps unsurprisingly, Weber places little emphasis upon its ludic dimension, and indeed seems to think that 'playing' is of little value. 'In the field of its highest development, in the United States, the pursuit of wealth, stripped of its religious and ethical meaning, tends to become associated with purely mundane passions, which often actually give it the character of sport' (Weber, 1976, pp. 181–2). The linkage of freedom and mind prevents Weber from regarding this play as 'really free'; it is not, to be sure, 'traditional' action, but it is still irrational. The central opposition for Weber is rather that between rationality and spirit. For Hegel, of course, the phenomenology of spirit culminated in philosophy. At the same time, access to philosophy could only be had through this phenomenology. Reason was the destiny of spirit. Now Weber set spirit against reason, or, more precisely, came to see reason, once the product of spirit, as subsequently turning against it and stifling it. In few areas was this process more self-evident than in the consequences of the institution of rational law.

Possibilities of Rationality, Residues of Spirit

I am conscious that I have thrown around these two terms – rationality (or reason) and spirit – in the loosest possible fashion. This is deliberate, because it is essential to grasp the very wide possible extensions of these terms in order to understand the plausibility of their applications across so wide a terrain as has in fact occurred. But I think these two ideas have a central organising core within the tradition of critical philosophy. Both terms give expression to an opposition between human consciousness and the world. Rationality, as we have seen, involves essentially the escape from or transcendence of the world in and through human thought. And since thinking, and the articulation of the products of thought, is a specifically and uniquely human attribute, rationality involves the full realisation of human potential. To live by a set of rational laws is merely one example of this; but it is a very important one at the same time, since few if any of the writers we have discussed here would have doubted that the laws under which one lives constitute a crucial dimension of the practical level of human existence. Spirit presupposes this rationality, but draws attention to the active dimension of the mental life of humans; it stresses the ability of humans – so often suppressed – to act and move in their world with no other cause than themselves, than their thoughts. This is not a condition which generally prevails; the whole point of the critique of the dogmatic slumber was intended to suggest that most people are impelled by the promptings of the world, not by the autonomous products of the purely and specifically human, viz. human thought.

And so with law. One must make its reason one's own in order to live as a free and completed individual. What Weber does is to insert a fundamental doubt into this scheme of representations. While retaining both emphases sketched above, he suggests that reason ceases to animate, and thereby becomes antithetical to spirit, to man as self-mover. Instead, reason imprisons, entraps, stultifies. Reason ceases to fuel life, and comes to make it dead. Weber's project is thus both enframed within the categories of Idealism and registers their final bankruptcy. In Weber, reason has ceased to be the means of attaining, and thus the expression of, human freedom from the world – of the attainment, that is, of an autonomous human condition in which humans are able to decide for themselves about the character of the world they wish to inhabit. Such decisions are, instead, handed over to a plurality of 'dark forces' – will, power, fanaticism and so on.

At this point, Weber's critical resources are almost exhausted, and it is perhaps not therefore surprising that no coherent or consistent critical theme can be extracted from his *oeuvre*. But how could it? Weber is one of the first with this problem but by no means the last. The reason for this is simple enough to state. Human reason once constituted the voice of freedom, the means through which, for the Enlightenment, the dark ages of superstition and dogmatism – and authoritarianism, up to a point[21] – could be dispelled. Man had within himself the ability to take control of his life and his destiny through the cultivation and use of the faculty peculiar to him, his reason. (Whether or not God underwrote the possession of this faculty is for present purposes irrelevant.) But what is to be done if reason becomes a new cage, a new tyrant? Suddenly a history of freedom becomes a history of domination, and the cunning of reason appears in less benevolent attire.

For Weber, then, what was, historically, the foundation of critique – rationality – slipped over into being the principal form of closure against which critique had to be directed. The problem – and the resulting incoherence, which echoes through the subsequent history of Franco-German thought – was what resources to deploy in such a critique.

Weber had two conflicting responses to this crisis of rationality. One could be called resignation. It was not quietism, but an austere, calculative, pessimistic politics which approaches decisions about the world with caution and circumspection. The other, more peripheral and yet somehow essential, was the resuscitation of spirit, the revival of some active life-force. 'Here I stand, I can no other' was a dangerous stance to take; but to exclude it entirely was to exclude life as an active principle in inner human existence.[22]

CONCLUSION

I have tried to give some sense above of the cultural baggage which Weber's writings, projects and categorial apparatus inescapably carry with them. As is always the case, to make use of such schemes as interpretive devices is never innocent in its consequences. What I have suggested so far is that, in essence, there have been two eras of critical thought. In the first, man sought, through reason, to take full possession of the world through the use of the faculty of reason.[23] Rational law was one exemplification of this critical process. In the second, the link between reason and freedom was problematised, and reason became part of the problem of domination instead of part of the process of its elimination. But in this second moment of the critical project, a new problem comes to the fore, and Weber exemplifies it. From what critical resources is a critique of reason to be undertaken, given that what seems to remain constant is the assumption that humans can only be freed through the strategic deployment of their own resources?

Since Weber, certain new and significant figures have appeared on the landscape of critique, generating new possibilities, most notably those inherent in the writings of Freud and Heidegger, where the ground of the thinking, rational subject is subverted through a somewhat paradoxical process of reflection. Weber's writings have not had comparable effects, and Weber has been enrolled in the Serious Scholar rather than Mystic chapter of the Hall of Fame. Yet so many of the problems which have proved so decisive for the postmodern project were compacted in Weber's notion of spirit and in his positioning of spirit in relation to rationality. If we pursued this path, I suspect we would find that the tracks Weber laid are very much those along which the journey has since been conducted, or, more exactly, that the point at which Weber stopped remains that around which much so-called postmodern thought has encircled. And this concerns the relationship between, to use Englished Weberian terminology, rationality and affectualism.[24] Weber was among the first to see and articulate the problems which have arisen because of the reversals which have occurred in the meaning and significance of reason. I doubt that we have made many advances since his time; in this sense, Weber still needs to be read in the present tense.

NOTES

1. For a different emphasis, cf. Habermas (1989).
2. For an attempt to endow these changes with world-historical significance, see Arendt (1958, ch. 2).
3. I owe this formulation to Hayo Krombach.
4. This is precisely the point at which Habermas takes up Fichte. The difference between Habermas and Fichte reveals with singular clarity the nature of what has changed and the problems of returning to the tradition: see Habermas (1974, pp. 256 ff.), Habermas (1987) and Dews (1987, pp. 19–34, 220 ff.).
5. This way of posing the opposition between freedom and necessity, read as one between the non-utilitarian and the utilitarian, is commonly supposed to have its forebears in Aristotle: see Arendt (1958, ch. 2).
6. See now Gorz (1989).
7. Cf. Godelier (1986).
8. There is a clear thematic continuity here from, say, 'On the Jewish question' through the 1859 'Preface' to the *Contribution to a Critique of Political Economy* to Lenin's *The State and Revolution* of 1917 (Marx, 1975, 1970; Lenin, 1965).
9. Here, cf. especially Gudeman (1986), Joyce (1987), Gorz (1989).
10. Whether collectivisation should be forced upon the peasants was treated as a tactical question, with most, including Lenin, favouring gradualism; but a peasantry was in principle incompatible with the new order which was to be established (see e.g. Medvedev, 1972; Nove, 1969). Historians may rightly make much of the differences between Lenin and Stalin here, but it is Lenin (1965, p. 123) who wrote: 'The whole of society will have become a single office and a single factory' and that 'there will be no getting away from it, there will be "nowhere to go"'; see also the essays collected in Lenin (1976).
11. Even to understand Pashukanis (1978) properly, one was thrown back to Rubin (1972).
12. See the closing remarks of the '1857 Introduction' (Marx, 1973, pp. 110–11).
13. Cf. Kant, 'Idea for a Universal History with a Cosmopolitan Intent', in Kant (1983), p. 29.

14. See, for example, the contrast drawn between the 'rational' and 'magical' elements in Indian law in Weber (1978a), p. 817.
15. See e.g. Adriaanssens (1980).
16. Luhmann (1989) provides a good example.
17. Unsatisfactory as the term 'romanticism' is, this mode of critique can be seen as culminating in Nietzsche, Heidegger and Weber himself.
18. Ersatz in that tradition as a product of the discipline of history is itself a by-product of rationalism. Savigny provides an example.
19. There is useful discussion in the essays collected in Iggers and Powell (eds) (1990).
20. Murphy and Roberts (forthcoming).
21. Cf. 'Only one ruler in the world says, "*Argue* as much as you want and about what you want, *but obey!*"' (Kant, 1983), p. 42).
22. See Hennis (1988), Murphy (1989).
23. Kant (1960) is especially revealing here.
24. In this century, such affectualism has taken two forms, one placing the accent upon poetics or music, the other reasserting the 'claims' of the body. For the former, see e.g. Bloch (1985), Bachelard (1969); for the latter, see Braidotti (1991).

REFERENCES

Arendt, H. (1958), *The Human Condition*, Chicago: University of Chicago Press.
Adriaanssens, H. P. M. (1980), *Talcott Parsons and the Conceptual Dilemma*, London: Routledge and Kegan Paul.
Bachelard, G. (1969), *The Poetics of Space*, Boston: Beacon.
Bloch, E. (1985), *Essays on the Philosophy of Music*, Cambridge: Cambridge University Press.
Braidotti, R. (1991), *Patterns of Dissonance*, Cambridge: Polity Press.
Dews, P. (1987), *Logics of Disintegration: Post-structuralist Thought and the Claims of Critical Theory*, London: Verso.
Dickey, L. (1987), *Hegel: Religion, Economics and the Politics of Spirit, 1770–1807*, Cambridge: Cambridge University Press.
Fichte, J. G. (1982), *The Science of Knowledge*, Cambridge: Cambridge University Press.
Gadamer, H.-G. (1979), *Truth and Method*, 2nd ed., London: Sheed and Ward.
Godelier, M. (1986), *The Mental and the Material: Thought, Economy and Society*, London: Verso.
Gorz, A. (1989), *Critique of Economic Reason*, London: Verso.
Gudeman, S. (1986), *Economics as Culture: Models and Metaphors of Livelihood*, London: Routledge and Kegan Paul.
Habermas, J. (1974), *Theory and Practice*, London: Heinemann.
—— (1987, *The Philosophical Discourse of Modernity*, Cambridge, Ma: M.I.T.
—— (1989), *The Structural Transformation of the Public Sphere*, Cambridge: Polity Press.
Hawthorn, G. (1976), *Enlightenment and Despair*, Cambridge: Cambridge University Press.
Hegel, G. W. F. (1967), *Philosophy of Right*, Oxford; Oxford University Press.
—— (1969), *Science of Logic*, London: George Allen and Unwin.

—— (1975), *Hegel's Logic* (tr. of the *Encyclopaedia Logic*, 1817, rev. 1827), Oxford: Oxford University Press.

—— (1977), *Phenomenology of Spirit*, Oxford: Oxford University Press.

Hennis, W. (1988), *Max Weber: Essays in Reconstruction*, London: George Allen and Unwin.

Iggers, G. G. and Powell, J. M. (eds) (1990), *Leopold von Ranke and the Shaping of the Historical Discipline*, Syracuse, New York: Syracuse University Press.

Joyce, P. (ed.) (1987), *The Historical Meanings of Work*, Cambridge: Cambridge University Press.

Kant, I. (1960), *Religion within the Limits of Reason Alone*, New York: Harper and Row.

—— (1983), *Perpetual Peace and Other Essays*, Indianapolis: Hackett.

Lenin, V. I. (1965), *The State and Revolution*, 2nd ed., Peking: Foreign Languages Press.

—— (1976), *The Agrarian Question and the 'Critics of Marx'*, 2nd ed., Moscow: Progress.

Luhmann, N. (1989), *Ecological Communication*, Cambridge: Polity Press.

Marx, K. (1970), 'Preface', in *A Contribution to the Critique of Political Economy*, Moscow: Progress.

—— (1973), '1857 Introduction', in *Grundrisse*, Harmondsworth: Penguin.

—— (1975), 'On the Jewish question', in *Early Writings*, Harmondsworth: Penguin.

McLemore, L. (1984), 'Max Weber's defense of historical inquiry', in *History and Theory* 23, 277.

Medvedev, R. (1972), *Let History Judge: The Origins and Consequences of Stalinism*, London: Macmillan.

Murphy, W. T. (1989), 'Reason and society: the science of society and the sciences of man. Durkheim and Weber', in P. Windsor (ed.) *Reason and History*, Leicester: Leicester University Press.

Murphy, W. T. and Roberts, S. (forthcoming), *The Question of Law: A Sociological Perspective*.

Nove, A. (1969), *An Economic History of the USSR*, Harmondsworth: Penguin.

Pashukanis, E. B. (1978), *Law and Marxism: A General Theory*, London: Ink Links.

Rubin, I. I. (1972), *Essays on Marx's Theory of Value*, 3rd ed., Detroit: Black and Red.

Sainte Croix, G. de (1981), *The Class Struggle in the Ancient Greek World*, London: Duckworth.

Veyne, P. (1988) *Did the Greeks Believe in Their Myths?*, Chicago: Chicago University Press.

Weber, M. (1976), *The Protestant Ethic and the Spirit of Capitalism*, 2nd ed., London: George Allen and Unwin.

—— (1978a) *Economy and Society: An Outline of Interpretive Sociology*, 2 vols, ed. G. Roth and C. Wittich, Berkeley: University of California Press.

—— (1978b), 'Politics as a vocation', in *Weber: Selections in Translation*, ed. W. G. Runciman, Cambridge: Cambridge University Press.

5

The Illusions of the 'I':
Citizenship and the Politics of Identity

ANNE BARRON

In recent years, as the implications of poststructuralist thought for the practice and theory of politics have begun to be assessed, the category that lies at the centre of liberal political and legal thought – that of the universal citizen/subject – has itself become vulnerable to reappraisal. In general, poststructuralism problematises the notion that the human subject can be conceived of as a unitary agent of intervention in the social world, where agency signifies the capacity to 'get behind' one's discursively constituted contexts of interaction to a privileged vantage point from which those contexts could be understood and controlled. Within liberal political theory, agency takes a particular form: citizenship describes the identity assumed by the subject as a participant within the political realm, and is conceived of in terms of a capacity for autonomous action which is shared by all. Rawls's theory of justice is exemplary here: it explicitly identifies the rational and autonomous citizen as the very source of political and legal authority, and thus highlights the centrality of this conception to the legitimation of the liberal state. So it is that Ronald Dworkin, applying Rawls's insights to the legal enterprise, has argued that since human nature is essentially rational and autonomous – each person fundamentally has the capacity to form and act upon intelligent conceptions of how her/his life should be lived – the true point or value of law is to 'capture' and give effect to the 'rights that people in fact have' as a consequence of this, rights to equality of concern and respect in the design and administration of the political institutions that govern them. For Dworkin, the recognition of the basic and natural right to equal concern and respect (the primacy of which, he argues, is assumed within Rawls's theory of justice) is the presupposition of contemporary legal and political institutions, the underlying purpose which explains the coherence, unity and rationality of legal doctrine (Barron, 1992). To the extent that positive law fails to respect and give effect to this right, it is unjust and requires amendment.

Clearly, then, the invocation of the rational, autonomous subject as the foundation of political legitimacy is capable of serving a critical purpose. For Rawls and Dworkin alike, this subject is the vehicle through which social conflict can be at once articulated and resolved: it serves as a criterion against which the justice of social institutions can be assessed, and as such enables critical reflection upon, and assessment of, 'the basic structure of society' (Rawls, 1971, p. 7). Yet if this is indeed the category around which contemporary legal and political institutions are organised, then any engagement with these institutions, and in particular any invocation of the discourse of rights, would seem to enable only those claims that are proper to such a subject. The rational, autonomous, individuated citizen, that is, must be the necessary form of political subjectivity within liberal democracy, and the rights of this citizen inevitably the language of political expression. This is not a source of any great anxiety to either Rawls or Dworkin. Both identify the category of the universal citizen as a mechanism of inclusion, and both emphasise the emancipatory implications of their celebration of the rights implied by the freedom and equality of all persons. Poststructuralism, on the other hand, suggests an orientation towards the liberal subject that is suspicious of its capacity to include and accommodate all perspectives and all claims, and focuses instead upon what is negated and denied in the process of its construction: a poststructuralist critique of the totalising narratives of liberal political and legal thought would therefore expose how the latter tend to constitute the domain in which the subject may express itself politically in such a way as to effect a closure around the realm of the political itself.

This chapter situates itself within the space opened up by that critique[1]: it seeks to explore the processes of exclusion upon which the liberal subject of rights is founded and upon which it depends. Its immediate focus is Rawls's conception of the 'moral person', chiefly because the latter embodies the features which liberal thought holds to be essential to political agency. I therefore begin with a brief account of the moral person and describe how it achieves its identity as an autonomous being through a separation from what it is not, a separation effected by the imposition of a barrier, the veil of ignorance. For Rawls, the veil of ignorance symbolises that which distinguishes the subject appearing within the political domain from what cannot be signified politically: it is the very mechanism of exclusion. As such, it will be argued, it recalls the repression which Freud identified as constituting the structure of the human ego, and suggests an analogy between this ego and the Rawlsian moral person. Yet the central insight of Freudian psychoanalysis is that the repression upon which the ego is founded also constitutes the unconscious as the locus of whatever is denied access to consciousness. Further, the unconscious cannot be seen as the effect of an absolute exclusion, for it constantly manages to evade the ego's censorship, speaking through and against the latter's 'rational' discourse. The remainder of the chapter, then, explores the implications for political theory of this understanding of the subject as perpetually divided against itself, inhabited from within by what it negates. It will be argued that Althusser's account of the 'interpellation' of the individual as a subject usefully appropriates Lacan's reading of Freud for a critique of liberalism, for it explicitly equates the liberal political subject with the ego of psychoanalytic theory. Althusser's work therefore invites an exploration of the repressed unconscious that shadows the political 'ego' (the citizen) and its forms of expression, and it would tend to expose the figure of the citizen as the effect of a rigorous policing of political identity and speech that, however vigilant, is never entirely successful. Nonetheless, in identifying the agency of interpellation as ideology – a unified and cohesive discourse – Althusser is driven to insist upon the univocity and stability of the subject as interpellated. He therefore defuses the significance of the unconscious and so leaves out that dimension of political identity which is, in Lacanian terms, 'beyond' interpellation. Ultimately, then, Althusser accepts the claim to integrity and coherence that Rawls and Dworkin make on behalf of the liberal political tradition and the subject that lies at its centre: his argument that the latter functions only as ideology in no way undermines its efficacy as an autonomous and unified agent. A recuperation of those aspects of Lacanian – and Freudian – psychoanalysis that Althusser ignores help, on the contrary, to expose the precariousness of the liberal subject of rights, the fact that it is inhabited from the start, and threatened always with disruption, by its other.

THE MORAL PERSON: METAPOLITICAL, NOT PHYSICAL

How are the institutions, discourses and practices of the liberal state to be explained and justified? Rawls's answer to this question is elaborated through the deployment of the metaphor of the original position. This is the space occupied by the moral person – or rather an association of such persons, whose task it is to devise the fundamental terms of their association. It is a hypothetical state of nature, the parties to which inhabit a situation of complete equality and sameness: they are indistinguishable from each other in their essential freedom and rationality. Knowledge of the particular facts that might set them in opposition – differences of race, class, sex and social status, of natural assets and abilities, and of values, aims and conceptions of the good – is denied to them because these details, in Rawls's view, are morally irrelevant. The only characteristic that can be brought behind the 'veil of ignorance' is the capacity for autonomous action, the ability to formulate and pursue a rational plan of life, for it is this capacity which alone is definitive of moral personality

(1971, p. 23). A person acts autonomously when the principles governing action are self-imposed: 'liberty is acting according to a law that we give ourselves' (ibid., p. 256). Autonomy and constraint are thus not irreconcilable: those principles which have been chosen by a subject are capable of exerting moral authority with respect to that subject. Likewise, those norms which would have been chosen jointly by free and rational persons in a situation of equality will legitimately regulate an association of such persons. 'By acting from these principles persons are acting autonomously: they are acting from principles that they would acknowledge under conditions that best express their nature as free and equal rational beings' (ibid. p. 24).

Rawls's debt to Kant is evident here: the original position is intended to generate universally valid norms in a manner akin to Kant's categorical imperative. However, it would appear that for Rawls, the original position functions not merely to create a space for the reflections of an individual conscience, but to facilitate intersubjective communication. The process of elaborating a conception of justice for a given society must in principle involve the participation of all members of that society, and a universal tenet of political morality is one to which all participants could agree to submit. The idea of a social contract at once respects the Kantian notion that choice is the source of obligation, and emphasises that political morality in a plural society rests upon a collective choice. On one level, this interpretation of Kant represents an apparent shift of emphasis away from the transcendental subject as the origin of normative principles, and instead seems to highlight the ethical significance of participation, with others, in discursive practices. Commentators have therefore pointed to the commonalities between Rawls's work and the 'communicative ethics' of Habermas, Apel and Alexy:

> Instead of asking what an individual moral agent could or would will, without self-contradiction to be a universal maxim for all, one asks: What norms or institutions would the members of an ideal or real communication community agree to as representing their common interests after engaging in a special kind of argumentation or conversation? The procedural model of an argumentative praxis replaces the silent thought experiment enjoined by the Kantian universalisability test. (Benhabib, 1990, p. 1)

Rawls's position, on this view, reflects a fusion of contractarian and Kantian influences: his universal norms are not given a priori to the asocial moral agent, but rather are the outcome of a process of discussion which terminates with the participants' agreement. The principles of justice yielded by the original position are universalisable because they express a universal consensus, and for no other reason. Yet, as a number of commentators have remarked (see e.g. Sandel, 1982; Benhabib, 1987), the parties to the original position are in fact identical to each other. It follows that any conception of justice yielded by their meditations cannot be the result of an argument between persons differently situated, whose differences are the focus of discussion. Rawls's principles of justice, no less than Kant's universal moral law, proceed not from discussion but from the lonely reflections of a singular self. As Habermas has remarked, the procedure that Rawls envisages is entirely monological: 'in the role of a party in the original position, [I] determine what admits of universal approval from the perspective of that role (thus, from my perspective)' (Habermas, 1990, p. 38). *A Theory of Justice*, in short, stands or falls with the conception of the subject on which it is based.

Now, it could be argued that the interpretation of moral personality which informs the original position bypasses controversial ontological claims, primarily because it is not identified with the pursuit of any particular conception of the good. Yet, as Michael Sandel has demonstrated, in a brilliant reading of the account of the self hidden within the description of the moral person, Rawls's equation of citizenship with a capacity for action, a rational will, requires that one see this citizen as having some characteristics rather than others (Sandel, 1982, pp. 15–65). It is identifiable through its capacity to choose, not the objects of its choices, for 'the self is prior to the ends which are affirmed by it' (Rawls, 1971, p. 560). Thus, although ends may vary and conflict within and between persons, the self 'behind' those ends remains unified, stable and the same for all persons. As such, the self retains a certain distance from its attributes, aims, desires and environment: they do not define the subject, but are of the subject. Further, the Rawlsian self is not only prior to its ends, but also to its relationships with others. Persons are 'mutually disinterested' (ibid., p. 13), not in the sense that they are necessarily selfish, but because any ties of affection or solidarity that they may have must be objects of the will: they are chosen and possessed by the subject rather than being the subject. Groups of persons, therefore, can only be understood as associations, constituted by the voluntary activity of their individual members: the 'community' that inhabits the original position is clearly characterised by Rawls as an association in this sense (cf. I. Young, 1990, pp. 42ff.).

Rawls, however, devotes considerable effort in some of his later work to refuting the suggestion that his conception of justice depends upon claims about 'the essential nature and identify of persons' (Rawls, 1985, p. 219) or that the original position involves a 'metaphysical doctrine of the nature of the self' (ibid., p. 231). There are two aspects to Rawls's response to these interpretations of his earlier work. The first involves the claim that the account of the moral person 'is not a moral ideal to govern all of life' (ibid., p. 245) but merely describes the person insofar as s/he appears in the public realm of politics: it is a conception of the person as *citizen*. In his or her 'non-public' dimension, the individual may well be consumed and defined by experience, lacking a sense of self beyond the roles contingently inhabited and the ends pursued. As a citizen, however, the person is entitled to claim an identity which is 'independent from and not identified with any particular conception of the good or scheme of final ends' (ibid., p. 241), and which therefore is not affected by changes over time in his or her conception of the good:

> For example, when citizens convert from one religion to another, or no longer affirm an established faith, they do not cease to be, for questions of political justice, the same persons they were before. There is no loss of what may be called their public identity, their identity as a matter of basic law. (ibid.)

There is a second sense, too, in which this identity is to be understood as political. As well as being proper only to the discrete realm of politics, it has been *elaborated* politically, in and through the practices and principles by which the public political culture of a constitutional democratic regime is given expression. Thus, the person occupying the original position does not reflect the necessary form of political identity as such, but is merely an interpretation – although for Rawls, the only plausible interpretation – of what the liberal political system takes her/him to be. Likewise, the notion that political life consists in a series of interactions between such persons is a reconstruction of the 'intuitive ideas' embedded within liberal political culture: as such, it captures the 'overlapping consensus' (1985, p. 225; 1987; 1989) sustaining contemporary political institutions and accurately reflects 'premises that we and others publicly recognise as true' (1985, p. 225). But these apparently modest claims disguise a number of problematic assumptions: that such a consensus is discernible on any level, that it takes shape around the particular ideas and values that Rawls identifies as fundamental to public life, and that the public realm itself can therefore be ordered, unified and rendered coherent by reference to these ideas. In changing the form of his argument, then, Rawls does not avoid controversy (1987, p. 8), but merely shifts it onto a new terrain. By conceding that the citizen whom he describes has been constructed within political traditions and practices, he eschews metaphysical speculation on the nature of being, but his essentialist interpretation of those practices reproduces the very ontology as to which he purports, in his later work, to be agnostic: the public realm can *only* be understood as producing the political subject in the image of the rational, autonomous individual.[2]

The central objective of Rawlsian liberalism, then, is clear: it sets out to show that what lies at the heart of political life is the idea of a sovereign consciousness. Political agency, or citizenship, consists in the capacity for self-determination, and the sole rationale for the liberal state and its law is that it respects and enables the realisation of that capacity. Yet the liberal commitment to the foundational status of the autonomous individual has been called into question by a range of anti-humanist discourses, all of which, whatever else might divide them, share a tendency to decentre this consciousness, and to interrogate the processes that bring it into being. The next section focuses upon Louis Althusser's attempt to connect two of these discourses by incorporating a version of the psychoanalytic account of ego formation within a Marxian framework. Althusser's invocation of Lacan's notion of the 'imaginary' deserves particular attention, for it is this that constitutes the link in his work between the Freudian understanding of the ego as an effect of repression and the Marxist understanding of the liberal political subject as an effect of ideology.

ALTHUSSER AND PSYCHOANALYSIS: SUBJECTIVITY AS MISTAKEN IDENTITY

Marxist critiques of liberal political philosophy have long sought to demonstrate the impossibility of the ideal of autonomy. Within the Marxist tradition, subjectivity is regarded as a function of one's place within the social formation, and the 'bourgeois' individual as an effect, in the last instance, of capitalist relations of production. Hence, to suggest that the 'man' of liberal thought occupies a position from which the social totality can be apprehended and understood disguises the partiality of 'his' perspective: the perspective of the dominant class. As far as some variants of Marxism are concerned, it follows that the consciousness celebrated within liberalism is merely false, a myth woven by ideology, and that the latter in turn is a bourgeois illusion, an empty distortion of real social relations. Yet this position mirrors the assumptions of the liberalism that it sets out to refute, for it too refuses to renounce the possibility of a true consciousness, an entirely unmediated (non-ideological) perception of reality (Hirst, 1979, pp. 22–39). For Althusser, on the contrary, the subject's relation to its real conditions of existence is never immediate, but is always necessarily an 'imaginary' relation, which is lived through the signifying practices by which societies sustain and reproduce themselves (Althusser, 1977a). Ideology therefore always precedes the subject: it is the process by which social meanings, and the forms of human identity that these require, are produced. It is not to be understood as a system of ideas interpreting or representing an existing and independent reality, for it is inscribed within material practices and has material effects. Through the process of 'interpellation', it equips the individual with an imaginary (but lived) self, one which makes choices, adopts beliefs, reflects, acts, initiates relationships with others, and which, in short, believes itself to be at the centre of its own world. It thus enables a recognition by the biological individual of itself as an autonomous subject. But at the same time, ideology hides from that self the conditions of its own emergence, the structures that have produced it. In particular, it disguises the biases that permeate those structures, and their tendency to yield only those subject positions which are appropriate to a particular social formation. Identities, ideas and values which appear to be freely chosen are in reality generated elsewhere – within institutions, rituals and practices that systematically validate and facilitate some possibilities while excluding others.

Law, as far as Althusser is concerned, is one set of institutions and practices through which ideology operates and in which it is concretised: it is an 'ideological state apparatus' which in a capitalist society plays a crucial role in reproducing capitalist relations of exploitation and consolidating the power of the dominant class. It achieves this in part by mobilising the forces of repression against the recalcitrant and the deviant. Yet, as an ideological practice, law must and does construct the figure of the free and responsible agent as a measure against which a refusal of the state's authority can be judged and found wanting. Far from being prior to law and the state, the sovereign will of the individual is generated in the process of law's functioning. It is required by the social relations of capitalism, relations which, because based upon ownership and exchange, depend upon a conception of the subject as one in possession of (as opposed to being identified with) a realm of objects, included in which is the body itself and its labour.

Althusser's deployment of the concept of the imaginary owes much to Lacan's account of the 'mirror stage' in the development of the individual. Indeed, in very general terms, Althusser and the interpreters of Freud unite around an insistence upon the *misrecognition* that is an inevitable part of the subject's perception of itself as autonomous. 'Just as in Althusser's thought the subject of ideology exists only through ignorance of its true conditions, so the paradox of Freud ... is that the subject comes into being only on the basis of a massive repression of its own unconscious determinants' (Eagleton, 1991, pp. 176–7). For Freud, the id produces – and threatens always to dethrone – the ego:

> Unconsciousness is a regular and inevitable phase in the processes constituting our psychical activity; every psychical act begins as an unconscious one, and it may either remain so or go on developing into consciousness, according as it meets with resistance or not. (Freud, 1912, p. 264)

Yet even 'wishful impulses' that have been repressed can generate effects that reach consciousness and destabilise the efforts of the rational mind to engage in autonomous moral reflection: conscious mental life is thus continually subverted by 'drives' which arise outside it and remain beyond its comprehension or control. The realm to which the ideational representations of these drives are banished – the id – 'knows no judgements of value: no good and evil, no morality' (1933, p. 74). True, the renunciation of instinctual satisfaction, and the elaboration of moral norms justifying this renunciation, is made possible through the operations of conscience: the 'higher, moral, supra-personal side of human nature' (1923, p. 35). Yet conscience, or the superego, is nothing more than the internalisation of parental (specifically, paternal) authority: 'As the child was once under a compulsion to obey its parents, so the ego submits to the categorical imperative of its super-ego' (ibid., p. 48). For Freud, the moral voice is merely a trace – albeit a particularly powerful and lasting one – of the same processes that produce the ego: the introjection of the id's abandoned object choices, such that the latter are 'set up again inside the ego' (ibid., p. 28) and the ego itself becomes the object of libidinal investment. The superego, 'a special agency in the ego' (ibid., p. 48), is a residue of the id's earliest object cathexes – the child's parents. As such, it is the 'heir of the Oedipus complex, and thus it is also the expression of the most powerful impulses and the most important libidinal vicissitudes of the id ...' (ibid., p. 36).

The recognition that desire and its repression, organised within a structure of identifications, is *internally* related to the development of a sense of moral autonomy casts doubts upon some of the central assumptions of liberal political thought. According to the Freudian interpretation of the categorical imperative, for instance, the argument that human beings can release themselves from the effects of socialisation and thereby realise the capacity for moral action refuses to acknowledge the very forces that enable moral action. It fails to recognise that this capacity develops not despite, but because of the individual's entry into the social order: it is a precipitate of the individual's 'first and most important identification' (Freud, 1923, p. 31) with other human beings. To equate moral personality with the sovereignty of the ego is therefore to deny the *subjection* (to the cultural norms thereby introjected) that is an inescapable part of every act of moral choice. But further, it is to obscure the constitutive role played by desire in sustaining the structures of social power. In suggesting that desire motivates the identifications forming the superego, 'Freud's work powerfully undercuts traditional philosophical notions that posit the possibility of a transcendental law or rational authority' (Elliott, 1992, p. 42). Far from being 'higher' than the rational mind, the superego is sustained by the vicissitudes of desire: it 'reaches deep down into the id and for that reason is farther from consciousness than the ego is' (Freud, 1923, p. 49). Moreover, not only does it find its roots in the id, but its efficacy is continually undermined by the latter's recalcitrance. The superego issues a command and does not ask whether it is possible for people to obey it. On the contrary, it assumes that a man's ego is psychologically capable of anything that is required of it, that his ego has unlimited mastery over his id. This is a mistake; and even in what are known as normal people the id cannot be controlled beyond certain limits. (1930, p. 143)

If this is so at the level of the individual, then it may also have implications for the way in which the polity is understood, for a community's system of law and the political morality that underpins it can, Freud implies (ibid., pp. 141–3), be represented as the demands of a sort of cultural superego upon the members of that community. As such, it would seem always to be vulnerable to subversion and resistance from a cultural/political 'id', a collective unconscious which is never quite repressed by the association of sovereign subjects that constitutes the political realm. Nonetheless, the potential of orthodox Freudian psychoanalysis for a critique of liberal political morality is ultimately limited by the apparent biologism of Freud's account of the drives which structure the unconscious – for the effect of this is to naturalise the phenomenon of resistance – coupled with Freud's own conception of the proper aim of psychoanalysis: the conquest of the drives by the ego (Dews, 1987, p. 86). And although Althusser recognises that potential in general terms, he too ultimately defuses the implications of the unconscious for such a critique. By giving the name 'ideology' to Freud's cultural superego,[3] Althusser suggests that social processes beyond the nuclear family may be responsible for the production of the norms concretised within the structures of the liberal state (Althusser, 1977b, pp. 194–5, 199), and this in turn enables an explanation of the latter as the object and effect of a range of social (as opposed to purely familial) struggles. Yet Althusser's (imaginary) subject submits readily and unproblematically to the demands of this superego: the possibility of rebellion by the unconscious is simply left out of Althusser's account (Eagleton, 1991, pp. 144–5). In this respect, Althusser's deployment of psychoanalytic theory obscures some of its most subversive implications for liberal political thought.

THE RETURN OF THE UNCONSCIOUS: LACANIAN PSYCHOANALYSIS

An assessment of these implications necessitates a closer look at Lacan's rereading of Freud than Althusser's treatment of it can afford. Lacan foregrounds what had remained only partially developed in Freud's work (see e.g. Dews, 1987, pp. 55–7; Grosz, 1990, pp. 24–31; Elliott, 1992, pp. 30ff.) – the importance of narcissistic processes of identification to the formation of the ego – and in so doing reinterprets the Freudian theory of the ego in terms of the Hegelian dialectic of self and other: 'consciousness can grasp itself only through its reflection in and recognition by the other, yet ... an inherent aspiration towards autonomy repugns against the dependency which this relation implies' (Dews, 1987, p. 53). In thus emphasising that self-identity is a fragile effect of processes of intersubjective negotiation, which in turn are propelled by a desire for recognition in/by the other, Lacan rejects Freud's (actual or perceived) tendency to reduce ego development to a series of biologically determined stages, and desire to a derivative of instinctual stimuli (Freud, 1915). For Lacan, '[t]he social and linguistic orders function in place of the instinctual in human existence' (Grosz, 1990, p. 33).

Lacan's 'mirror stage' (1977, pp. 1–7) – that phase in the development of the human subject when the child begins to recognise its image in the mirror[4] – inaugurates a process that recurs with every attempt by the subject to represent itself both to itself and to others. The reflection *anticipates*, in the realm of the imaginary, that which has yet to be realised in actuality: the infant's mastery of its body. Captivated by what it sees in the mirror – the body as a unified totality – the child jubilantly identifies with this image, although its own experience of its body is one of fragmentation and dependence. It is through an identification with this ideal-ego, Lacan argues, that the ego itself is constructed as unified and autonomous, the procedure being repeated subsequently through the individual's relationships with other persons. However, the ego thus formed is founded upon an imaginary representation of the subject, which in turn divides the subject against itself. The difference between experience and image is precisely what enables an identification to take effect – it explains the child's fascination with its mirror image – yet the otherness of the image is overlooked in the perception of sameness. Thus, the sense of identity and autonomy that the subject derives from its ego is the deceptive outcome of a persistent denial of the alterity that brings it into being and upon which it depends. The ego, in short, is constituted in and through this otherness, or difference, yet the imaginary is 'an order of representation which misrepresents difference as the image of identity' (Weber, 1991, pp. 105–6). Nevertheless, this process of dissimulation is never entirely successful. The unifed ego itself 'is the means by which the individual retains an active memory of his earliest sense of physical disarray' (Bowie, 1991, p. 26), and aggressiveness is the behavioural manifestation of this 'return' of the fragmented body in the form of fantasies of mutilation and disintegration (Lacan, 1977, pp. 8–29).

If the imaginary order effects an alienation of the subject from itself, then a second 'splitting' of the subject occurs with its entry into the symbolic order through the acquisition of language. The subject of the statement, the 'I' which appears in language, purports to reflect the true subject, the subject of enunciation, the 'I' which makes use of language in order to represent itself. Yet (like the child's mirror image), it is never entirely adequate to the task. Language can only be said to represent the subject of enunciation if it is understood as a set of correspondences between signifiers (sound-images) and signifieds (concepts), the latter being prior to, and determining, the former. But for Lacan, language, on the contrary, is a system of differential relations between signifiers (1977, pp. 146–78). As one commentator explains – in a suitably metaphorical mode:

> [a]nyone who goes in search of meaning at its source, or in its essential forms, has no choice but to travel by way of language, and at every moment on this journey variously connected signifiers extend to the horizon in all directions. When the signified seems finally to be within reach, it dissolves at the explorer's touch into yet more signifiers. (Bowie, 1991, p. 64)

Recognition of the subject can only be achieved through language, yet a subject constituted through its combinatory 'play' can never be the self-identical entity presupposed by the imaginary order. The operations of language always leave an irreducible residue, something which is unpresentable; hence, whatever the subject is represented as being will be characterised by a lack, an absence.[5] It is this very lack that constitutes the existence of the subject of enunciation as a desiring subject, and that motivates the continuing flux of the signifying process (Lacan, 1977, pp. 292–325). The truth of the subject is therefore to be found not in the signified but in the spaces between signifiers (Dews, 1987, p. 100; Benevenuto and Kennedy, 1986, p. 118), simultaneously fading and becoming through a paradoxical juncture of retroactivity and anticipation. 'There where it was just now, there where it was for a while, between an extinction that is still glowing and a birth that is retarded, "I" can come into being and disappear from what I say' (Lacan, 1977, p. 300).

Lacan interprets the separation of the ego from the unconscious in terms of this split between the subject of the statement and the subject of enunciation. The unconscious, characterised, as Freud had demonstrated, by the primary processes of condensation and displacement, exhibits the same polysemy and the same sliding of meaning as the signifying function itself (Lacan, 1977, pp. 146–78). However, the very existence of the subject depends upon its recognition as such by other subjects, and this in turn requires the assumption of a site of intentionality within language – language here being understood as a set of determinate meanings, existing for a subject who intends those meanings. Hence, the subject is forced into a separation from the movement of the primary processes: conscious thought (the secondary process characteristic of the ego) is the outcome of this separation. So too is the resolution of the Oedipus complex: the acquisition of a place within culture is the child's 'reward' for its acceptance of paternal authority and its renunciation of desire for the mother. However, in Lacan's account of the Oedipus complex, the child's submission is not to a real, biological father, but to the Other, the symbolic father, the author of the law governing the symbolic order: '[i]t is in the *name-of-the-father* that we must recognise the support of the symbolic function, which, from the dawn of history, has identified his person with the figure of the law' (ibid., p. 67). In identifying with the position of this father, the child identifies with the possessor of the phallus, the signifier of that which satisfies desire, or, in Lacanian terms, of that which controls the signifying process itself. The superego is born through the internalisation of the symbolic father's authority, and it is through the superego that the infant's imaginary relation with the (m)other is disrupted: desire for the (m)other, or, in Lacanian terms, for the recognition that the (m)other can bestow, is repressed and displaced onto the phallus. The 'resolution' of the Oedipus complex thus consists in an acknowledgement of the phallus as the ultimate guarantee of meaning/ identity/recognition, of the mother's (and the child's) lack of the phallus, of the father's possession of it, and of the prospect that through intro- jecting the father's authority the child too will eventually gain access to it.

The subject of the signified/statement emerges at this point, yet the repression which brings it into being also establishes the unconscious as the subject of the signifier/enunciation. It follows from Lacan's concep- tion of the symbolic order that the Other 'does not exist' (ibid., p. 323): the position of the Other, and with it the phallus, is unattainable, which is to say that the desire for recognition, for a stable position within language, is insatiable. The unconscious is the locus of this desire. It is therefore the unconscious that guarantees the ceaseless motion of the signifying proc- ess, its discourse manifesting itself in the inevitably metaphoric and metonymic structure of conscious thought and speech through which repressed signifiers constantly interfere with, subvert, and evade the censorship of, the subject of the signified (ibid., pp. 146–78). In this sense, it 'provides the most rigorous criticism of the presupposition of a consistent, fully finished subject' (Coward and Ellis, 1977, p. 94). Yet in a manner anticipated precisely by the mirror stage, the ego denies the inevitability of the gap between the subject reflected in language and that which exceeds representation. Just as the mirror stage involves a misrecognition by the child of itself as autonomous in relation to its body, the acquisition of language permits the speaking subject to misrecognise itself as the author and master of its speech (possessor of the phallus), and speech itself as the transparent medium of its relations with others. For Lacan, psychoanalysis, far from seeking to strengthen the alienating and inert form of the ego, should aim at helping the analysand to accept his/ her desire, and the lack of which it is a manifestation, and relinquish the ultimately self-destructive commitment to plenitude and autonomy.

It is precisely the operations of the unconscious that are obscured by Rawls's invocation of the original position in *A Theory of Justice*. Clearly, to the extent that the moral person describes an essential human nature, the original position signals Rawls's commitment to an ontology which refuses the possibility of the unconscious altogether, for the moral person is simply the ideal-ego, a (mirror) image of the ego, and the basis for the subject's perception of itself as a unified entity, determined solely by its capacity for rational and autonomous action. In Lacanian terms, the original position can only be the realm of the imaginary. Yet for the 'later' Rawls, as we have seen, the original position is to be understood as reflecting a truth which is 'political, not metaphysical' (1985, p. 219): it is not to be taken as representing the essential form of human agency as such but merely the vision of political agency, and of the public realm, that is immanent within 'the political institutions of a constitutional democratic regime and the public traditions of their interpretation' (ibid., p. 225). The apparent shift in Rawls's position here, towards an acknowledgement that the identify of the political subject is an effect of political practices and the ideas concretised within them, is reminiscent of the progression of Lacan's work from a preoccupation with the formation of the ego in the register of the imaginary to a concern with language as constitutive of the subject: Rawls's later work clearly attests to the constitutive force of the 'symbols' through which the political domain is organised. Moreover, the condition of access to this domain is analogous to that described by Lacan in relation to the subject's entry into culture. For Rawls, the position of author (of the law), which is the original position, is occupied by the moral person, and the citizen is brought into being through an identification with this author, the bearer of the 'phallus' (the capacity for autonomous action). And since that identification in turn can only be achieved through submission to the restrictions imposed by the veil of ignorance, the latter effectively sets up the condition that must be fulfilled if the subject is to 'signify' within the normative order of institutionalised politics. The desire for (political) recognition, that is, propels the subject into an assumption of the identity of the citizen, and the person attains a place within the political order only to the extent that he or she can achieve this identification.

For Rawls, however, this process is inherently unproblematic. Unlike Lacan, for whom the perception of a stable and unified subject position within language is an effect of *méconnaissance*, sustained only by the operations of the ego, and continually interrupted by the playfulness of language (the discourse of the unconscious) itself, Rawls regards the signifying practices that constitute liberal political culture as capable of being 'organised' (Rawls, 1985, p. 229) into a coherent whole. Hence, the acknowledgement that the political subject is discursively produced does not operate to shatter its imaginary unity: the agency of its production, the 'language' of public life, is itself unified. The 'fundamental intuitive idea' structuring these institutions and practices is that of the political community as an association of free and equal persons who are the architects of the norms by which they are governed. Therefore, as far as Rawls is concerned, the only conception of political agency that can be said to be true (i.e., publicly recognised as true) for a constitutional democratic regime is that of the citizen as author.

It is this notion that Althusser exposes as the imaginary effect of the process of interpellation, one which operates not to reveal but to obscure the true conditions of the individual's existence in a liberal capitalist society. For Althusser, what Rawls insists on describing as '*our* public political culture ... the *shared* fund of implicitly recognised basic ideas and principles' (Rawls, 1985, p. 228; emphasis mine) is an ideological apparatus which disguises its true function – the reproduction of capitalist relations of production and of the dominance of the ruling class within capitalism – and enables the individual to *mis*recognise him/herself in its speculary structure as the author of its laws and underlying norms. Nevertheless, although the influence of Lacanian psychoanalysis is evident here, Althusser's reading of Lacan's œuvre as a whole is highly selective. For Lacan, there can be *no* position 'behind' language which would constitute its point of origination – the author, prior to difference, fixed, stable: that which can control the movement of the signifier. Yet, while Rawls reserves this position for the autonomous individual, Althusser seems to permit 'the ruling class' to occupy it in relation to ideology. Language is reduced to ideology,[6] and the latter in turn is conceived of as a seamless web of coherent meanings: 'the ideology by which [the ISA's] function is always in fact unified, despite its diversity and its contradictions, *beneath the ruling ideology* which is the ideology of "the ruling class"' (Althusser, 1977, p. 139; emphasis in original). Consequently, Althusser can recognise no split between the subject interpellated in ideology and that which exceeds interpellation, the unconscious: in place of a separation, he posits an absolute alienation of the subject in ideology. His silence with respect to the unconscious, in turn, is an effect of his dismissal of the Lacanian real, that 'kernel resisting symbolic integration-dissolution' (Zizek, 1989, p. 3) which is the object-cause of desire. Althusser focuses upon Lacan's account of the formation of an autonomous ego through the subject's identification with an imaginary representation of itself in the symbolic forms by which capitalist social relations are sustained. Yet he sees the subject interpellated in 'language' (ideology) as simply that which the imaginary represents it to be – unified, self-contained, and self-identical. In this respect, Althusser ultimately allies himself with none other than Rawls.

Althusser and Rawls concur in conceiving of the liberal political subject as one produced by, rather than being prior to, the institutions, practices and discourses of the liberal state; Dworkin performs a similar manoeuvre in relation to the subject inscribed within law. Indeed, like Althusser, Rawls acknowledges that there may be a split between the public identity which is allotted to the person in law and his/her lived experience: the veil of ignorance serves as a metaphor for the boundary separating the 'public' from the merely 'private'. But further, Althusser, Dworkin and Rawls all unite around a conception of that (public) subject as the stable, unified, non-contradictory effect of these processes of 'interpellation', and of the discourse of rights as a coherent and unitary medium in which it addresses its demands to an imaginary counterpart, an 'other' which is nothing more than a reflection of itself. To adapt Lacan's insights to an analysis of the political domain is, however, to recognise that the splitting that accompanies the construction of the subject of rights, the subject of the statement, at the same time produces the subject of enunciation, and the desire which exceeds the fulfilment of (political) demand. In other words, the very process by which the citizen is constituted and inscribed constantly generates something akin to a political 'unconscious', identities and voices which are repressed within but nonetheless ineradicable from the categories and structures of liberalism: the 'beyond of the demand' which is at the same time 'hollowed within' it (Lacan, 1977, p. 265). In the words of Zizek, '[i]f the Name-of-the-Father functions as the agency of interpellation, ... desire ... marks a certain limit at which every interpellation necessarily fails' (Zizek, 1989, p. 121). The final section will sketch the terrain occupied by this 'other scene', and argue that its continuing significance lies in its disruption of the liberal citizen's capacity to exhaust the meaning of political identity and political expression.

THE PLACE OF THE OTHER

Lacan's account of the denials upon which the ego is founded suggests an approach to the category of the citizen that asks *how* it achieves its unity and identity: what is excluded in the process of its construction? It draws attention to the negations upon which Rawls's vision of the political subject is founded, and which are structured by his insistence upon the autonomy of the rational will as the characteristic feature of the moral person. The citizen is autonomous, not heteronomous; unified, not plural; static, not shifting; individual, not collective; abstract, not material. Above all, however, Rawls's moral person is characterised by its will, rather than its bodily existence. The body here can be understood as a metaphor for everything that the Rawlsian subject is not: it signifies 'embodiment', that which situates the person in time and space, equips the person with a perspective on the world which is necessarily limited, though mobile, and differentiates the person from others (Bordo, 1990). Bodily characteristics also link individuals with one another: it is by appealing to shared physical attributes such as gender, skin colour and age that people identify with others in the context of social groups (I. Young, 1990, pp. 122–55). Finally, the body is the site of desire, impulse and sentiment: 'the passions', as Hobbes would have put it. The will, on the other hand, is disembodied and transcendent, and thus stands outside of and opposed to everything the body represents. Action originates with the will, which thus frees the person from the determinations of bodily existence. It reduces the heterogeneous needs, inclinations and perspectives of the body to the unity of a personality: the subject realises itself as a subject by conquering the body through its capacity for rational choice and responsibility. It is individual, yet possessed by everyone in the same way, and thus enables, while being prior to, relationships with others.

It is the existence of a barrier separating those attributes which are proper to the citizen from those which are not that constitutes citizenship as a mechanism, not of inclusion, but of closure. Given that it defines the characteristics that qualify the person for participation in public life, the category of citizenship marks out a boundary between that which properly belongs within the realm of politics and that which is eliminated from it: as Iris Young in particular has shown, it purports to determine who can be a political subject, and thereby guarantees that only those issues appropriate to that subject, as defined, can count as political issues. To attribute the status of citizenship to the individual rather than to the group, for instance, is to refuse the notion that identity is an achievement of inter-subjective negotiation: it is to represent the individual as prior to any groups to which s/he belongs, the group as, at most, the result of an act of choice that leaves the self intact, and the needs that groups take to be definitive of their shared identity as nothing more than claims of right asserted by their individual members. Again, the identification of the individual in terms of the will rather than the body has the effect of disqualifying from the public realm those who are deemed incapable of rational thought and action because determined by the bodily and affective aspects of existence. Feminist analyses of the public/private distinction have explained the denial of political rights to women until relatively recently in the history of the liberal state as an effect of precisely this antinomy between reason and desire. More fundamentally, feminists have argued that the exclusion of women from citizenship persists, albeit not in formal legal terms, by the association of traits culturally defined as masculine with the capacities that privilege the citizen as a universal subject. Thus the public realm of citizens achieves its unity and universality only by defining the civil individual in opposition to that which is identified as feminine: everything which embraces the body (see e.g. Pateman, 1988, 1989; A. Young, 1990; Phillips, 1991; Dietz, 1992).

It is as a rational person, as pure will, abstracted from the empirical conditions of lived experience, that one is 'capable ... of a sense of justice' (Rawls, 1971, p. 12) and therefore entitled to a political voice. The freedom of the individual citizen, which is the project of liberal politics, is articulated in terms of liberation from external constraints, and the discourse of rights is the language in which this project is properly expressed. Yet Dworkin's account of the political subject as a subject of rights can be understood as calculated to censor rather than to enable the articulation of claims, in that it dispels those claims which are appropriate to a subject that falls on the wrong side of the divide separating the rational autonomous citizen from what it is supposed not to be: a subject of need or desire. Further, this censorship, since it is the very condition of the subject's political 'speech', cannot itself be signified within the idiom of liberal discourse. The perspective of the universal citizen is deemed to be equally available to all, and from that perspective, politics 'begins' only when the will of the individual is coerced; when the capacity for rational action is interfered with in some determinate way. The processes that constitute both the rational citizen and its rejected others remain inaccessible to explicitly political intervention.

The free, rights-bearing individual functions in liberal political theory as the pre-eminent 'anchoring point' within the montage of signifiers that constitute the political domain. By means of this (phallic) category, 'the political institutions of a constitutional democratic regime and the public traditions of their interpretation' (Rawls, 1985, p. 225) can be totalised into a coherent structure of meaning and equipped with a defining essence. Yet Lacan's conception of the symbolic order suggests that meaning cannot be regarded as immanent within a given discursive field, but is rather a retroactive effect of the relational interplay between signifiers, an effect, moreover, which is illusory in its consistency. The node around which these elements are articulated – the original position, the place of the Other/Author – is not the repository of truth, but another signifier, itself implicated in the play of differences: the embodiment of a fundamental lack. The fantasy of the veil of ignorance, through which the closure of the political realm can be achieved and the latter represented as coherent and complete, is the screen which masks this lack, represses everything that recalls it, and 'sutures' the insufficiency of the signifier by displacing the lack to another place. Yet the attempt to encircle the real place of the political reveals not a presence but a failure of representation, and it is through this failure that 'desire' makes itself known. The symptoms of desire, in this context, manifest themselves in the irruption of political subjectivities that cannot be captured by the category of the citizen, and by forms of political and legal expression which exceed the logic of right:[7] the subversive power of the repressed other of liberalism consists precisely, then, in its 'refusal of a unitary construct of citizenship as exhaustive of the political tasks of the present' (McClure, 1992, p. 123). The attempt to argue for the institution-alisation of a reworked notion of citizenship that could accommodate these identities and claims, and for mechanisms and structures within or linked with the state that might entertain them, now constitutes an identifiable trend within postliberal political theory (see e.g. Keane 1984, ch. 5; Melucci, 1989, ch. 8; I. Young, 1990, ch. 6). Yet to eradicate the symptom is an impossibility, for it is an inevitable expression of the antagonism that constitutes, sustains and finally limits the discursive field of the political. Lacanian psychoanalysis demands a constant awareness of this surplus of the real over every attempt at symbolisation; it requires a coming to terms with what remains always beyond accommodation; and it serves as a reminder that every description of the just society bears witness to the unpresentable. Justice, in short, has no guarantee. It 'remains to be attained: it is ahead of us' (Lyotard, 1985, p. 83).

NOTES

1. This is so despite the problematic relationship that is said to exist between Lacanian psychoanalysis – the source of many of the themes of this chapter – and poststructuralism: see e.g. Dews (1987, ch. 3) and Zizek (1989, ch. 5).
2. Dworkin's argument that legal truth is to be found not in some objective set of moral principles of which law is merely declaratory, but in the coherence of the values and purposes embedded within the legal enterprise, obeys the same logic as Rawls's political concep-tion of justice, and meets with the same objections: see Dworkin (1977, ch. 6) and cf. Barron (1992, pp. 150–3).
3. This move was in fact anticipated by Freud himself in a paper entitled 'The dissection of the psychical personality' (Freud, 1933, p. 67).
4. It should be noted that the mirror stage can be understood as a metaphor for the child's pre-Oedipal relationship with its mother.
5. In his later work, Lacan theorises this lack in terms of the *objet 'a'*, that dimension of the subject which is proper to a third order, the real. The real subsists beyond any attempt at its reflection/represen-tation in the register of the imaginary or the symbolic. The glossary added to the English edition of *Ecrits* by its translator, Alan Sheridan, defines it elegantly as 'that which is lacking in the symbolic order, the ineliminable residue of all articulation, the foreclosed element, which may be approached, but never grasped ...' (Lacan, 1977, p. x).
6. Thus, 'the Law of Culture, which is first introduced as language and whose first form is language, is not exhausted by language; its content is the real kinship structures and the determinate ideological formations in which persons inscribed in these structures live their functions ...' (Althusser, 1977b, p. 194, n. 4).

7. The correlate of the symptom in liberal legal theory is the Dworkinian concept of the 'mistake'.

REFERENCES

Althusser, L. (1977a), 'Ideology and ideological state apparatuses', in *Lenin and Philosophy and Other Essays*, 2nd ed., London: NLB.

——— (1977b), 'Freud and Lacan', in *Lenin and Philosophy and Other Essays*, 2nd ed., London: NLB.

Barron, A. (1992), 'Ronald Dworkin and the challenge of postmodernism', in Hunt, A. (ed.), *Reading Dworkin Critically*, Oxford: Berg.

Benhabib, S. (1990), 'In the shadow of Aristotle and Hegel: communicative ethics and current controversies in practical philosophy', Kelly, M. (ed.), *Hermeneutics and Critical Theory in Ethics and Politics*, Cambridge, Ma: MIT Press.

——— (1987), 'The generalised and the concrete other', in Benhabib, S. and Cornell, D. (eds), *Feminism as Critique*, Minneapolis: University of Minnesota.

Benvenuto, B. and Kennedy, R. (1986), *The Works of Jacques Lacan*, London: Free Association Books.

Bordo, S. (1990), 'Feminism, Post-Modernism and Gender-Skepticism', in Nicholson, L. (ed.), *Feminism/Postmodernism*, London: Routledge.

Bowie, M. (1991), *Lacan*, London: Fontana.

Coward, R. and Ellis, J. (1977), *Language and Materialism*, London: Routledge.

Dews, P. (1987), *Logics of Disintegration*, London: Verso.

Dietz, M. (1992), 'Context is all: feminism and theories of citizenship', in Mouffe, C. (ed.), *Dimensions of Radical Democracy*, London: Verso.

Dworkin, R. (1977), *Taking Rights Seriously*, Cambridge, Ma: Harvard University Press.

Eagleton, T. (1991), *Ideology*, London: Verso.

Elliott, A. (1992), *Social Theory and Psychoanalysis in Transition*, Oxford: Basil Blackwell.

Freud, S. (1912), 'A note on the unconscious in psychoanalysis', in Strachey, J. (ed.), *The Standard Edition of the Complete Psychological Works of Sigmund Freud*, vol. 12, p. 257.

——— (1915), 'Instincts and their vicissitudes', *Standard Edition*, vol. 14, p. 117.

——— (1923), 'The Ego and the Id', *Standard Edition*, vol. 19, p. 12.

——— (1930), 'Civilisation and its discontents', *Standard Edition*, vol. 21, p. 64.

——— (1933), 'The dissection of the psychical personality', *Standard Edition*, vol. 22, p. 57.

Grosz, E. (1990), *Jacques Lacan: A Feminist Introduction*, London: Routledge.

Habermas, J. (1990), 'Justice and solidarity: on the discussion concerning "Stage 6"', in Kelly, M. (ed.), *Hermeneutics and Critical Theory in Ethics and Politics*, Cambridge, MA: MIT Press.

Hirst, P. (1979), *On Law and Ideology*, London: Macmillan.

Keane, J. (1984), *Public Life and Late Capitalism*, Cambridge: Cambridge University Press.

Lacan, J. (1977), *Ecrits. A Selection* , London: Tavistock.

Lyotard, J.-F. (1985), *Just Gaming*, Manchester: Manchester University Press.

McClure, K. (1992), 'On the subject of rights: pluralism, plurality and political identity', in Mouffe, C. (ed.), *Dimensions of Radical Democracy*, London: Verso.

Melucci, A. (1989), *Nomads of the Present*, London: Radius.
Pateman, C. (1988), *The Sexual Contract*, Cambridge: Polity.
—— (1989), *The Disorder of Women*, Cambridge: Polity.
Phillips, A. (1991), *Engendering Democracy*, Cambridge: Polity.
Rawls, J. (1971), *A Theory of Justice*, Cambridge, Ma: Harvard University Press.
—— (1985), 'Justice as fairness: political not metaphysical', in *Philosophy and Public Affairs* 14, 219.
—— (1987), 'The idea of an overlapping concensus', *Oxford Journal of Legal Studies* 7 (1), 1–25.
—— (1989),'The domain of the political and overlapping consensus', *New York University Law Review* 64 (2), 233–55.
Sandel, M. (1982), *Justice and the Limits of Liberalism*, Cambridge: Cambridge University Press.
Weber, S. (1991), *Return to Freud*, Cambridge: Cambridge University Press.
Young, A. (1990), *Femininity in Dissent*, London: Routledge.
Young, I. (1990), *Justice and the Politics of Difference*, Princeton: Princeton University Press.
Zizek, S. (1989), *The Sublime Object of Ideology*, London: Verso.

6

After the Law

NICK LAND

There are peculiar difficulties associated with any philosophy of law, due in large part to the inevitability that any attempt at a transcendent evaluation of law finds itself enacting a parody of judicial process. Ever since the trial of Socrates (if not already with the fragment of Anaximander), philosophy has affirmed its vocation only insofar as it has fantasised a supreme tribunal: an ultimate court of appeal or ideal form of justice. The vindication of Socratism is inextricable from a retrial, both exculpation and counterlitigation, the forum of which remains the unstable *issue* of metaphysics. As for its 'own' or 'inner' law, logic has never been anything other than the distillation of juridical procedure, the abstract form of inclusion or non-inclusion of a case under a law (species under genus), which has been predominantly thematised as *judgment*, although a language of *propositions* has more recently risen to prominence. Philosophy and judicial authority find themselves bound together in a discourse upon real legitimation. Appearances (cases) are to be judged from the perspective of a generic reason at a superior level of reality, identified in the premodern period with an ideality whose final term is the intellect of God. Aristotle consummates a categorial – accusatory – sense of form, and the Augustinian collision of Platonism with Judaeo-Christian eschatology and Christian *logos* has only entrenched this complicity.

This chapter cuts into two episodes or intersections of the occidental juridico-philosophical complex, in an attempt to dramatise the broadest tendency of its process: that of collapse towards immanence, or evaporation of the transcendent. There is nothing peculiarly occult or mysterious about such a tendency, since it finds its most highly accelerated phase in our contemporary marketisation of social transactions: the phased transition from traditional theopolitical authorisation or *legitimacy* to an impersonal, cybernetically automated *efficiency*. The commodity 'form' is a transmutational matrix, and not a static (synchronic) order of economic liberalism. Insofar as capital is still interpreted Platonically – according to legitimation criteria – there is an overt paradox or contradiction emergent in this process, a paradox whose disappearance is epitomised by the figure of Georges Bataille, who offers *an operational description of law*. Bataille no longer offers a juridical procedure of any kind, but only a tactics of recoding that converges upon the outside of human history (where everything functions without respect or legitimacy).

Those seeking to defend the human management of social processes (where 'man' speculatively unites with the God of anthropomorphic monotheism) can have no project but to restore a *history* whose ideal sense would reconnect with the *meaning of the West*, such as those proffered by Plato, Aquinas and Hegel. Such restoration is a modernist aspiration which strikes me as incredible. To drag Plato and Bataille before the tribunal of philosophy has ceased to be anything but entertainment, yet I dedicate this text to the few remaining political animals of the planet Earth, as an experiment in the tenacity of philosophy, or as a jest.

PLATO AND THE TRIAL OF SOCRATES

Plato's *Apology* is initiated by submission to the political, in which civic obedience and justificatory discourse are fused. Rebellion is not Socratic, and the principle of authority – or right to judge – is never radically interrogated; only its source is in question. In attempting to contest the charge that he 'makes the weaker argument defeat the stronger' (Plato, 1969, p. 47), it is not long before Socrates invokes the 'unimpeachable authority' (Plato, 1969, p. 49) of Apollo, and narrates the journey of his disciple Chaerephon:

> one day he actually went to Delphi and asked this question of the god – as I said before, gentlemen, please do not interrupt – he asked whether there was anyone wiser than myself. The priestess replied that there was no one. (Plato, 1969, p. 49)

To interpret this statement as a submission of evidence would be to efface the fracture line between the sacred and the profane across which Socrates steps. It is precisely the resistance to evidentiality that lends to this message its oracular force, and the paradoxical gesture at the heart of Socrates' defence is that of deploying the privilege of the unknown on behalf of knowing.

The mystery of the oracular message is registered within the order of judgment as an underinterpretation. The priestess's words require translation, beyond that of their reworking into verse that occurs at Delphi itself. They pose a problem that can be construed as exegetical, as an insufficiency of commentary and resolution. Words are oracular precisely insofar as they suspend intelligence, whether in the sacred abandonment to unknowing which is their source, or in the profane detour of philosophy that becomes their destination. Socrates' discourse is the site of a crossing from inspiration to anticipated wisdom.

It is not only words of the Delphic oracle that are at stake here, since they resonate with the more intimate counsel of Socrates' δαιμων or 'spirit'. Later in the *Apology*, we are told by Socrates that:

> I am subject to a divine or supernatural experience, which Meletus saw fit to travesty in his indictment. It began in my early childhood – a sort of voice which comes to me; and when it comes it always dissuades me from what I am proposing to do, and never urges me on (Plato, 1969, p. 64)

The interference between the sacred and the profane, the unknown and knowing, is in its sacred sense a gateway opening onto death, and in its profane sense a hesitation: interruption as the edge of time or as a delay within time, death as the outside or as the deferred, the threshold of death as a brink or as a moment. Later in the *Apology*, Socrates reports that 'I am now at that point where the gift of prophecy comes most readily to me: at the point of death' (Plato, 1969, p. 73). This remark connects strangely with the earlier comment that

> I soon made up my mind about the poets too: I decided that it was not wisdom that enabled them to write their poetry, but a kind of instinct or inspiration, such as you find in seers and prophets who deliver all their sublime messages without knowing in the least what they mean. (Plato, 1969, p. 51)

Poets and prophets explore the zero-degree of judgment, a zone at the edge of the great zero that Socrates tentatively sketches, but only rarely approaches. His own sense of 'preparation for death' is the path of wisdom rather than intoxication, aligning himself with a knowing that is compared to its inadequate instances, rather than succumbing to the unknowing beyond comparison beside which all knowing is inadequate. Comparing himself to his fellows, Socrates elaborates the oracle as suggesting that 'I am wiser ... to this small extent, that I do not think I know what I do not know' (Plato, 1969, p. 50). This is the edge of the unknown, but always there is the gesture of recuperation to knowing, to judgment, to the tribunal, justice and authority: 'real wisdom is the property of God, and this oracle is his way of telling us that human wisdom has little or no value' (Plato, 1969, p. 52). If human wisdom has little or no value, where do the dogmatic assertions about God and his wisdom stem from? Why should they be trusted? Is not the figure of God indistinguishable from the claim that we know it is knowledge that matters, that the unknown is something we know, something we can populate with our feverish anthropomorphisms? Does Socrates not exhibit God as the eclipse of religion, the surrender of knowing as a submission to ... knowing? It is thus that religion is buried beneath the icon of a supreme judge.

The figure of Socrates, as sketched for us by Plato – his advocate – is that of philosophy on trial. It is in crossing this judicial threshold that philosophy comes to delight in the voluptuousities of persecution. Yet the drama of Socrates' condemnation distracts from the more far-reaching process whereby philosophy succumbs to the order of the courtroom, and with this process Socrates is deeply complicit. He could even be said to have forged a new alliance between knowledge and condemnation, as well as becoming the first philosophical *case*.

How could one imagine an *Apology* for a Herakleitus, an Empedokles, or a Parmenides? To whom would they be attempting to justify themselves? To the *people*? The thought is absurd. For what does the opinion of the people matter? It was precisely as an escape from the opinion of the people that philosophy emerged! To philosophise and to ignore popular opinion are scarcely differentiable. If the Presocratics speak in terms of cosmic justification – as Anaximander already does – it is as a concession, in order that the people will at least understand the surpassing of human judgment, if not that by which it is surpassed. The harsh 'justice' of fate is the ironisation of human litigation, and not its inflation to the absolute (monotheism).

With Socrates, things are different. Philosophy becomes dialectical; which is to say justificatory, political, logical, plebeian. Truth is identified with irrefutability, evidentiality and educated belief, beginning its long subsidence into the forms of human credence, as if its acceptability were in any way a criterion.

The *Apology* focuses a multiple interweaving of death and judgment. There is first of all the sense in which death fulfils judgment in the sentence of death, even if this is an injustice – or misjudgment – such that Athens is condemned in the tribunal of the Platonic text, whose judgment in this case becomes a massively influential precedent. There is a nesting of judgments; that of Socrates, that of Athens and that of Plato, with each level subsuming the antecedent one as an item or case to be judged.

Judgment is the subsumption of a case under a principle or law. It is classificatory or categorising, according to a discursive order which is simultaneously juridical and logical. The very word 'category' is derived from the Greek word χατηγορος, or accuser. Judgment is thus an image of thought, and Plato's entire philosophy can be read as an appeal to a higher court, as an obsessive retrial, as well as a counteraccusation against Socrates' executioners. The democracy which sentenced Socrates to death is not merely vilified by Plato, it is also categorised within a taxonomy of political forms, brought to an ulterior site of judgment and included within an expanded system.

A second integration of judgment with death is suggested at this point. If Athens misjudges Socrates, it is because it misjudges death and the death sentence, by construing death as a punishment. Death is judged from the perspective of a restricted arena – that of the Athenian court and democratic polity – which is subordinate in principle, logically and juridically, to a tribunal that includes such an arena as a case, item or species. It is in this way that Plato comes to interpret sensible existence as a specification of intelligence; as a restricted forum demarcated within the total field of intelligibility. Death is a boundary which isolates sensible intelligence from the general system of knowing, the species from the genus, the case from the principle of Idea. The juridical advantage of the philosopher – qualifying him to rule in an ideal republic – is that he 'frees his soul from association with the body (so far as is possible) to a greater extent than other men' (Plato, 1969, p. 109). Death is no longer being thought as a consequence of judgment, but as its justifying condition. Judgment is disqualified by its specification to sensibility, since the sensible instance or case is comprehended by the superior generic order of the ideal, which is unrestricted by the sensible limit of death.

In its migration through a succession of bodies, the soul crosses and recrosses between life and death, passing in and out of restricted spaces, although never escaping the irreducible atom of self. One might accept Socrates' depiction of life as the phase during which the soul is 'chained hand and foot in the body, compelled to view reality not directly but only through its prison bars, and wallowing in utter ignorance' (Plato, 1969, p. 135), and still want to insist that the soul is a cage which is even more insidious, constricting and wretched than the body. The soul is the fantasy of a separation from death that persists in death, a kind of corporeal telepresence by which the body projects its servile categories into the unknown. But this is to interrupt Socrates' account.

The thought of knowledge as a recollection reaching beyond birth is most fully developed in the *Phaedo*, where the complicity between his conception of death and that of an adequate tribunal is emphatic. The approximation to wisdom under the specifications of life can only be a preparation for death, an anticipatory harmonisation with the escape from sensible existence:

> If at its release the soul is pure and carries with it no contamination of the body, because it has never willingly associated with it in life, but has shunned it and kept itself separate as its regular practice – in other words, if it has pursued philosophy in the right way and really practised how to face death easily: this is what 'practising death' means, isn't it? (Plato, 1969, p. 133)

According to the judgment of death, by which all human judgments are judged, only the philosopher is just, because only he recognises the specificity of all sensible judgments, and their subsumption within a higher genus of wisdom: 'no soul which has not practised philosophy, and is not absolutely pure when it leaves the body, may attain to the divine nature; that is only for the lovers of wisdom' (Plato, 1969, p. 135). The strongest expression of this though is probably to be found in an earlier passage from the *Phaedo:*

> the wisdom which we desire and upon which we profess to have set our hearts will be attainable only when we are dead, and not in our lifetime. If no pure knowledge is possible in the company of the body, then either it is totally impossible to acquire knowledge, or it is only possible after death ... (Plato, 1969, p. 111)

This introduces a third integration between judgment and death, through which Socrates decides against the sacred and in favour of the profane, because death is to be judged. This is to say that death is only to be an issue from the optic of knowing, from that of the philosopher or wise judge rather than the poet or the visionary. Here we arrive at the most mysterious and fateful twist in Socrates' interpretation of the oracle:

> to be afraid of death is only another form of thinking that one is wise when one is not; it is to think that one knows what one does not know. No one knows with regard to death whether it is not really the greatest blessing that can happen to a man; but people dread it as though they were certain that it is the greatest evil; and this ignorance, which thinks that it knows what it does not, must surely be ignorance most culpable. This, I take it gentlemen, is the degree, and this is the nature of my advantage over the rest of mankind; and if I were to claim to be wiser than my neighbour in any respect, it would be in this: that not possessing any real knowledge of what comes after death, I am also conscious that I do not possess it. (Plato, 1969, p. 60)

By interpreting contact with the unknown as the deferral of judgment by the subject, translating the positivity of sacred confusion into the negativity of epistemic uncertainty, Socrates initiates the proper history of the West. The Socratic sophism runs: either one already knows death (since it is only the cessation of life), or death is a higher knowing. Death is either the extinction that makes it nothing except what life knows of it, or the immortality of the soul that preserves knowing in death as entry into knowledge of the Ideas. If death is the unknown, it is only insofar as we do not know that there is nothing to know; but, were there an unknown other than as a hidden or forgotten knowledge, it would still only be what we already know as the end of knowing. This is Socrates' own reading of his claim to be conscious that he does not know: a repression of the unknown.

While ultimately returning the problem of death to knowing (philosophy to sophism), this passage is not without its sceptical openings. Most importantly, it suggests that the conception of personal mortality is an icon of death that must be ironised from the perspective of unknowing. In this way, the optic of the court is momentarily refused, and death prised away from its punitive sense. Socrates mocks those who act as if 'they would be immortal if you did not put them to death!' (Plato, 1969, p. 68).

The court is no more capable of judging death than judging Socrates, since it is in both cases ignorant as to its own ignorance, and therefore iconic. It lacks even the space of the question, having satisfied itself over-hastily with an array of pseudo-knowledges or unexamined opinions that substitute for difficulties. As Socrates interprets things, the Athenian court, having judged the punishment as incompetently as the defendant, accidentally rewards an innocent man, rather than persecuting a guilty one. Death has been judged badly, but Socrates does not conclude from this that it escapes judgment; it is rather that it requires a more appropriate tribunal: a philosophical forum open to the perfect evidence of the intelligible, uncluttered by the deceit and confusion of the sensible world. It is this conjunction of philosophy with death – philosophy as the fair trial of death which avoids precipitate condemnation – that completes the inversion of the Athenian trial. It is no longer that death confirms the judgment of the city; instead, it carries the philosophical dialectic for-wards to its destination:

> Ordinary people seem not to realise that those who really apply themselves in the right way to philosophy are directly and of their own accord preparing themselves for dying and death. If this is true, and they have actually been looking forward to death all their lives, it would of course be absurd to be troubled when the thing comes for which they have so long been preparing and looking forward.
> (Plato, 1969, p. 107)

If Socrates is in part an ironist and an iconoclast, he is also a zealot and a dogmatist. He disrupts one trial in order to replace it with another, mocks human judgment in order to replace it with divine judgment, subverts sophistry in order to replace it with a higher sophistry, and disengages himself from this world only to bind himself more tightly to another; to 'the unseen world' (Plato, 1969, p. 136) or 'the next world' (ibid., p. 179), to the realm of that which 'is invisible and hidden from our eyes, but intelligible and comprehensible by philosophy' (ibid. p. 133). Socratism is the mobilisation of unknowing on behalf of knowing; sub-ordinating irony to dialectic, confusion to judgment, and the sacred to a subtilised profanity.

There is a sense in which Socrates already floats a fourth – and far more corrosive – integration of judgment and death, according to which death is the suspension of judgment. Death is a problem that interrupts the judicial process, switching it into a dialectical detour which prolongs the path before arrival at a verdict. Resisting sensible evidentiality, death contests the conventional procedures of its trial. Typically enough, Socrates moralises this issue into a farce, asking whether death is good or evil. Nevertheless, death suspends justice in a hesitant unknowingness, even if this is only a dialectical vacillation between pre-established alternatives. For Socrates, death is recuperable to judgment, in a movement by which it is transcended by the idea; but this return of interruption to due process is not without its limit.

BATAILLE AND THE TRIAL OF GILLES DE RAIS

Whereas Plato is a midwife of the profane, establishing the intellectual coordinates of a transcendent reason that will dominate the juridico-philosophical discourses of post-Hellenic societies for two millennia, Bataille is driven by a passion for (and from) the sacred to explore the most extreme formulations of a philosophy of immanence. In a broadly Nietzschean fashion, he interprets law as the imperative to the preservation of discrete being. Far from expressing a transcendent ideality, law summarises conditions of existence, and shares its arbitrariness with the survival of the human race as sovereign autonomy (an expression that Bataille seeks to exhibit as an oxymoron). The word which Bataille usually employs to mark the preserve of law is 'discontinuity', which is broadly synonymous with 'transcendence', or the space of judgment. Discontinuity – read immanently or genealogically – is the condition for transcendent illusion or ideality, and precisely for this reason it cannot be grasped by a transcendent apparatus; by the interknitted series of conceptions involving negation, logical distinction, simple disjunction, essential difference, etc. Discontinuity is not referred in the direction of a separated or metaphysical realm, but in that of a precarious distance from death: a space of profane accumulation that is juxtaposed messily with the sacred flow into loss. Religion is thus extricated from theology in order to be connected with an energetics or 'solar economy', according to which the infrastructure of discontinuity inheres in the obstructive character of the Earth, in its mere bulk as a momentary arrest of solar energy flow, which lends itself to hypostatisation. When the silting-up of energy upon the surface of the planet is interpreted by its complex consequences as rigid utility, a productivist civilisation is initiated, whose culture involves a history of ontology and a moral order; persistent being and judgment. Systemic limits to growth require that the inevitable recommencement of the solar trajectory scorches jagged perforations through such civilisations. The resultant ruptures cannot be securely assimilated to a metasocial homoeostatic mechanism, because they have an immoderate, epidemic tendency. Bataille writes of 'the virulence of death' (1987, p. 70). Expenditure is irreducibly ruinous because it is not merely useless but also contagious. Nothing is more infectious than the passion for collapse.

In *The Accursed Share*, Bataille outlines a number of social responses to the unsublatable wave of senseless wastage welling up beneath human endeavour, which he draws from a variety of cultures and epochs. These include the potlatch of the sub-Arctic tribes, the sacrificial cult of the Aztecs, the monastic extravagance of the Tietans, the martial ardour of Islam, and the architectural debauch of hegemonic Catholicism. Reform Christianity alone – attuned to the emergent bourgeois order – is based upon a relentless refusal of sumptuary consumption. It is with Protestant-ism that theology accomplishes itself in the thoroughgoing rationalisation of religion, marking the ideological triumph of the good, and propelling humanity into unprecedented extremities of affluence and catastrophe. It is also with Protestantism that the transgressive outlets of society are deritualised and exposed to effective condemnation, a tendency which leads to the explosions of atrocity associated with the writings of the Marquis de Sade at the end of the eighteenth century and, almost three centuries before that, with the life of Gilles de Rais.

Bataille describes his 1959 study of Gilles de Rais as a tragedy, and its subject as a 'sacred monster', who 'owed his enduring glory to his crimes' (Bataille, 1987, p. 277). The bare facts are quite rapidly outlined. Gilles de Rais was born towards the end of the year 1404, inheriting the 'fortune, name and arms of Rais' (ibid., p. 345) due to a complicated dynastic intrigue involving his parents, Guy de Laval and Marie de Craon. Even by the standards of his times and rank, de Rais dissipated vast tranches of his wealth with abnormal extravagance; in Bataille's words, 'he liquidated an immense fortune without reckoning' (ibid., p. 279). At the battle of Orléans, he fought alongside Jeanne d'Arc, 'acquiring renown as "a truly valiant knight in arms" which survived right up to the point of his condemnation to infamy' (ibid., p. 354). It has been suggested that the two warriors were friends, but Bataille expresses reservations about this hypothesis (ibid., p. 356). On 30 May 1431, Jeanne d'Arc was burnt by the English. In the years 1432–3, de Rais began to murder children. His preferred victims were males, with an average age of eleven years, there was occasional variation in sex and considerable variation in age (ibid., p. 426). At least thirty-five murders are well established, although the number was almost certainly a great deal higher; the figures suggested at his trial ranged up to 200.

In a somewhat inelegant passage from this study, Bataille recapitulates the (quasi-Weberian) general economic background to his researches:

> We accumulate wealth in the prospect of a continual expansion, but in societies different from ours the prevalent principle was the contrary one of wasting or losing wealth, of giving or destroying it. Accumulated wealth has the same sense as *work*; wealth wasted or destroyed in tribal *potlatch* has the contrary sense of *play*. Accumulated wealth has

nothing but a subordinate value, but wealth that is wasted or destroyed has, to the eyes of those who waste it, or destroy it, a *sovereign* value: it serves nothing ulterior; only this wastage itself, or this fascinating destruction. Its *present* sense: its wastage, or the gift that one makes of it, is its final reason for being, and it is due to this that its sense is not able to be put off, and must be *in the instant*. But it is consumed *in that instant*. This can be magnificent those who know how to appreciate consumption are dazzled, but nothing remains of it. (Bataille, 1987, pp. 321–2)

The tragedy of de Rais, which Bataille extends to the nobility as a whole, was that of living the transition from sumptuary to rational sociality. He was dedicated by birth to the reckless militarism of the French aristocracy, which Bataille summarises in the formula: 'In the same way that the man without privilege is reduced to a worker, the one who is privileged must wage war' (ibid., p. 314). He is emphatic on this point: 'The feudal world ... is not able to be separated from the lack of measure [démesure], which is the principle of wars' (ibid., p. 316), and also: 'primitively war seems to be a luxury' (ibid., p. 78). That honour and prestige are incommensurable with the calculations of utility is an insistent theme in Bataille's work, as pertinent to the interpretation of potlatch among the Tlingit as to the blood-hunger and extravagance of Europe's medieval nobility. The context of Christianity and courtly love should not mislead us here.

The paradox of the Middle Ages demanded that the warrior elite did not speak the language of force and combat. Their mode of speech was often sickly-sweet. But we shouldn't fool ourselves: the goodwill of the ancient French was a cynical lie. Even the poetry that the nobles of the XIVth and XVth centuries affected to love was in every sense a deception: before everything the great lords loved war, their attitude differed little from that of the German Berzerkers, whose dreams were dominated by horrors and slaughter. (ibid., pp. 303–4).

For Socrates, war is understood as civic duty: a preservative function of the city. When the city wages war, it is to be judged as a moral act, following the dictates of reason to a greater or less extent. This is the dialectical image of war, fostered by the Church, and exercising a fascination over Hegel (not to mention post war American administrators). There is a principle of commensurability that binds military and judicial violence, permitting both to follow from a logically orchestrated procedure of political judgment. Bataille's suggestion is quite different, since his figure of war is a zone of disappearance, a passage to the unknown, through which the city communicates with its ultimate impossibility. It is not that war is treated as a metaphor by Bataille (any more than by

Nietzsche), but rather that all historical and intelligible evidence is a metaphor for war as an energetic function of death (descent to the unknown = degree zero). War exceeds judgment, since every judicial apparatus is a petrified war, just as every 'case' of war is a domestication politicised, utilitarianised, Clausewitzeanised. At the end of war there is only senseless death, where judgment counts for nothing.

The feudal aristocracy held open a wound in the social body, through which excess production was haemorrhaged into utter loss. In part, this wastage was accomplished by the hypertrophic luxuriance of their leisured and parasitic existence, which echoed that of the Church, but more important was the ceaseless ebb and flow of military confrontation, into which life and treasure could be poured without limit. De Rais embraced this dark heart of the feudal world with peculiar ardour. Bataille writes of

his entire – his mad – incarnation of the spirit of feudalism which, in all of its movement, proceeded from the games that the Berzerkers played: he was tethered to war by an affinity that succeeded in marking out a taste for cruel voluptuosities. He had no place in the world, if not the one that war gave him. (ibid., p. 317).

He continues: 'Such wars required intoxication, they required the vertigo and the giddiness of those that birth had consecrated to them. War precipitated its elect into assaults, or suffocated them in dark obsessions' (ibid., p. 317).

During the fourteenth and fifteenth centuries, the epoch of feudal warfaring reached a crescendo, due to exactly the same processes that were leading to its utilitarian reconstruction. Power was being steadily centralised in the hands of the monarchy, and changes in military technology effected a gradual shift in the social composition of the military apparatus. In particular, Bataille points to the way in which the development of archery supplanted the dominant role of heavy cavalry, and to the fact that with the increasing importance of arrows and pikes came an accentuation of military discipline. War became increasingly rationalised and subjected to scientific direction. This evolution was not rapid, but de Rais was personally touched by it. The battle of Lagny in 1432 was the last to plunge him into the heat of conflict, after which his position as a marshal of France – which he had occupied since July 1429 – detached him from the military cutting edge. Bataille's interpretation of these tendencies is emphatic:

[A]t the instant where royal politics and intelligence alters, the feudal world no longer exists. Neither intelligence nor calculation is noble. It is not noble to calculate, not even to reflect, and no philosopher has been able to incarnate the essence of nobility. (ibid., p. 318)

War is progressively disinvested by the voluptuary movement passing through the nobility, increasingly becoming an instrument of rational statecraft, calculatingly manipulated by the sovereign. A process was under way that would lead eventually to the tightly regimented military machines of Renaissance Europe, led by professional officers and directed by their operations in accordance with political pragmatics. Bataille considers this transition from warlord to prince to be crucial in de Rais's case:

> To the eyes of Gilles war is a game. But that view becomes less and less true: to the extent that it ceases to be predominate even amongst the privileged. Increasingly, therefore, war becomes a general misfortune: at the same time it becomes the *work* of a great number. The general situation deteriorates: it becomes more complex, the misfortune even reaching the privileged, who become ever less avid for war, and for games, seeing in the end that the moment has come to lend space to problems of reason. (ibid., p. 315)

Where the Church erected cathedrals in a disfigured celebration of the death of God, the nobility built fortresses to glorify and to accentuate the economy of war. Their fortresses were tumours of aggressive autonomy; hard membranes correlative with an acute disequilibrium of force. Within the fortress, social excess is concentrated to its maximum tension, before being siphoned off into the furious wastage of the battlefield. It was into his fortresses that de Rais retreated, withdrawing from a society in which he had become nothing, in order to bury himself in darkness and atrocity. The children of the surrounding areas disappeared into these fortresses, in the same way that the surplus production of the local peasantry had always done, except now the focus of consumption had ceased to be the exterior social spectacle of colliding armies, involuting instead into a sequence of secret killings. Rather than a staging post for excess, the heart of the fortress became its terminus; the site of a hidden and unholy participation in the nihilating voracity which Bataille calls 'the solar anus', or the black sun.

The words 'no philosopher has been able to incarnate the essence of nobility' are a concise anti-Socratism. There is no nobility in judgment or accusation, but rather an impoverishing separation from the inarticulacy of death. It cannot be a matter of a retrial therefore, as if a higher judgment were to redeem a victim of injustice: de Rais is almost perfectly indefensible. No case could be more clear-cut. Perhaps one short passage will suffice in lieu of detailing these monstrosities. Early in his study, Bataille remarks:

> His crimes responded to the immense disorder which inflamed him, and in which he was lost. We even know, by means of the criminal's confession, which the scribes of the court copied down whilst listening to him, that it was not pleasure that was essential. Certainly

he sat astride the chest of the victim and in that fashion, playing with himself [se maniant], he would spill his sperm upon the dying one; but what was important to him was less sexual enjoyment than the vision of death at work. He loved to look: opening a body, cutting a throat, detaching limbs, he loved the sight of blood. (ibid., p. 278)

An *Apology* for de Rais is an absurdity. He cannot be justified, and picking over his case can only be a nauseous reaffirmation of profane justice, or a vertiginous descent into the madness of the sacred. Among the problematic features of this passage, for instance, is the fact that it slices violently across the terms of Bataille's writings, where the prevailing sense of 'work' is exactly that of a resistance to death. He describes work as the process that binds energy into the form of the resource, or utile object, inhibiting its tendency to dissipation. This difficulty is exacerbated by the central role allocated to vision in Gilles's atrocities. Work constrains the slippage towards death, but it conspires with visibility. Scopic representation and utility are mutually sustained by objectivity, which Bataille understands as transcendence; the crystallisation of *Things* from out of the continuum of immanent flow. There is a virtual inanity to Gilles's aberration, therefore, which is attested by the fact that it is not the taste or smell of death that he seeks, but its sight, or representation.

Is not de Rais, at this moment, portrayed as an experimental Socrates, as an autonomous subject who would open a tribunal, collate evidence, judge a death that he transcends? Where is the military furor, the black-out intimacy with death, through which an unsupportable separation is collapsed into solar immanence? It is not merely a case that judgment stumbles upon here, but a ruinous metaphor for itself.

De Rais on trial is only Socrates becoming Baconian, which is why the 'object' of Bataille's text is the sumptuary current of feudalism – that which was unsocialisable by precommoditocratic civilisation – and not the accused person through which this movement found an outlet. Death has no representatives, which is to say that crime has no real subject. There is only the sad wreck whom Nietzsche calls 'the pale criminal', de Rais at his trial for instance, terrified of Satan, separated from his crimes by an unnavigable gulf of oblivion. The truth of such criminality, at once utterly simple and yet ungraspable, is that evil does not survive to be judged.

The profound criminality that Bataille sometimes names 'transgression' is not merely culpable or antisocial behaviour, insofar as this latter involves private utility or the occupation by a subject of the site of proscribed action. It is rather the effective genealogy of law, operating at a level of community more basic than the social order which is simultaneous with legality. Transgression is only judged *as such* in the course of a regression to a prehistorical option which was decided by the institution of justice. At this point, the sedimentation of energy upon the crust of the earth becomes normatively reinforced by an affirmation of social persistence. Nietzsche explores exactly this issue in § 9 of the second essay of his *Genealogy of Morals*, in which he describes the primitive response to transgression:

> 'Punishment' at this level of civilization is simply a copy, a *mimus*, of the normal approach toward a hated, defenceless, prostrated enemy, who has not only lost every right and protection, but is also deprived of all mercy; *vae victis* as the right of war and festivity of victory, in all its ruthlessness and cruelty – from which it is clear why war itself (including the warlike cult of sacrifice) has provided all the *forms* under which punishment has emerged throughout history. (Nietzsche, 1981, p. 813)

War is irreducibly alien to a collision of rights, so that it is war that bears down on the one who violates right as such. Transgression is not a misdemeanour, even if this is the necessary form of its social interpretation. It is rather a solar barbarism, resonant with that of the Berzerkers, and of all those who fathom an abysmal inhumanity on the battlefield, becoming derelicted conduits of the impossible. There is no tragedy without an Agamemnon, or some other mad beast of war, whose nemesis preempts the discourse of the juridical institution, and whose death is thus marked by a peculiar intimacy, even though it is never commensurable with propriety. For we would not recognise this war that comes from beyond the city and after the law, this movement without essence or precedent which is perhaps already guiding us, a movement without utility, ideology or motivation, forsaking melodrama for the true violence of the *insidious*; of infiltration, subversion, larval metamorphosis and phase-change. After the law, across the line of unknowing, where tribunals count for nothing, Socrates is silent, and accusation is dissolved into the sun. De Rais is merely the botched and humane anticipation of a tragedy which is no longer ours:

> *Tragedy is the impotence of reason.* ... This does not signify that Tragedy has rights against reason. In truth, it is not possible for a right to belong to something contrary to reason. For how could a *right* be opposed to reason? Human violence however, which has the power to go against reason, is tragic, and must, if possible, be suppressed: at least it cannot be ignored or despised. It is in speaking of Gilles de Rais that I come to say this, for he differs from all those for whom crime is a personal matter. The crimes of Gilles de Rais are those of the world in which they they are committed, and these ripped throats are exposed by the convulsive movements of such a world. (Bataille, 1987, p. 319)

CONCLUSION

In its virtual truth, law has already disappeared from the Earth. What remains of 'law' is a dissolving complex consisting of relics from political sociality, nostalgic media-driven theatre, and pre-automatised commodification protocols. All appeals to a 'criminality' irreducible to the impersonal consequences of social/psychological pathology have degenerated to the level of television evangelism. Among the educated, 'freedom' has lost all its Christian-metaphysical pathos, to become the stochastic market-intervention patterns of desolidarised (contractually disaggregated) populations. The legal suppression of the sex and drugs industries, for instance, is increasingly exhibited as an overt farce perpetrated by the economically illiterate, and leading only to perverse effects such as the growth of organised crime, the corruption of social institutions, deleterious medical consequences and a rapidly growing contempt for the legislature, judiciary and police by groups whose consumption processes are incompetently suppressed. The post civilisational pragmatism of immanence to the market (anonymous resource distribution) reiterates its own juridical expression as an increasingly embarrassing archaism, preserving law only by functionalising legality in terms that subvert its claim to authority. As domination loses all dignity, the state becomes universally derided, exhibited as the mere caretaker for retarded sectors of behavioural management.

It is in the context of such runaway immanentisation that the contemporary cult of the 'serial killer' – prefigured by Bataille's portrait of de Rais – is to be understood. The psychopathic murderer is both the final justification for law and the point of transition from evil to pathology from the criminal soul of political societies to the software disorder of commodity-phase population cybernetics. Bataille's Gothic aesthetic cannot hide the distance traversed in two-and-a-half millennia of erratically developing 'Socratism', or rationalistic desolidarisation. While Plato's Socrates is a judge *because he might have been a criminal* Bataille's de Rais is an economic control malfunction.

REFERENCES

Bataille, G. (1987), *Oeuvres Complètes*, vol. 10, Paris: Gallimard.
Nietzsche, F. (1981), *Werke*, vol. 3, Frankfurt am Main: Ullstein Materialien.
Plato (1969), *The Last Days of Socrates* (transl. Tredennick), Harmondsworth: Penguin.

The translations from Bataille and Nietzsche are my own.

7

Fate as Seduction:
The Other Scene of Legal Judgment

PETER GOODRICH

Fate ... is a great wooden vessel which among Brewers in London is
ordinarily used at this day to measure Mault by, containing a Quar-
ter, which they have for expedition in measuring.

Cowell, 1608/1627

What is law?
 Destiny, Sir. Destiny.

Peake, 1976

The defining feature of legal modernity lies in the attempt to make law
self-founding. Unable or unwilling any longer to justify or found law upon
nature, justice, right or contract, modernist jurisprudence has been forced
to seek the legitimacy of law, the justification of judgment and the
criterion of legality, within law itself. The science of law was thus
predicated upon closure.[1] It sought to replace a jurisprudence based upon
theocracy, nature or ethics with a secular conception of a self-regulating
system of norms or rules. The crisis of legal modernity and of its
hermeneutics, its interminable theories of interpretation, lies in its failure
to address the issues that were previously posed in terms of canons, nature
or ethics, in terms of legal foundation, of ultimate causes or reasons. As
the metaphor of closure suggests, a self-regulating science is shut up or
enclosed, it is silent or at least cannot speak of foundation but must rather
presuppose it.[2] In etymological terms, it is not simply a question of
circularity: the Latin root of closure, *claudo*, not only means to close, end,
terminate or finish – to die – but also refers to something crippled, lame or
defective, and so by implication it refers to something approaching its fate
or coming towards death. To invoke the problematic of legal closure is
necessarily to address the question of death as the repressed object of
institutional structure: the end or terminus of law refers both to the
finality of the institution as the legal structure or limit of personality, and
equally to the modern, positivised conception of law as an autonomous

form of judgment enclosed by its self-appointed criteria of normative legitimacy.[3] In the ensuing analysis, I will examine first the latter, broader meaning of the death of law itself, the closure or death of an institution whose very protocols of enactment or enforcement sever its relation to the lifeworld by constituting that world of mundane sociality as its outside or other. It is a question of addressing the death of law as the fatality of that institution which both represents the call of the dead in the form of the pre-existent structure of historical being, the image or mask of law, and the fate of individuality as subject to an inevitable progress or call towards a prospective death.

DEATH AND LAW

In an immediate and frequently observed sense, the death of law refers to the demise of a particular tradition and meaning of legality, or more specifically of legal judgment. Classical jurisprudence had historically associated law with both an origin and an end or goal, a fatality, which exceeded its merely positive status and norms.[5] The life of law belonged to a reason, art or cause which preceded and survived its mere administration or simple acts of judgment. To separate law from its cause was to separate law from life, and more particularly it was to divest it of the possibility of becoming, of creating new meanings for itself. The positivised conception of law as the brute fact of a system of norms was simultaneously a repression of the possibility of its having a conscious meaning, an indeterminacy, which would relate the system of fatality of law to its temporal presence and application. In this sense, its death was hermeneutic: bereft of reason, cause or essence, the law is without life or without a relation to life and can neither be defined nor valued. To take an example from the early era of modern law, we thus find a proleptic criticism of common law, in the mid-seventeenth century, posed in the dual terms of geographical and hermeneutic closure combining to produce the exile and abandonment of justice conceived as the reason and art of law. A nation such as England, which casts classical jurisprudence and its conceptions of universal reason and supranational justice out of its territory, 'plainly puts out the light of [its] own laws, and does abandon and exile that mother, of which [its] own laws, for so much as is good in them, are but the off-spring'.[6] A law founded upon closure or internal to a nation and its system of positive – and all too human – law, a system of purely municipal regulation, is dead in the sense of being irreversibly estranged from the reason, justice and art of universal law. Common law, by virtue of its particularity and its limited territory, is here depicted as 'fitted for the climate of one people only, and serves for the exigencies and occasions of the state, and varies at times and occasions – [it] commands rather than teaches – [and] has an eye more to what is profitable to the public, than for what is just or equitable' (Wiseman, 1664, p. 168).[7] The art of law, by contradistinction, 'understands some more universal law, that is commonly embraced and allowed by the best and most potent nations; that is full of equity and true reason, and being grounded upon dictates of nature and common reason, is unchangeable; whose method is to teach and instruct by certain rules and principles orderly and hand-somely digested ... it is the only necessary art' (ibid., p. 168). Without justice, without the learning and knowledge of a reason of law (*ultima ratio*), judgment depends upon 'the wandering fancies and imaginations of men only: ... under how many several shapes and forms must it needs appear, when the apprehensions and conceptions of men ... are as different as their visages be?' In short, law dies in the sense that it ceases to be recognisably law because it lacks any referent, justification or foundation beyond its simple existence as judgment, its act of self-positing: 'the professors of municipal law must acknowledge that their Book cases (the only learning of their law) must needs fail them here ... ' (ibid. p. 167).[8] That failure is an ethical one and is correlated both to the insularity of a positivised system and to the hermeneutic abdication of the meaning of law as a practice of judgment which, to be just or ethical, must exceed the terms and constraints of merely positive or municipal rule.

Closure entails loss, in the sense that death is not only absence but is also, in its transitive form, privation. It is also failure, the breakdown of a system. In its more complex connotation, the death of law is not simply its restriction or self-limitation to the plural and changing needs of municipal regulation, but also its 'shutting up', its failure to speak to the issues of justice and judgment, reason and nature that are historically its proper jurisdiction. In the absence of a criterion by reference to which it is possible to judge law and to define its 'lawfulness', it is not simply impossible to criticise or evaluate law, but it is equally impossible to know what law is.[9] The death of law becomes synonymous with the arbitrariness of legal judgment: to the extent that law becomes no more and no less than what lawyers do ... or jurists recognise ... within any given field of legal regulation, the defining feature of law is its non-definition and correlatively the absence of any constraint or limit upon the content, proliferation or practice of such regulation.[10] The death of law in this sense ironically signifies the hyperinflation of legal practices or of legal regulation: it signifies the death of judgment, death, in Blanchot's terms, being 'the utterly indeterminate, the indeterminate moment and not only the zone of the unending and the indeterminate' (Blanchot, 1982, p. 99). Indifferent in terms of value, purposeless in terms of need and irrational or merely technical in terms of practice, the death of law here refers to the absorption of legality into a series of pragmatic, actuarial and disciplinary administrative practices which subordinate or 'cripple' legal judgment and the value of law to a series of overriding bureaucratic and normalising concerns: 'nothing can any longer claim identity for itself. Everything changes, unceasingly. The social bond can no longer have the form of an original contract, whose terms would be invariable; these terms can only be continually negotiated and renegotiated' (Ewald, 1988, p. 44).[11]

In the discussion which follows, I will be concerned less with the positivity of legal closure, the various specifications of legal normativity in terms of theories of sources of law, systematicity or autoregulation, than with the loss of meaning and the repression of sensibility or judgment that such closure entails. In a stronger and more specific sense, I am concerned with the problematic of judgment which legal modernity repressed, and so too with reconstructing such a problematic or form of discourse in the languages of fate and destiny, cause and chance, in which they received their classical expression. As will become clear, the motive or deceit underlying such a reconstruction relates to the possibility that the reformulation of the discourses of judgment or the speech of the Fates can serve to reinstate the question of justice, the question of absolute indeterminacy, as the essential and explicit question of the history and practice of law. The function of law is in this respect bound to death both as the limit and as the constraint represented by the image of law as human fatality and as that indeterminacy of becoming which will always speak the failure of law. To represent that indeterminacy is not to reinvoke a lost universal but rather to recognise an absent object of desire, a law of indecision, of that failure, gap or lapse which marks all closure as provisional.

LAW AND FATE

The thesis of the death of law can either be posed in terms of the twilight of legal ideals, and so characterised in terms of the loss of legal *universalia*,[12] or alternatively it can be approached as a question relating to the decay of legal reason, and specifically to the demise of certain forms of speaking about or invoking legal judgment.[13] In either case, it is first a matter of death and of what it means for an institution to die. Hermeneutically, it is initially a paradox insofar as institutions are by definition legal fictions that do not die: institutions such as religion, law or economics are deep structures embedded in the *longue durée*, they are the forms of (social) life and as such they cannot die: individuals or those that hold offices may die, but structures or forms of sociality are passed on in the indefinite and durable time of tradition.[14] In consequence, to speak of the death of law is to appropriate a metaphor (rhetorically *aposiopesis*) which is contradicted by the classical principle of *lex aeternitas* and the maxim *dignitas [ius] non moritur*. It is also, however, and as a consequence of this paradox, a matter of mixing genres: to speak of the death of law is not only to raise the question of the relation of law to temporality but also to juxtapose law and literature, symbolic and imaginary, and to suggest that there is a very precise relation of repression between the two genres. Death is the object and end of literary discourse, it is the subject of poetics and the aesthetic principle of philosophical writing: to the extent that each literature in its turn endeavours to produce an impossible staging or image of the other, of that which cannot be represented because it does not yet exist, it attempts to present the unpresentable in an imaginary (phantasmatic) or symbolic (legal) form. Literature precedes law and subsists within it, marking its history as a narrative of choices or exercises in the language of power and the expression of the choices of fate. Yet law cannot recognise the literary without confronting the possibility of its own demise. Death belongs in this sense to the biography of law, and as a literary or metaphoric figure or attribution it is to be understood not as an external force threatening legality but as an internal quality, as an active principle of disintegration, as a figure of escape, which would be formulated in rhetorical (or aesthetic) terms as *vanitas* or decadence and in psychological terms as an instinct or drive negating both pleasure and reproduction. Philosophically, it would be the death of the soul, of the spirit of law: an extinction which in metaphysical terms is represented as closure or the failure to create, and in mundane terms as injustice in the precise sense of *ressentiment*, passivity or existential inauthenticity, namely a being in flight from death.[15] Literature, in short, threatens law by recognising the play of language to which law is also subject and by virtue of which it is possible to imagine worlds other than that of the juristic institution. Literature imagines an end of law, a death already signalled by the impermanence of legal forms and the ambiguities of their transmission. Before examining these various terms in detail, it is necessary to establish a more diffuse relation between law, death and fate or *amor fati*.

It has been suggested so far that the theme of the death of law necessarily engenders a problematic which exceeds the closure of law and evokes the language of poets, literature and the philosophy of aesthetics. These are simultaneously the first forms of law and the first objects of regulation. For the western tradition, language is the primary institution and is classically aligned with nature as the condition for any contract or for the earliest species of civility. Language is the first institution held in common; it is the universal law prior to Babel; it is the invisible writing of law in the heart, prior to writing; it is the only inscription of law which can escape the idolatry of other signs. These facets of language form the exemplar or origin of that commonality which later gains expression in conceptions of unwritten custom, common law or immemorial practice as the natural though hidden basis of legality as such. These are primary affinities, and they can be rendered more specific by examining the cross-cutting values of necessity and chance, interiority and exteriority, tradition and accident, pleasure and suffering to which both poetry and law would speak *through their death* or *in articulo mortis*.[16]

In immediate logical terms, law masks death in the sense that the institution of tradition is concerned precisely with the passing-on of structures across and against the blandishments of time. To the extent that law constitutes and transmits traditions as meanings, as persons, things and actions,[17] it establishes the very form of survival as repetition and in a stronger sense as eternal recurrence. In passing on – and it is not accidental that passing on is also a metaphor for death – the deep structures or forms of social reproduction, the legal tradition is bound classically to expressing or imagining death as the incident of inheritance, as the structure of sociality. In posing the question of language, literature raises the question of the possibility of sociality and so also of its eventual decay. Death is what passes, what succeeds, unacknowledged, from father to son. Death, which, as an event, cannot be contained and so cannot have a value or price,[18] is that which makes containment possible. Death is the condition of possibility of sociality, precisely because it limits and so also delimits the subject and in consequence displays the necessity of the social.

In historical terms, the imaginary status of death, its unassimilable quality or irreducibility, made the event or meaning of death the repressed reality of the symbolic or legal form. In that it was imaginary, it was associated, like all images, with the literary and with femininity: it was feminine in this sense not simply by virtue of its futurity, but also because, being defined by the imaginary, by the soul or *anima*,[19] it was associated with a being which both sows and reaps and is in consequence the appropriate gender and metaphor for creativity as both birth and death, production and destruction of a life which will be over soon.[20] In theological terms, death confuses meaning and sense, spirit and flesh. The great fear associated with death in the western tradition of repressed materiality is precisely a fear of the feminine, of contingency, contact and the irreducibility of corporeal habitus. In Christian terms, death destroys the inessential, the egoistical, the ornament or shell of living; it shatters the image and so dissociates the soul from the mundane capture of mortal forms. Femininity is thus either essential to the realisation of undying forms or it distracts from a spirituality that can only ever be confused by the false representations and pleasures of the flesh (see Goodrich, 1993).

In historical terms, the paradoxical relation between law and the feminine gender is tied to images of justice and of judgment which express that which exceeds, mitigates or abrogates, and so defines legal rule. The necessity of law is matched classically with the accident of an indefinable justice conceived as harmony, mercy or lesbian rule.[21] Even or especially within the common law tradition, justice is a woman, and the origin of law is represented in the Furies, the Godesses of a fateful justice derived from the *Oresteia* (Aeschylus, 1953 ed.). The Furies, or *Semnai-theai* (venerable Goddesses), are referred to by Selden as the first law-giver. The avenging Goddesses, repulsive maidens, 'sit upon the skirts of the wicked: but the Eumenides, that is, the kind Goddesses ... do attend the good and such are blameless or faultless ... [whereby] we see out of the most ancient Divine among the Heathens, how judges and the Dispensers of law pass under the notion of these venerable goddesses' (Selden, 1610, pp. 4–5). In Britain, Selden, following Camden, finds evidence of the *semnai* as the original judges of English law in references and inscriptions addressed to mother Goddesses or *Deis Matribus*, to which he adds 'nor let it be any hindrance, that so splendid and so manly a name is taken from the weaker sex, to wit, the Goddesses' (Selden, 1610, p. 5; Camden, 1586). The figures of a vengeful and unconscious femininity, the justices who are also the daughters of night, the harbingers of death, represent the political Fates whose task is to assure that in life, as in death, judgment will take place according to the indefinable, feminine and fateful will of the divine justices. The Furies inscribe the dictates of fate upon the human soul. It is a fate which kills, but it is also a figuration of truth, an affective representation of necessity as a law to which the soul, the emotions, are bound (Hachamovitch, 1993).

Remaining with the historical relations between law and death, justice and fate, the tradition drawn upon by classical law runs from the Stoics to Cicero and Boethius. Law conceived as necessity or nature is ideally aligned to the tragic pronouncements of the Fates, the *moirai* or *fata*, the daughters of necessity who are born with and who dictate each human life from beginning to end. The Fates are the figure of the judgment and justice of providence; they represent in legal terms the speech of irreversible necessity or of ultimate causes which link past (*Lachesis*), present (*Clotho*) and future (*Atropos*) from an indefinite temporal perspective (eternity) external to them.[22] In one sense, the space of legal speech is thus coincident with a series of 'inaugural' or prescient discourses, and the founding act of law is to appropriate the human expression of fate to the representatives of law. The founding definition of law is one which distinguishes law from divination, soothsaying, magic, astrology and witchcraft not because the speech of law differs from those discourses or practices in terms of its concerns or objects but precisely because it belongs to the same order and is the only socially legitimate expression of them (Legendre, 1989, pp. 29–30; Goodrich, 1990, pp. 139–42). Law enacts the symbolic form of human relationship and gives effect to those unconscious forces which would otherwise remain in the hands of the magician, the soothsayer, the diviner or the evil women who invoke the powers of Satan to perform impossible acts or to represent an invisible order of past and future causes.[23] Law claims to be the sole legitimate representation of the social order of fate; it is the human speech of providence and knows that no science can fully apprehend the plenitude of absolute causes or the preordination of causal relations. Fate, in Cicero's depiction of Chrysippus' argument, is providence, namely the pre-existent but unknowable order of absolute and unchanging causes: to the extent that phenomena and events are said to have causes, 'you are bound to admit either that everything takes place by fate (*fato*) or that something can take place without a cause' (Cicero, 1942, ed. p. 233). So, too, future events are fated in that they will in retrospect be seen to have had causes: 'is it possible for anything to have happened that was not previously going to be true? For just as we speak of past things as true that possessed true actuality [*vera fuerit instantia*] at some former time, so we speak of future things as true that will possess true actuality [*vera erit instantia*] at some following time' (ibid. p. 223). Fate predetermines irrevocably but it does so through the medium of causes and their interconnection (Schopenhauer, 1898, pp. 389–90; Deleuze, 1990, p. 270). The event is predetermined as the consequence of preceding causes, but the unity of those causes is unknown, an argument formulated by Boethius in terms of a distinction between 'providence [which] embraces all things, however different, however infinite; [and] fate [which] sets in motion separately individual things, and assigns to them severally their position, form, and time ... providence is the fixed and simple form of destined events, fate their shifting series in order of time' (Boethius, 1897, ed., p. 201).

It is thus the task of those who would know or love their fate, the task also of lawyers who apply the dictates of the Fates, to understand and interpret the invisible interconnection of causes. It is an unknowable providence which determines the movements of all manifest causal series, for it is this underlying series of unitary providence 'which renews the series of all things that are born and die through like successions of germ and birth; it is its operation which binds the destinies of men by an indissoluble nexus of causality, and, since it issues in the beginning from unalterable providence, these destinies also must of necessity be immutable' (ibid, pp. 204–5). On the other hand, such destinies, or such interconnectedness of all things, are unknowable; they are the accidents of a fate, which is without reason, consideration or pretext. To love fate, to act fatefully, is to accept chance or fortuna's spin as the necessary grounds of action: 'Thou deemest *fortuna* to have changed towards thee; thou mistakest. Such were ever her ways, ever such her nature. Rather in her very mutability hath she preserved towards thee her true constancy' (ibid., p. 44). The crucial relation in existential terms is thus between chance and choice, the one implying the other in the irrevocable choice, the necessary fate invoked and imposed by acting in the world, by living according to the ethical or aesthetic dictate of making something of one's lot.

Fate, in assigning to individuals their manifest place, their position and time, assigns human destiny in the form of a structure or place, and in legal terms it dictates the institutional form of social existence as the fatality into which the individual is born. To speak of destiny or fate is to talk of the institution of life in the precise sense of the preassignment of individual and social places. It is to speak of the predetermined familial and political places that await an individual before birth. In Freudian terms, fate constitutes *the other scene* of human life, the unconscious, in the form of the juridical categories of father and son (familial fate) and claim and due (political fate).[24] These categories give form to the unconscious and to its demands: far from being accidental, or a veneer imposed upon human reality, these categories stake out the structure of human life, its destiny, namely its place and its truth. Two features of fate deserve particular comment in this context. Formulated in terms of the unconscious as the 'discourse of the other', and in legal terms as the will of the sovereign Father in whose name law judges, fate is exteriority. It is that into which the individual is born and in relation to which the individual acquires an identity: it is, in Lacanian terms, the figure of the mirror phase (Lacan, 1977, pp. 2ff.), while in more classical terms it is the structure of narcissism, the prohibition through which the individual enters the genealogical line (Legendre, 1985, pp. 55–6). Conceived as exteriority, the *Fata* 'are the speeches of foundation, they take hold of life, they are the speeches which make [*fabriquent*] us, as is suggested by the word *tyche* [literally: luck] used by Sophocles, and translated as destiny. Consider also the Greek *daimon*, the other equivalent of destiny, some inner demon: by this word, Oedipus addresses himself in uncovering his parricide' (Legendre, 1989, p. 29).

The exteriority of the Fates represents the exteriority of the order of institutional causes and of political organisation: 'humanity is spoken in advance, it enters an instituted life' (Legendre, 1989, p. 51). Such exterior institution, which bewitches or fascinates, which fabricates subjectivity as a place of predetermined possibilities or common destiny, is also, however, the place of interiority. The external law of the institution is at the same time the law of interiority, the institution of a personality adjusted to its culture (Papageorgiou, 1990, pp. 56–9). In this second sense, the Fates or *moirai* are depicted as a foreign will within, an interior exteriority (Levinas, 1969, p. 226). What is at issue is a process of identification or internalisation; it is the function of law to make necessity recognisable as limitation:

these received determinations are themselves synthetic and internal, since they are always directed to a future end, and they represent a constant enrichment and an irreversibility of time, they proceed not from analytical Reason or the laws of exteriority but, if one is not to prejudge them, from an external law of interiority ... this law might of course be referred to as destiny, since an irresistible movement draws or impels the ensemble towards a prefigured future which realises itself through it. (Sartre, 1976, pp. 179–80)

Necessity is experienced as contingency, as accident or chance, the distribution of lots. It is the function of law to intimate the irreversibility of such predeterminations and so to represent the singular and irreversible relation of the indefinite time of tradition to the passing time of individual life. As a discourse of foundation, law makes the individual as exteriority; the legal subject enters the social as other to herself, as a signification of self or a legal sign within the system of legal signs or within the objectivity of destiny: 'all of us spend our lives engraving our maleficent image on things, and it fascinates and bewilders us if we try to understand ourselves through it, although we are ourselves the totalis[ing] movement which results in *this* particular objectification' (Sartre, 1976, p. 227). In short, we meet our fate, again and again, in each and every image that we inscribe upon the world.

FATE AND JUDGMENT

The space of legal judgment or of the art of law is predicated upon an ignorance: 'the *Fata* are the echo of the abyss [*l'abîme*] and, at the same time, to take up a formulation of Seneca's defining destiny, they are the will of the sovereign Father' (Legendre, 1989, p. 29). In representing necessity or the force of exteriority, the speech of the Fates is intrinsically tied to law in both its objective and its subjective dimensions. One and the same discourse of fate speaks as providence both to the institution of the subject and to the institution of sociality. At the level of the subject, 'the discourse of the *Fata* can be defined as the discourse of foundation, that is to say, as that which should provide the young subject with the subjective means of surviving the horror of a subjective division inaugurated by its separation from the first incestuous object, that is to say from the mother – from the biological mother, but above all from the mythological Mother of the order of representation ... No one escapes the law of separation, of which the biological father, himself also a child of the mythological Mother' is also a subject, until such time as he identifies himself with, and takes up his place as, the image of the Father and transposes biological paternity into the role of transmitting social fate through the image of the Father, through entry into the symbolic. Once the infant enters into the parental discourse, she finds herself subject to its law, a law which requires the child to detach herself irrevocably from her physical reality as a surface of pleasure and excitation, and to identify herself with the signifier which carries her into discourse and so also into law (Legendre, 1990, p. 218). The institution, as that which fabricates human existence and engenders the human as a 'speaking being', is both an interior and an exterior governance establishing legitimacy, father (*patria potestas*) and sovereign (*regia potestas*), as both a familial and a political relation to others and to exteriority: 'The law is the word of the father. The father intervenes to counter the phantasm of maternal omnipotence with the potency of his word. Its force is not that of the pain of a real fear effectively produced. Subjection to the word of the father … [is subjection to a] speech [which] is not only indicative but also imperative: speech itself orders … It functions to put a sign in the place of reality – the phallus in the place of the penis. It makes the infantile surfaces into signs' (Lingis, 1989, p. 79).

The discourse of fate is the oracular representation of a life which will be over soon. It is a life which must in consequence be governed by laws of reproduction: the Fates must bring each child before the law and inscribe, in conscious and unconscious forms, upon the body and upon the soul, the narratives of the *longue durée*, of a before, during and after which both comprehend (include) and survive the individual life: 'all production, creative or symptomatic, cultural or pathological, only ever emerges at the point of the opening of the structure, which is also the point of its failure' (Papageorgiou, 1990, p. 33).[25] What is crucial to an understanding of fate as judgment is the indissoluble tie between interiority and exteriority, the commonality of destiny in an institutional existence that is both outside and within: 'the most private, the most intimate, that which is at the heart of the concept of a subject, to know the fantasm, is already marked by the seal of the genealogical order. All subjects carry with them, if I can express myself in this way, the institutional under the primary form of familial institution' (Papageorgiou, 1990, p. 56). The first myths or representations of fate are thus narratives of a necessity which captures the subject for law, for transmission across the generations, for reproduction. That which until recently did not exist has to be inscribed with individuality and with personality or citizenship. It is in this respect no accident that the inaugural narrative of law takes the emblematic form of a legend of the family expressed in terms of genealogical forms. The story of Oedipus thus recounts the tragic unravelling of a subjectivity which defied genealogical prohibition, in which the subject who infracts the rules of kinship, and specifically the interdictions of parricide and of incestuous descent, pays the absolute price first of madness and then of annihilation.[26] In the *Oresteia*, divine vengeance in the form of the Furies (the repulsive maidens) is visited again upon one who does harm to their kin. Apollo orders Orestes to kill his mother,

Clytaemnestra, and must then protect Orestes from the Furies.[27] These are the Goddesses who punish all crimes against kin, of which murder of the parent is the most absolute and sacrilegious in that it steals the power of the Gods and puts it into human hands (Spelman, 1632). The first and principal crime is precisely one which challenges fate by attempting to arrogate destiny and, in specifically legal terms, to expedite the speech of the Gods (*fata properaverit*).[28] Those who commit such a crime against the genealogical order are pursued by the Furies, Goddesses who are invisible to all but their victims and whose approach drives the victims mad. They strike, in other words, at the soul.

Death, in Heidegger's terms, is not extinction without recompense, but the condition for the possibility of every significance and every value. 'Death then is nowhere else than in the world, and in throwing ourselves into the world we are casting ourselves into death; death is the world as pure openness or clearing in which beings are distinguishable and phosphorescent, [it is a] reservoir of possibility for beings and for nothingness' (Lingis, 1989, p. 185). The institutional form of reproduction is one which inscribes a pattern of repetition upon the unconscious of the subject: 'there is transmission, because there is repetition' (Papageorgiou, 1990, p. 49); indeed, Freud specifically designates instinct as an urge for repetition, for the restoration of 'an earlier state of things', and fate is likewise defined as the repetition of infantile experiences which are explicitly depicted as possession by a 'malignant fate' and as an internal 'daemonic power' (Freud, 1961 pp. 30–1, 15–16). Fate refers, in other words, to the inscription of a pattern upon the empty space of the unconscious, and at a collective level it refers to what Heidegger terms destiny (*Geschick*), the historicisation of being. *Dasein* has fate (*Schicksal*) inscribed in it; it is fate to the extent that it is authentic to its destiny, to the recurrence of inherited possibilities: repetition hands down, it is the means of historicality, for 'in repetition, fateful destiny can be disclosed explicitly as bound up with the heritage which has come down to us. By repetition, *Dasein* first has its own history made manifest' (Heidegger, 1962, p. 438). Fate is here the handing-down of inherited possibilities, and particularly the anticipation of the events of birth and death as the implicit object, the other scene, of all transmission. It is, in Heidegger's terms, being-towards-death, or the finitude of temporality, that joins the subject to history and so also to repetition as the means of entering history, as *amor fati*: 'when historicality is authentic, it understands history as the recurrence of the possible, and knows that a possibility will recur only if existence is open for it fatefully ... in resolute repetition' (ibid., p. 444).

A final step in the argument is taken in the conception of *amor fati* as the manner in which possibility is realised, and necessity lived as chance.

Where Schopenhauer suggested quiescence in the face of fate, and Kierkegaard offered redemption as the end-product of repetition, poststructuralist thought – which is itself the expression of a certain contemporary sense of fatality – addresses the active principle of *amor fati* as the precondition of all creativity or becoming.[29] It derives its inspiration from Nietzsche's conception of eternal recurrence as the principle of becoming predicated not upon causality but upon chance, not upon law but upon judgment as the justice of play and the will to affirm fortune or *fortuna* as she stands. The authentic thought of finitude, of being towards death, is predicated upon an historical conception of fatality as the irreversibility of chance: 'my formula for greatness in a human being is *amor fati*: that one wants nothing to be different, not forward, not backward, not in all eternity. Not merely bear what is necessary, still less conceal it – all idealism is mendaciousness in the face of what is necessary – but *love* it' (Nietzsche, 1881, p. 258). It is the irreversibility of the past, of the dice-throw of necessity, that dictates both the circumstances and the *persona* or identity of present action. Neither could be other than they are, because history – necessity as chance – has made them such as they are: 'becoming must be explained without recourse to final intentions; becoming must appear justified at every moment', and similarly, 'the present must absolutely not be justified by reference to a future, the past by reference to the present' (Nietzsche, 1882–8, p. 377).

Formulated in Nietzsche's terms, destiny or providence takes the form of eternal return as the structure of all action the repetition of life or more specifically of action in the form of the unique coupling of chance and necessity or chance and destiny. It is the fate of law to act 'as if' each act will return eternally, 'as if' each judgment were unique. The necessity or law that governs each decision is precisely the necessity of judging: it is the fate of law to have to decide, to be decided upon deciding while knowing that nothing can be absolutely determined. Necessity imposes choice, chance dictates both discrimination and decision; law expresses the need to act upon the circumstances, the facts which fate flings to judgment. In one sense, the eternal return is the categorical imperative of each act of judgment. Destiny produces both the necessity – the historical circumstances – and the person who acts, and they must act or judge in the knowledge that their act will return eternally, namely that no rewriting of the past, nor future intention nor afterlife will ever change that action: the categorical imperative of judgment expresses both the irreducibility of judging and the universality of judgment. In Nietzschean terms, *amor fati* refers both to the positive force that affirms the uniqueness of each act of judgment – that closure creates openness – and to a responsibility, that each act determines the fate of the soul. It is of the essence of judgment as fate that while the impact of judgment – of eternal recurrence – may escape codification and may indeed be inexpressible, it is nonetheless remembered and inscribed. The soul of the judge is marked by judgment. While others may not perceive or judge the act of judging, the judgment is indelible nonetheless: judgment (discrimination and taste) traces and defines the subject that judges, and the body carries the corpus or product of judgment. The eternal return is thus the return of the same in the substantive form of becoming or difference (Deleuze, 1983, pp. 25–9). In this respect, the eternal return

> is not the effect of the Identical on a world which has become the similar [*semblable*], it is not an exterior order imposed upon the chaos of the world, the eternal return is, on the contrary, the internal identity of the world and of chaos ... it is not the same which returns, it is not the similar that returns, but the Same is the return of that which returns, that is to say of the Different, the similar is the return of that which returns, that is to say of the Dissimilar ... of simulacra. (Deleuze, 1969, p. 382).

The history of return is thus the history of the image, of the representation or simulation of the same, the image of resemblance conceived as if the return of the same was an exterior force, a trace of a vanished difference or division. At an ontological level, the return of the same is the motive principle of closure; the image of the same is conceived juridically in terms of a reference to an absolute cause (*causa causans*) or vanished unity towards which human judgment endeavours to approximate or refer. In this respect, closure is a principle of passivity or reaction to a determinant exteriority or external force and law which has already decided, already judged and already spoken the way. Closure is the history of an infinitely extended error in which finite representation is predicated upon an eternal principle of correspondence to exterior identity. It excludes the force or active principle of becoming in which it is simply the return that both returns and passes on; returning is the being of that which becomes: 'that everything recurs is the closest approximation of a world of becoming to a world of being' (Nietzsche, 1882–8, p. 617). The eternal return is being as becoming, a principle of passage or synthesis of past, present and future states, of diversity and its reproduction. In Nietzsche's later writings, the same principle of return is expressed existentially and politically in terms of an aesthetic of judgment, a theory of affectivity as the object of ethics and of justice. *Amor fati* is an aesthetic principle of judgment and of action: the aesthetic is the criterion of ethical action insofar as authentic being survives the truth – fate or law – through artistic endeavour, through dramatising and transfiguring an inexorable yet unknown order of providential fate into an act of will. The ecstasy of authenticity is the necessity of self-determination and its pleasure or its play lies in the ethical and in many senses theatrical will to become the appropriate expression or vehicle of that which fate dictates.

JUDGMENT AND LAW

The concept of the eternal return, of fatality or destiny as law, is also an application of judgment to all genres or aspects of existence. It should be recollected that 'Dionysus is a judge' (Nietzsche, 1882–8, p. 541) and that the jurisdiction of judgment is a singularity which is connected in Stoic terms to all being. The eternal return indicates precisely the relation of destiny to finitude and imposes the necessity of judgment upon every act, the inescapability of a choice between reaction and affirmation, *ressentiment* and *amor fati* in relation to all discourses: 'the overriding aim is to combat the historical and philosophical effacing of the connections between law and morality ... Instead a text is designed which makes explicit and visible the historical connection between law and morality for the sake of "justice" (*die Gerechtigkeit*). Zarathustra's discourse is the jurisprudence of this law beyond the opposition of the rational versus revealed' (Rose, 1984, p. 90). For Nietzsche, too, it transpires that law is dead in the sense that it has lost its value, that in its closure as scientific jurisprudence it has embraced an internal principle or logic of separation. Through denying connection as fate, it has consequently been forced also to deny its relation to judgment and to destiny as the interconnectedness of ethics and law. It has ceased to judge, it has ceased to be of value; it remains as no more than passivity, lethargy or brute repetition: a law or *logos* without *nomos*, namely a law which no longer produces measure or value.

The distinction between *logos* or law and *nomos* is instructive. In classical terms, *logos* refers to that speech which lies at the basis of the legal bond or *legere*, that which ties a being to its proper form. The *logos* is the basis of the symbolic, of law in its broad sense of enforcement or prohibition. *Nomos* refers to the qualitative principle of measure; it is law but it is also movement in the sense of nomadism, of that transhumance or itineration that marks out territories according to the contingent criteria of seasons and foods or the availability of markets (Braudel, 1976). In Nietzschean terms, it is a question of two different principles of theoretical organisation. The legalistic (Apollonian) model is scientific and operates upon the basis of extracting constants or of establishing invariant forms for variable matter. Its foundation lies in calculability in the sense that the essential feature of legal science lies in reproduction, in iteration and reiteration within defined territories. *Logos* formalises and separates so as to reproduce the same: 'reproducing implies the permanence of a fixed point of view that is external to what is reproduced' (Deleuze and Guattari, 1988, p. 372); it searches for a form, a constancy, which law itself will extract from variation. *Nomos*, by way of distinction is Dionysian and expressive of individuation and heterogeneity. It is founded upon difference and itineration; it is what Deleuze terms 'an ambulant science' (ibid., p. 372) which does not reproduce but rather follows contingent singularities. Where the ideal of reproduction pervades the science of law and reduces difference to variation, the nomadic science searches for 'the singularities of a matter, or rather of a material ... that consist in following a flow in a vectorial field across which singularities are scattered like so many accidents' (ibid., pp. 372–3). It expresses forces, which come like fate, without reason, consideration or pretext, another justice, another movement, another space-time.

Translated into jurisprudential terms, the distinction between *logos* and *nomos* as principles of science is equivalent to that between law and justice.[30] The legalistic model seeks reproduction and self-reproduction within a defined territory, an autonomous sphere or field. The surrealistic principle of nomadism is different in that it follows the particularity of the event. More specifically, the legal model charts the calculability of rule and extracts the constancy of norm or of principle from the variability of rule-application or precedent. In either case, the form of law remains separate from its matter or particular instances. The destiny of law becomes unspeakable or closed in the sense that questions of form, of the immutability of law, are conceived as strictly distinct from those of the circumstances of its expression. In its positive formulation, law follows rules and not events, norms and not values. The event of judgment escapes law; it is the point of its failure. It is also the moment of excess, of a variability which exceeds the stability of a system and faces the judge with the aporia of judgment, with facts which appear like fate, without reason, consideration or pretext. A logic or science which follows the irreducibility of the event is a nomadic science of shifting jurisdiction or theoretical openness. The competence to speak of the event is based upon the ability to move from a field of reproduction or of law to a field which is demarcated around the event and which by virtue of its externality shatters the pre-existent sentence or competence.

In classical jurisprudential terms, awareness of the event to be judged was theorised in terms of an opposition between judgment and law, *nomos* and *logos*. Law was perceived to err where it rested upon no more than prior sentence or precedent: 'those that do succeed, may be by many degrees more eminent in wisdom, reason, knowledge and experience, than those that sat in the same tribunals before them; for there is in this world an undoubted wheeling in all things' (Wiseman, 1664, p. 39). That wheeling, whether chance or accident, is formulated in terms of an aporia of judgment to the effect that *argumentum ductum a simili est multum fragile et infirmum; nec procedit, quando datur dissimilitudo etiam parvai.*[31] The maxim founds the rule in the Justinian *Code* that judges are bound to pursue strictly Truth, Justice and the Laws and 'not in judging to take their example from the most solemn sentences of the highest and most eminent judges in the whole Empire'. The principle upon which such an ordinance of judgment is based is nomadic and predicated at first upon the simple perception of the eternal return of difference:

> in so many ages, and in such multitude of cases that have occurred, there has not been found one wholly like another; for indeed the dissimilitude and difformity that is amongst ourselves and the whole offspring of man not in outward form, visage, lineaments, or stature only, but even in our natures, tempers, inclinations, and humours, also makes all the matters we deal in, and the actions that flow from us, disagreeing too. Also in other productions of nature, and the accidents that are commonly ascribed to chance and fortune, there is such a strange and wonderful variety that nothing is acted, produced, or happens like another, but that in some circumstances or other that does diversify it and make it differ. (Wiseman, 1664, p. 41)

From fate, which is without reason, consideration or pretext, there flows difference, and no amount of law can erase that difference save by evacuating the otherness of justice and abandoning the event. Again,

> the Emperor makes it a strange and unwonted thing in Rome that judgments had between other parties should either profit or prejudice those who were neither present then in court nor ever called ... Neither will any likeness of one case to another, involve an absent person in such accidents as have fallen upon the men ... though the cases are never so much the same, yet a third person that never was a party, shall sustain no detriment by what hath been done between those that were. (ibid., p. 43)

The itinerant singularity of judgment, or the face-to-face quality of justice, leads to the appointment of the Roman judge being made subject to a rule of indeterminacy; he is to have equity always before his eyes: *semper aequitatem ante oculos habere*. By *Code* 1.8, the point it repeated: in all things, there ought to be a greater consideration of right and equity than of strict and exact rule: *placuit in omnibus rebus praecipuam esse justitiae aequitatisque quam stricti juris rationem.*

The principle of judgment elaborated in terms of the indeterminacy of the event to be judged should be read in an extreme way. Nature binds destiny to death and faces the judge with a choice. The judge either acts reactively with a resentful passivity towards death and so reproduces a past state of affairs according to the 'grave sentences' already handed down, or the judge acts affirmatively and creatively and suspends those sentences so as to do justice in the face of fortune. The nomadic judgment is the expression of *amor fati* and remakes the law in each judgment. It is a quality of judgment which is curiously captured by Schopenhauer in linking *fortuna* to *synderesis*, the conscience of the judge who dreams or at least imagines a future which will ever repeat his judgment in its singularity, for each judgment is the last judgement for those that are judged (Schopenhauer, 1890 ed., p. 113). To judge is to discern, to discriminate, to move: '*synderesis* is a natural power or motive force of the rational soul ... moving and stirring it to good and abhorring evil ... this *synderesis* our Lord put in men to the intent that the order and connection of things should be observed ... And this *synderesis* is the beginning of all things that may be learned by speculation or study' (St German, 1528, p. 81). What is learned is an openness to the irresistibility of fate, to a fate which since the Stoics has been inscribed in human conscience as the interconnectedness of all things or phenomena, an interconnectedness that is only apparent through the failure of scientific systems and of legal reproduction, that precisely destroys science and rule through attention to the exigency of singularity. It is in a further sense translation which begins from and follows the specific speech or face of those subject to or appearing before the law (Boyd White, 1990).

Law, as the discourse of fate as judgment, becomes a discourse of seduction. Fate seduces in the form of singularity, and it is the task of an itinerant judge to follow that which fate, which is without reason, consideration or pretext, has presented to be decided. To judge, in this perspective of *nomos* against *logos*, is to follow the eccentric logic of matter and to recognise that the judge 'finds himself therefore in the pagan situation of having a kind of 'fate' inflicted upon him by his utterance' (Lyotard and Thebaud, 1985, p. 42). The judge is seduced by his fate; his role is to love fate, to create a law that is ethical, which is to say a law which is appropriate to its circumstance. Where literary theory has suggested that rhetorical figures be interpreted according to the language of the genre from which they are drawn, that floral figures require recourse to botanical vocabularies, metaphors of light to discourses of optics, the judge must render judgment in a similar manner of appropriateness to its genre, that is to say, a judgment adequate to its circumstances. In Derrida's depiction, the philosophical is 'carried away' each time that one of its products – in this instance, the concept of metaphor – attempts to include under its own law the totality of the field, namely rhetoric, to which its product belongs: 'one then would have to acknowledge the importation into so-called philosophical discourse of exogenous metaphors, or rather of significations that become metaphorical in being transported out of their own habitat. Thus, one would classify the places they came from: there would be mataphors that are biological, organic, mechanical, technical, economic, historical, mathematical'. As Derrida's argument progresses, it becomes apparent that metaphor is both the seduction and the fate of philosophical discourse; it cannot escape figuration save by abandoning language. It is in consequence fated either to police arbitrarily the boundaries of proper and non-proper metaphors or to follow the logic of metaphor itself.

In jurisprudential terms, a similarly ethical reading of the legal text would be equally 'carried away' by the irreducible connections, the sensibility and the excess, of events themselves. Legal memory, or precedent in such a context, is no more than an image (*phantasiai*) of desire (*epithumia*): in Platonic terms, the representation, the image or the memory of the thing gives pleasure and so activates the soul.[32] In medieval terms , *affectus* or emotion is bound to *intellectus,* and *memoria* to *cogitatio*: 'desire begins the ascent to understanding by firing memory, and through memory's stored-up treasures the intellect is able to contemplate'.[33] The phantasms of memory provide both the stimulus, the desire, that will move the will to action and also the images of likeness (*simulacrum*) that will guide reason from one scene to the other. Both memory and desire appertain to the soul, or, in a more recent terminology, to the unconscious, and are the phantasmatic motive forces of what Bodin terms the 'execution' of law, namely its fateful acts of judgment, its soul (Bodin, 1580, p. 760). In the same text, indeed, we are taught that 'the law without equity, is a body without a soul, for that it concerns but things in general, and leaves the particular circumstances, which are infinite, to be by equality sought out according to the exigence of the place, times and persons' (ibid., p. 763). The ethical judge pursues precedent as the lingering memory of past desires, as the images or phantasmata of value, as *amor fati* or the laws (*nomoi*) which, without reason, consideration or pretext, the singular judgment must connect.

Legal closure may be addressed finally as a nihilism which refuses fate. In more specific terms, it is an account of judgment which denies the value, force, desire and art of judgment. While it is undoubtedly ironic to reinvoke a classical or indeed medieval conception of judgment as an antidote to the closure of law, it is precisely the hermeneutic significance of the tradition, the place of history, which is in question. In a striking variety of forms and metaphors, the medieval reception of Roman law attempted both to accommodate and to revise the inheritance of universal law. Theories of 'harmonicall judgment' (Bodin, 1580, p. 760; Lambard 1591, p. 72), geographical variation of constitutions (Bodin, p. 547), lesbian artifice (Lambard, p. 70) and of a precedence of desire (Bodin, p. 559) all served a comparable function of providing a supplement for laws which 'experience and time doth beger' (Lambard, pp. 66–7). The science of the supplement can be interpreted as a science of *nomos*, a postmodern pursuit of the simulacrum, a path paved by memory and by desire, by fateful speech and an art of smooth spaces, vague essences and singular indeterminacies. The integrity of law lies in a logic of disintegration, in the paradoxes and aporia that inevitably accompany the pursuit of similitude, likeness or the 'semblable' into the infinite variety or changes of circumstance, of persons, places, times and their connections. It is a singularity beyond the jurisdiction of any laws; it follows circumstances or events 'which [in their] infinite varieties can in no laws, no tables, no pandects, no books, be they never so many or so great, be all of them contained or comprehended' (Bodin, 1580, p. 776). The pursuit of the supplement extends beyond both rule and jurisdiction; it is a quest for images of particularity, for an ethics of the singular, for an impossible justice.

In consistently contemporary terms, we may speak of the aesthetic of judgment as the being of law towards death. The historicisation of law first presents judgment with the requirement of an ethics. A judgment which is embedded in the world and appropriate to the event necessarily follows singularity and, much as the leaden rule of the 'lesbian artificer' would 'bow to every stone of whatever fashion' (Lambard, 1591, p. 70), it loves its fate sufficient to judge according to the historical possibilities of the matter before it. In Aristotelian terms, it is an ethics or practice of virtue, 'an energy of the soul according to reason, *or not without reason*', a transformation which establishes character and happiness, and expresses *synderesis* (Aristotle, 1826 ed., pp. 19–20). It is also a species of responsibility, which at a political level denies that it is possible to judge within the closed framework of an autonomous law or to think law without justice. Its injunction is that the judge should not 'remain enclosed in purely speculative, theoretical, academic discourses, but rather [should] aspire to something more consequential, to *change* things and to intervene in an efficient and responsible though always, of course, very mediated way, not only in the profession but in what one calls the city, the *polis* and more generally the world' (Derrida, 1990, pp. 931–3). The irony of *nomos* as a science of law is that it is fated to a tradition which it inherits without reason, consideration or pretext. It is equally fated to love and to change that world or tradition in ways which it cannot predict or foresee. Judgment in this respect is Kant's 'law without law' (Kant, 1952 ed., p. 76); it is an aesthetics, sensibility or style. It is both the fate and the face of history as judgment. To be ethical or to be just, it must respond to the plurality of faces and fates with which history confronts it. It must follow so as to direct, or more simply it must both seduce and be seduced.

NOTES

1. For a sophisticated introduction to the senses of legal closure, see Stewart (1987, p. 908; 1990, p. 279) distinguishing practical reason, as the prescriptive function of will, from the Kantian idea of purity as following 'from [a] firm adherence to the logical law of identity, that

each thing is what it is and not something else. Any statement of something, therefore, must state it as what it is and without admixture. Such a statement will be pure.' Contemporary European debates around the issue of legal closure have tended to centre around Luhmann's conception of autopoiesis, depicted by Ewald (1988), as an extension of Kelsen's Kantian thesis: 'To be sure it rejects the hypothesis of the fundamental norm in favour of the idea of an interaction, of a correlation, of some solidarity among norms. But this is a secondary proposition by comparison with the reconfirmed thesis that law can have no other reference than itself.' For a recent statement of Luhmann's own view, see Luhmann (1990).

2. On the transcendental logical presupposition, see Kelsen (1967, p. 75): 'By defining law as a norm and by limiting the science of law to the cognition and description of legal norms and to the norm-determined relations between norm-determined facts, the law is delimited against nature, and the science of law as a science of norms is delimited against all other sciences that are directed toward causal cognition of actual happenings'. For a different view of foundation in self-reference, see Fish, 'Denis Martinez and the uses of theory', in Fish (1990).

3. Kafka, 'The Parable of the Law', in Kafka (1976). See, for jurisprudential commentaries, Derrida, 'Préjugés, Devant la Loi', in Derrida et al. (eds)(1985); Legendre (1983, p. 107); see also Stewart (1981) in Fryer (ed.)(1981); and Douzinas and Warrington (1991).

4. For typical statements of this thesis, see Legendre (1988); Ewald (1986); Donzelot (1986). In each case, the death of law refers to the demise of any conception of a law of law: '*the* law does not exist; that which one calls "law" is a category of thought which does not designate any essence, but rather serves to qualify certain practices: normative practice, practices of constraint and of social sanction no doubt, political practice certainly, practices of rationality as well. These are capable of being very different from each other; the law is in its entirety, without remainder, in each of these practices, without any possibility of anywhere supposing the permanence of an essence' (Ewald, 1986, p. 30). Similarly, 'we have shattered the seals of the message of the Laws and established that they contain nothing. God the legislator and Nature have ended by disappearing as a setting, or alternatively, as maintained at a distance in the manner of the founding texts of the American constitution, blurred in the aura of a halo' (Legendre, 1988, pp. 29–30). For a lengthy elegy, see Legendre (1982), especially pp. 212 ff.

5. For a series of interesting essays on this sense of legal fatality, conceived as the loss of any rational means of evaluating law, see Sarat and Kearns (eds)(1991) p. 12, who opine that 'perhaps it is the ironic fate of law to be reconstructed or revitalized by those very ideas, for example, compassion, engagement, even politics, that law has for so long tried to exclude'.

6. Sir Robert Wiseman (1664, p. 167). For a similar view, see Duck (1679, pp. 300–2), arguing that what was good in common law was what had been borrowed from the Roman.

7. For a similar argument, see Bodin (1580/1606, pp. 555–60).
8. For similar views expressed from a perspective partially external to law, see Fraunce (1588, pp. 119–20).
9. This point is taken up at great length by Ewald (1986, pp. 33–43), see especially the discussion on pp. 433–4 of the failure of justice any longer to define or constrain law: 'The law (loi) was [historically] judged in the name of a law of law (droit); as if one conceived the possibility of a control of law (loi) by the law of law (droit). That has disappeared entirely now: the law of law (droit) is now confounded utterly with positive law; in place of the classical delimitation of the law of law we find substituted a study of sources of law. That is law which is stated as law. A formalism which implies that in place of the control of law by a law of law there is substituted a control of the constitutionality of laws and the jurist is forbidden any critical attitude in the name of law. With regard to the statement of the law, jurists become technicians, practitioners of a law which itself becomes ever more technical. Their task is simply to put the indefinite proliferation of a more and more complex legislative and regulatory arsenal into order. But it is no longer their task to orientate us as to the definition of a politics of law. They are no longer the guardians of law.'
10. For an important analysis of this sense of the failure of law, see Jacobson (1989) and its development in Jacobson (1992). For a development and application of Ewald's thesis in relation to British administrative regulation, see Barron (1990).
11. For an introduction to the logic of risk management, see Simon (1988); see further Simon, 'Insurance and Risk', in Burchell et al. (eds)(1991).
12. The *universalia* of law are classically associated with laws of nature: 'they are not discovered by stress of arguments or logical demonstrations, but ... by induction, by the assistance of the senses and the memory', per Sir J. Fortescue (1460, pp. 13–14).
13. On the conception of a rule of judgment, see Ewald (1986, pp. 33–40); also Ewald (1991). See also Boyd White (1990), on a comparable theme, namely the absence of an ethics of judgment, the emergence of a purely technical jurisdiction which exists simply to order regulation without reference or recourse to the rhetorical arts of judgment as translation, character and communal speech.
14. For a striking expression of the indefinite time of tradition, see Favour (1619). See, more generally, Braudel (1980). For further discussion, see Goodrich (1992).
15. For a lucid account of *ressentiment* see Deleuze (1983, pp. 111–19).
16. On the concept of speech *in articulo morits*, see Legendre (1983, pp. 106–10).
17. For discussion of such a point, see particularly Kelley (1990); W. T. Murphy (1987). For attempts to classify and systematise common law according to such divisions, see Sir Matthew Hale (1713); Cowell (1605); Finch (1627).
18. In strict terms, it cannot thus have a meaning or 'inter-pretium', and thus in classical Roman law there was no civil liability for death, on the ground that a life in its entirety could not be valued or priced. A

similar position obtained in common law until reforming legislation of the late nineteenth century.

19. On the duality of *animus* and *anima*, see Bachelard (1984); and de Beauvoir (1975).

20. On the femininity of fate more generally in its relation to philosophy, see Boethius (1897, ed.), Book 1.

21. For legal commentaries on Aristotle's conception of justice as lesbian rule, see Lambard (1591, pp.68–72; J. Bodin (1580/1606, pp. 760–5).

22. Plato (1963 ed.), Book X, 617 c–d: 'And there were three others who sat round about at equal intervals, each one on her throne, the Fates, daughters of Necessity, clad in white vestments with filleted heads, *Lachesis*, and *Clotho*, and *Atropos*, who sang in unison with the music of the Sirens, Lachesis singing the things that were, Clotho the things that are, and Atropos the things that are to be'.

23. For an interesting depiction of the evidential dimension of the legal proof of such crimes, see Perkins (1610), a work dedicated and addressed to Sir Edward Coke.

24. Legendre, 'Analecta', in Papageorgiou (1990, pp. 216–17). See also Deleuze and Guattari (1977), pp. 12–16, 51–6.

25. One register of such transmission is clearly biological but should not for that reason be seen as any more determined or determining than other aspects of fate: see, for a recent example, Gibson (1992).

26. The Freudian account of the Oedipus tragedy takes it as an instance of the founding murder of the father. See Freud (1962); also Freud (1936) for the earlier version of this thesis. For criticism of this interpretation for its failure to recognise the underlying figuration of a principle of blood, see Legendre (1989), and Papageorgiou (1990).

27. *The Eumenides*, at lines 66–93.

28. Justinian, *Code*, 9.17, under the title: *De his qui parentes vel liberos occiderunt* (of those who have killed their parents or their children.).

29. Sartre (1976, pp. 551–2) offers conceptions of praxis and of groups in fusion as the realisation of an interiority which can transcend the practico-inert. A history which is conscious of itself can be critical to the extent that it can make and unmake an exteriority which is otherwise perceived as a serial and necessary exterior totality. If the law of exteriority escapes us, we are powerless to act upon it. In this respect, Sartre's *Critique* comes close to Nietzsche's conception of *amor fati*.

30. Derrida (1990, p. 955) 'One must be *juste* with justice, and the first way to do it justice is to hear, read, interpret it, to try to understand where it comes from, what it wants of us, knowing that it does so through singular idioms (*Dike, Jus, justitia, justice, Gerechtigkeit* ...) and also knowing that this justice always addresses itself to singularity, to the singularity of the other, despite or even because it pretends to universality'. For a distinctive manipulation of a comparable theme, see Cornell (1992).

31. [An argument drawn from a like case is very weak and fragile; it falls to the ground when the smallest dissimilitude is found.] Quintilian, *Instituto Oratio*, 5.2.

32. Plato, *Philebus*, 34b ff. See also the discussion in Foucault (1985, pp. 38–47).
33. Carruthers (1990, p. 201). She subsequently cites Gregory the Great: 'We devour the book when with eager desire we clothe ourselves with the words of life'.

REFERENCES

Aeschylus (1953 ed.), *Oresteia*, Chicago: Chicago University Press.
Aristotle (1846 ed.), *The Nicomachean Ethics*, Oxford: J. Vincent.
Bachelard, G. (1984), *The Psychoanalysis of Fire*, New York: Harper.
Barron, A. (1990), 'Legal discourse and the colonisation of the self in the modern state', in A. Carty (ed.), *Post-Modern Law*, Edinburgh: Edinburgh University Press.
Beauvoir de, S. (1975), *The Second Sex*, Harmondsworth: Penguin.
Blanchot, M. (1982), *The Space of Literature*, Lincoln: University of Nebraska Press.
Bodin, J. (1580/1606), *De Republica*, London: Knollers.
Boethius (1897 ed.), *The Consolation of Philosophy*, London: Elliot Stock Books.
Boyd-White, J. (1990), *Justice as Translation*, Chicago: Chicago University Press.
Braudel, F. (1976), *The Mediterranean World*, New York: Viking Books.
—— (1980), *On History*, Cambridge, MA: Harvard University Press.
Burchell, C. et al. (eds) (1991), *The Foucault Effect*, Hemel Hempstead: Harvester Wheatsheaf.
Camden, W. (1586/1695), *Britannia sive florentissimorum regnorum, Angliae, Scotiae, Hiberniae chorographica descriptio*, London: F. Collins.
Carruthers, M. (1990), *The Book of Memory: A Study of Memory in Medieval Culture*, Cambridge: Cambridge University Press.
Carty, A. (ed.), (1990), *Post-Modern Law*, Edinburgh: Edinburgh University Press.
Cicero, (1942 ed.), *De Fato*, London: Heinemann.
Cornell, D. (1992), *Philosophy of the Limit*, New York: Routledge.
Cowell, J. (1605), *The Institutes of the Laws of England, Digested into the Method of the Civil Law*, London: Roycroft.
—— (1608/1627), *The Interpreter: Or Booke Containing the Signification of Words*, London: W. Sheares.
Deleuze, G. (1969), *Différence et Répétition*, Paris: Presses Universitaires de France.
—— (1983), *Nietzsche and Philosophy*, London: Athlone Press.
—— (1990) *Logic of Sense*, London: Athlone.
Deleuze, G. and Guattari, F. (1977), *Anti-Oedipus*, New York: Viking Books.
—— (1988), *Mille Plateaux*, translated as *A Thousand Plateaux*, London: Athlone.
Derrida, J. (1982) *Margins of Philosophy*, Brighton: Harvester Press.
—— (1985) 'Préjugés, Devant la Loi', in Derrida et al. (eds), *La Faculté de Juger*, Parls: Editions de Minuit.
—— (1990) 'Force of Law: the mystical foundation of authority', *Cardozo Law Review* 11, 920.
Derrida, J. et al. (eds) (1985), *La Faculté de Juger*, Paris: Editions de Minuit.
Doeuff Le, M. (1989), *The Philosophical Imaginary*, London: Athlone Press.
Donzelot, J. (1986), *L'Invention du Social*, Paris: Fayard.
Douzinas, C., Goodrich P. and Hachamovitch, Y. (eds), (1993), *The Legality of*

the Contingent,, London: Routledge.

Douzinas, C. and Warrington, R. (1991), 'A well-founded fear of justice', *Law and Critique* 4, 146.

Duck, A. (1679), *De Usu et Autoritate Juris Civilis Romanorum in Dominiis Principum Christianorum*, London: Rivers.

Ewald, F. (1986), *L'Etat Providence*, Paris: Grasset.

—— (1988), 'The law of law', in G. Teubner (ed.), *Autopoietic Law*, Berlin: Walter de Gruyter. (1988).

—— (1990), 'Norms, discipline and the law', in R. Post (ed), (1991).

Favour, J. (1619), *Antiquitie Triumphing over Noveltie*, London: Richard Field.

Finch, H. (1627), *Law or a Discourse Thereof in Foure Bookes*, London: Society of Stationers.

Fish, S. (1990), *Doing What Comes Naturally*, Oxford: Oxford University Press.

Fortescue, Sir J. (1460), *De Laudibus Legum Angliae*, London: R. Gosling.

Foucault, M. (1985), *The Uses of Pleasure*, New York: Pantheon.

Fraunce, A. (1588), *The Lawiers Logike, exemplifying the praecepts of logike by the practise of the common lawe*, London: W. How.

Freud, S. (1936), *Totem and Taboo*, London: Hogarth.

—— (1961), *Beyond the Pleasure Principle*, London: Hogarth Press.

—— (1962), *Moses and Monotheism*, London: Constable.

Gibson, S. (1992), 'Law representing life: towards a Darwinian jurisprudence', *Law and Critique* 3, 244.

Goodrich, P. (1990), *Languages of Law: From Logics of Memory to Nomadic Masks*, London: Weidenfeld and Nicolson.

—— (1992), 'Poor illiterate reason: history, nationalism and common law', *Social and Legal Studies* 1, 7.

—— (1993), 'Antirrhesis: on the polemical structures of common law thought', in A Sarat and Kearns (eds), *The Rhetoric of Law*, Ann Arbor: Michigan University Press.

Hachamovitch, Y. (1993), 'Clouds: an essay on the obscure object of judgment', in C. Douzinas, P. Goodrich and Y. Hachamovitch (eds), (1993), *The Legality of the Contingent*, London: Routledge.

Hale, Sir Matthew, (1713), *The Analysis of the Law: Being a Scheme or Abstract of the Several Titles of the Law of England, Digested into Method*, Savoy: J. Nutt.

Heidegger, M. (1962), *Being and Time*, Oxford: Basil Blackwell.

Hogan, J. (1984), *A Commentary on the Complete Greek Tragedies*, Chicago, Chicago University Press.

Jacobson, A. (1989), 'Hegel's legal plenum', *Cardozo Law Review* 10, 919.

—— (1992), 'Law and the unconscious', *Cardozo Law Review* 13, 1213.

Kafka, F. (1976), *The Trial*, Harmondsworth: Penguin.

Kant, I. (1952 ed.), *The Critique of Judgment*, Oxford: Oxford University Press.

Kelley, D. (1990), *The Human Measure: Social Thought in the Western Legal Tradition*, Cambridge, MA: Harvard University Press.

Kelsen, H. (1967), *The Pure Theory of Law*, Berkeley: University of California Press.

Lacan, J. (1977), *Ecrits: A Selection*, London: Tavistock.

Lambard, W. (1591), *Archeion or Discourse upon the High Courts of Justice in England*, London: Seile.

Legendre, P. (1982), *Paroles Poétiques Echappées du Texte*, Paris: Seuil.

—— (1983), *L'Empire de la Vérité*, Paris: Fayard.

—— (1985), *L'Inestimable Objet de la Transmission*, Paris: Fayard.

—— (1988), *Le Désir Politique de Dieu*, Paris: Fayard.
—— (1989), *Le Crime de Caporal Lortie: Traité sur le Pére*, Paris: Fayard.
—— (1990). 'Analecta', in A. Papageorgiou, *Filiation: Fondement Généaloglque de la Psychanalyse*, Paris: Fayard.
Levinas, E. (1969), *Totality and Infinity*, Pittsburgh: Duquesne University Press.
Lingis, A. (1989), *Deathbound Subjectivity*, Bloomington: Indiana University Press.
Luhmann, N. (1990), *Essays on Self-Reference*, New York: Columbia University Press.
Lyotard, J. F. and Thebaud, J. L. (1985), *Just Gaming*, Manchester: Manchester University Press.
Murphy, T. (1987), 'Memorising politics of ancient history', *Modern Law Review* 50, 384.
Nietzsche, F. (1881/1984 ed.), *Daybreak*, Cambridge: Cambridge University Press.
—— (1882–8), *The Will to Power*, New York: Vintage.
Papageorgiou, A. (1990), *Filiation: Fondement Généalogique de la Psychanalyse*, Paris: Fayard.
Peake, M. (1976), *Titus Groan*, Harmondsworth: Penguin.
Perkins, W. (1610), *A Discourse of the Damned Art of Witchcraft*, Cambridge: C. Legge.
Plato (1963 ed.), *Republic*, Baltimore: University of Princeton Press.
Post, R. (ed.) (1991), *Law and the Order of Culture*, Berkeley: University of California Press.
Rose, G. (1984), *Dialectic of Nihilism*, Oxford: Basil Blackwell.
St German, (1528/1974 ed.), *Doctor and Student*, London: Selden Society.
Sarat, A., and Kearns, T. (eds), (1991), *The Fate of Law*, Ann Arbor: Michigan University Press.
—— (eds)(1993), *The Rhetoric of Law*, Ann Arbor: Michigan University Press.
Sartre, J. P. (1976), *Critique of Dialectical Reason I*, London: New Left Books.
Schopenhauer, A. (1890 ed.), *Parerga and Parilipomena*, partially translated in Schopenhauer, *Counsels and Maxims*, London: Constable.
—— (1898 ed.), *The World as Will and Idea*, London: Kegan Paul.
Selden, J. (1610/1683), *Jani Anglorum Facies Altera*, London: T. Bassett.
Simon, J. (1988), 'The ideological effects of actuarial practice', *Law and Society Review* 111.
—— (1991), 'Insurance and risk', in C. Burchell et al. (eds), *The Foucault Effect*, Hemel Hempstead: Harvester Wheatsheaf.
Spelman, Sir Henry, (1632/1695 ed.), *The History and Fate of Sacrilege*, London: J. Hartley.
Stewart, I. (1981), 'Sociology in jurisprudence', in B. Fryer (ed.), *Law State and Society*, London: Croom Helm.
—— (1987), 'Law and closure', *Modern Law Review*, 50, 908.
—— (1990), 'The critical legal science of Hans Kelsen', *Journal of Law and Society*, 17, 273.
Wiseman, Sir Robert, (1664), *The Law of Laws, or the Excellency of the Civil Law* , London: Royston.

My thanks to Costas Douzinas, David Carlson and Yifat Hachamovitch for scrupulous readings of an earlier version of this article, which in many respects became the fate – the death mask – of their commentaries.

8

Reconstruction after Deconstruction: Closing in on Critique

NEIL   MACCORMICK

My focus in this chapter is American Critical Legal Studies (hereinafter 'CLS') in two of its programmatic statements, that by Mark Kelman (1987) and that by Roberto Unger (1986). I find CLS an engaging approach to law both for its iconoclastic spirit and for its social democratic tendencies in the political realm. Yet 'social democratic' is probably too pallid and tradition-bound a term wherewith to characterise the political posture of CLS, even though the political goals which I detect in many CLS utterances do not seem to go much beyond a fancy form of the western European welfare state. However that may be, it is on social democracy with all its pallidity that I would take my stand (MacCormick, 1982, ch. 1). Whether this amounts to a predisposition for or against CLS may remain an open question.

The iconoclasm of CLS has regard mainly to scholarly understandings and misunderstandings. The iconoclastic or 'trashing' activity of CLS fixes in its sights beliefs held by 'mainstream' legal academics and scholars about the determinacy, coherence and intelligibility of the law which they represent in their writings and tease out in their teachings. Where tradition finds coherence, CLS detects contradiction. Where solutions to issues are advertised as determinate, these are trashed as indeterminate. This trashing is achieved through a deconstructive analysis which reveals that in each supposed solution a counterprinciple has been overlaid by some privileged ruling principle, whereas the counterprinciple has quite as rational a title to govern the decision in question.

As stating or implying a general theory about law, however, CLS, or, rather, the two programmatic statements on which I here focus, seems to me seriously flawed. I want to argue for this view, not by sustained countertrashing, but by the more constructive procedure of advancing a sketch of a rival theory about law, and arguing for its preferability to that implicit in the Kelman/Unger approach. This may or may not amount to a general critique of CLS; but most probably it does not, since a broad tendency in legal scholarship ranges much more widely than the vision even of leading figures and programmatic proponents of the broad tendency. Whatever I succeed in refuting here, it will not be the whole of CLS, nor do I pretend that it is.

The argument has four parts, namely: one defining what I call 'legalism' and investigating the idea of law as a system of rules; a second, discussing whether sticking to law as rules is of any real value; a third, dealing with what (if anything) is wrong with CLS; and a fourth, which defends traditional legal scholarship as a practice of 'rational reconstruction'.

LEGALISM: LAW AS RULES – AND STANDARDS AND PRINCIPLES

My argument is that 'legalism' can be interpreted in a certain sense as a virtue, not the vice that it is commonly treated as being (MacCormick, 1989). The relevant sense of legalism is this:

> the stance in legal politics according to which matters of legal regulation and controversy ought so far as possible to be conducted in accordance with predetermined rules of considerable generality and clarity, in which legal relations comprise primarily rights, duties, powers and immunities reasonably clearly definable by reference to such rules, and in which acts of government however desirable teleologically must be subordinated to rules and rights. (ibid., p. 184)

Such 'legalism' is not the same as the 'Rule of Law', but involves an attitude of commitment thereto. Such an attitude is often dismissed by CLS scholars:

> in the emergence of liberal legalism from Blackstone's part-feudal, part-liberal construct, producers of legal thought attempted to purge their product of ambivalence or contradiction. Realms of freedom and necessity could ideally be readily distinguished; the world was neatly divided into the private sphere of contract and the collectively coercive but carefully delimited state. It may well have been that late nineteenth-century judges *believed* that they had done a reasonably thorough job of purifying law of both preliberal elements and postliberal redistributive fervor, but even then the enterprise was fundamentally collapsing, because the contradictory commitments could never be purged. (Kelman, 1987, p. 259)

My task is to find the good in that which is so casually dismissed. By reprivileging the deprivileged view, I wish to engage in that process of 'rational reconstruction' which can well be said to be the mark of legal scholarship well accomplished. Of rational reconstruction, more will be said later, in the final section.

My definition of legalism – as requiring that 'acts of government

however desirable teleologically must be subordinated to rules and rights'
– evidently supposes that it is possible for legal systems to comprise some
rules. There are indeed approaches to legal theory which define legal
systems as essentially and centrally systems of rules, rules which for
example require certain conduct in the form of legal duties subject to
civil remedies or penal sanctions for non-compliance, or enable the
establishment of legal relations by the exercise of legally defined and
conferred powers (Hart, 1961; Hohfeld, 1919; MacCormick, 1981).
Such approaches characteristically account for legal rights in terms of the
various ways in which a person's legal position may be favoured by such
rules, whether by the protection entailed through the duties laid upon
others, or by a release from or simple absence of duty, or by
empowerment, or by protection from putative exercises of legal power by
others. Legal rights – or some legal rights – can thus be envisaged as rights
conferred by legal rules; what makes a right legal is the quality of the
rule(s) under which it arises.

But it is important to acknowledge that, even if we do find it illuminating and accurate to characterise a settled legal order as comprising or
focusing upon some systematically interrelated sets of rules, this would
not warrant the conclusion that law is *exclusively* an affair of rules. For
rules to be intelligible, especially to be intelligible as forming ordered sets
and (sub)systems, we have to conceive of them as instantiations of
background principles and values of various kinds, and when we turn to
interpretation of the rules this can be of decisive importance. Rules
themselves, moreover, are statable at varying levels of generality or
specificity, and can exhibit more or less determinacy or indeterminacy
both at large in the abstract and in the concrete where one perpends
particular application to the complexity of a real-world case.

Thus for example, in dealing with commercial matters, lawyers quite
appropriately include terms such as 'reasonable', 'seasonable', 'special',
'proper' and the like as naming or invoking 'standards' within statutory
provisions.[1] Similarly, in the law of negligence, to demand reasonable care
is to set the law's standard of care; to demand proof beyond reasonable
doubt in the law of evidence is to set a standard of proof, and so forth.
This is sometimes taken as evidencing a difference of type between rules
and standards; but to take it so is a palpable error. The rule is that the
buyer in a commercial transaction may, with seasonable notice, acquire
the right within a reasonable time to re-tender goods conforming to
contract; the rule is that prosecutors must prove their cases beyond
reasonable doubt. It is by incorporation in a rule that the relevant
standard is made the law's standard. But for the rule incorporating it, it
would not be true that the criminal standard of proof is proof beyond
reasonable doubt; but for the rule in a commercial code, it would not be

true that the standard for timeousness of a buyer's due notification of intention to make a substituted tender is that of seasonableness – and so on. Hence there is no polar opposition between rules and standards. It takes a rule to make a standard legal; it may take a standard to make a rule satisfactorily workable. That there can be rules which do not incorporate standards does not show that standards can operate legally without incorporation in rules (or in formulations of legal principle).

One instance of the above-noted error is to be found in Kelman (1987, p. 17), where it is attributed to CLS generally as a fundamental insight:

> In every legal dispute about the appropriate resolution of a legal controversy, rule-like solutions, standard-based solutions, and intermediate positions will uncomfortably coexist, none fully dominating either day-to-day practice or *a fortiori* justificatory rhetoric.
>
> CLS adherents have been adept at reminding legal academics of the number of important controversies that can obviously be seen as instances of an irresolvable rules-standards conflict.

We have already seen that there can be no such irresolvable conflict, because there is no such polar opposition of types as the argument presupposes. Standards are not something apart from rules, but one possible component of rules. Rules can vary over a wide range in their degrees of determinacy and indeterminacy; in the range and kind of value judgments that their provisions make operative as conditions of rule-application. No rule can be so utterly determinate that in every possible case of its application the proper application is decidable without any regard to background principles or values. The broader the standards or other criteria a rule invokes, the less determinate in many concrete cases it will be.

Yet rules of any sort are in their nature apt to be very much more determinate than principles, such as the principle that there ought to be no liability without fault (with 'fault' itself being definable partly by reference to standards, such as that it is fault to fail to take such care as is reasonable in any situation of action). The task of the law-maker and, in a different way, of the analytical or critical (by 'critical' I do not mean only CLS) scholar is to find the most appropriate degree of determinacy in a given context across a wide range of possible variation. There is here no true opposition of polar opposites, far less any 'irresolvable conflict' – nor, still less, contradiction. My point here is perhaps open to being taken as merely verbal or conceptual. For, it could be said, a rule with narrowly stated operative facts, especially where enumeration is involved, as with speed limits or voting ages, does differ significantly from one which includes a 'standard' in its conditions of application. And that difference remains even if it might be analytically objectionable to speak as though standards operated outside of rules, rather than, as is so common, internally to them. My answer is that, for my purposes, analytical clarity matters a great deal, and it seems to me to be more important for this CLS argument than Kelman supposes. It is true that there is a spectrum ranging from the most tightly drawn and determinate of rules to particularly open-textured standard-stipulating rules; but some standard-stipulating rules are neither particularly broad nor vague, as witness those commercial code standards quoted above. To slide from the problematic character of choice among styles of rules into an 'irresolvable conflict' between rules and standards is to distort that truth beyond recognition.

In any case, my main present concern here is with establishing the possibility of a theory of law as a system of rules. One possible objection to such a theory might have been that it cannot accommodate standards. Evidently, it can; so this objection falls. Still, the necessary and omnipresent interpenetration of rules, standards, values and principles does exhibit why a conception of law as comprising rules *merely* would be false or at least misleading. For we make sense of rules as, and rules only make sense as, determinations or more concrete instantiations of coherently grasped principles of conduct and of social organisation; and the coherence of principles with each other and with rules depends on their being rationally geared to the realisation of some constellation of values (MacCormick, 1978, ch. 7; MacCormick, 1984; Nerhot, (ed.) 1990; Levenbook, 1984).

WHY RULES AT ALL?

If, however, rules are of little use save when animated by principles and values, it seems legitimate to ask why anyone bothers with rules at all. Why not just let the principles and values do their work without the seemingly useless interposition of rules at all? Why tie ourselves down with detailed and complex rules and statutory provisions, behind which we always have to make recourse to the underlying principles and values to sort out our ever-recurrent problems of interpretation which turn up whenever the legislation falls to be applied in actual cases? Could we not just handle the problems by intelligent case-by-case reflection upon the values which are at stake, and the principles which give normative expression to our pursuit of the values?

These questions are such old chestnuts as to be almost self-answering. Our pursuit of value is not single and unidirectional. Neither Benthamite happiness nor Dworkinian equality of concern and respect nor any other unitary summum bonum can be found which captures as a single target for pursuit all that we value (nor all that is of value). At the level of practical deliberation, we confront a plurality of values and of valued states of affairs, each in various settings partly incompatible with some other.

Even when we contemplate only a single principle or scale of value, we face always, as Fuller pointed out, a question of the point on that scale which we set as a minimum of required achievement – where shall we draw the line between mandatory duty and discretionary aspiration? Between cruelty or callous indifference to others and highly altruistic good neighbourliness or even saintly commitment to others' good, there are many gradations. But what is the minimum of concern for others that we shall actually *demand?* One solution is to say: 'for criminal law purposes, you must at least refrain from intentional and non-consensual physical interference with others; for civil law purposes, you must take reasonable care for their safety'. This answer has stood for a good long time, but the growth of various forms of strict liability indicates a concern to raise the standard of thoughtfulness towards others in at least some settings. The point here is not to commend one or another view in particular but to draw attention to the plain fact that somehow a view has to be taken.

So, reliance on raw values or principles would have two defects: even on a single scale of valuation, a line may have to be drawn as to that which is open to demand as a duty, and subject to some active sanctioning; and more than one scale of valuation is indeed often in play, so that we have to balance or reconcile the pursuit of several different values expressible in terms of a plurality of competing principles. Settling some rules of conduct through legislation, and further determining them through precedent, is the available method for striking a balance or securing a reconciliation. You can trace this through such legislation as that on road traffic or that on commerce. Sometimes the mode of settling rules as fixed points of general principle has been yet more reliant on precedent, as in the area of general doctrine about formation of contract or about liability for negligence.

In relation to this general sort of issue, John Finnis (1985) has to good effect redeployed St Thomas's concept of *determinatio*; Hans Kelsen's translator (Kelsen, 1967) used the term 'concretisation' to much the same effect. A *determinatio* or concretisation of a principle for a specific class of cases is not a deduction from it, nor a discovery of some implicit meaning; it is the act of setting a more concrete and categorical requirement in the spirit of the principle and guided both by a sense of what is practically realisable (or enforceable) and by a recognition of the risk of conflict with other principles or values, themselves concretised through other *determinationes*. Neither line-drawing between duty and aspiration nor achieving some standing balance or reconciliation of potentially conflicting values or principles is possible without some recourse to *determinatio*.

There are at least two reasons why this is important, and of value in itself. First, as a matter of interpersonal coordination: even if we belonged to a community all of whose members were profoundly agreed about the basic values of life and about the principles they mandated, there would be problems to be resolved both about priority in cases of competition or incompatibility of principles, and about line-drawing (fixing *duties*). This would require the determination of rules as a coordination device; all the more is this called for in a real world of at least partial disagreement about fundamental values and principles. Second, there is the issue of fairness or due process. Resort to coercive sanctioning, whether by way of civil remedy or as criminal penalty, justifies a demand for fair and clear notice in advance of the duties that are demanded, and, all the more, for exact and answerable forms of civil complaint or criminal charge. Without the *determinatio* of rules, a mere reliance on raw principles and values would conduce neither to reasonable interpersonal coordination nor to fairness or due process.

That rules are intelligible as *determinationes* or concretisations of principles is overlooked or at least under-regarded by analysts of law who focus on momentary systems of ordered rules. H. L. A. Hart's work (Hart, 1961; but see the opening sentences of ch. 7) is a case in point. Fuller, by contrast, places considerable emphasis on the rational and purposive activity of rule-determination, rather than on the rules which result from the activity (Fuller, 1969, pp. 74, 145–51). This he expressed in his repeated characterisation of law as 'an enterprise' – 'the enterprise of subjecting human conduct to the governance of rules'. His point is that our rules make sense in the light of what we are trying to do with them. Such an enterprise Fuller saw as fraught with difficulty, and as necessarily guided by the formal principles which he dubbed 'the inner morality of law'. These principles themselves defined the aspirations rather than the strict duties of the good legislator. They were in this view internally complex, and in their plurality capable of conflicting or pulling against each other in just the characteristic way we have already considered. So getting them right is as much art as science, and even the ideal legislator would have to be consciously aiming for some overall balance or compromise (ibid., pp. 41–94, especially 42–3, 91–4).

Fuller is, and rightly so, extremely anxious to portray the full internal complexity and problematic quality of each of his formal principles. Working out the proper interpretation and application of each one in law-giving is a difficult and value-laden enterprise in itself. Nor is that the whole of the problem. For there remains the yet more taxing enterprise of seeking to hold all in proper balance, despite their tendency to pull against each other in various settings – consider the tension between generality and clarity, and the difficult correlation of both with the demand for congruence. Again, we confront the problem of trying to secure the conjoint realisation of a plurality of values or principles where plurality implies a necessity for balance and compromise.

Legality is always a matter of more or less, not of absolutes; of aspiration, not simple duty. Certainly it is neither a matter of steering a mean between but two extremes, nor of balancing or choosing between simple polar opposites. It is a matter of attentiveness to an inevitably judgmental best-possible conjoint pursuit of a plurality of principles; and its realisation requires an orientation towards principles and values which are in a sense intrinsic to the enterprise itself, and which do constitute an important though not all-embracing set of politico-moral values.

What I call legalism is thus indeed an ethical and political stance about law, not an unimaginative attitude to its application nor an undue faith in the possibilities of literalism in legal interpretation. It commends that people should procure the governance of their countries in accordance with tolerably determinate rules, that is, tolerably determinate *determinationes* of otherwise infinitely contestable weighings and weightings of principles. The kinds and grounds of complaint laid against the corrupt regimes thrown out of office in recent revolutions should be enough to convince those who have doubted it that the Rule of Law in Fuller's sense is truly a moral value of fundamental political importance. Legalism is indeed not a vice, but an ethic.

It is in a way a positivistic ethic, expressive of what Tom Campbell (1988) has called 'ethical positivism', for the demand that there be clear and preannounced rules of law is also a demand that these laws, not the norms of either positive morality or ideal morality extraneous to law, nor indeed those of a dominant political ideology, be the grounds of state intervention in people's lives. To make a case for the Rule of Law can indeed be seen as a matter of making a 'moralistic case for a-moralistic law' (MacCormick, 1985).

SO WHAT IS WRONG WITH CLS?

The strand in cls doctrine with which I wish to take issue should now be clear. It is that strand whose substance is an elaborate denial that what I call legalism is either desirable or indeed possible (see Kennedy, 1976). The general picture presented of traditional or mainstream legal scholarship is in terms of such vices as inauthenticity, cynicism and self-deception or false consciousness. At the core of the critique is Unger's attack upon an 'objectivism' which appears to him quite unsustainable. By objectivism, he means the belief that 'the authoritative legal materials ... embody and sustain a defensible scheme of human association' or 'display, though always imperfectly, an intelligible human order' and are 'not merely the outcome of contingent power struggles or of practical pressures lacking in rightful authority' (Unger, 1986, p. 2). The falsity of objectivism is evidenced everywhere by the pull of principle and counterprinciple or by the omnipresence of contradiction, indeed of the 'Fundamental Contradiction' (Kelman, 1987, pp. 62–3; Kennedy, 1979, pp. 211–13), in the contents alike of case law and of legal doctrine, or 'legal dogmatics'. Contradictions include, for example, those between individualism and altruism in the law of obligations (Kennedy, 1976, pp. 1685–7), or between rules and standards (Kelman, 1987, pp. 62–3) or between freedom of contract and values of community (Unger, 1986, pp. 55–75).

Why does the tension of principle 'p' and counterprinciple 'cp' matter so? Kelman's thesis, also ascribed by him to central works in the cls canon, appears to be that every attempt to draw a line either judicially or academically in any case for decision falling within the sway of p leads *eo ipso* to a need for drawing the line on cp as well. But p and cp support different and competing possible decisions. Hence the line-drawing is legally arbitrary and only politically justifiable or explicable, since p and cp ex hypothesi supply sufficient legal ground for a decision either way. Any doctrinal (or dogmatic) depiction of the relevant body of law can as legitimately be in terms of cp subject to limitations or exceptions for p. The common privileging of p in terms of dogmatic expositions by traditional scholars reflects a conscious or unconscious suppression of a converse representation of law which is in truth equally supportable. The fact of the matter is that there is nothing in any kind of reified 'Law' which requires or justifies the relevant privileging. The preference or priority here rests in ideology or in political choice, not in any objective requirement of legal reasoning or general practical reason.

A further possible step is, then, as in Unger's *Movement*, to argue for the elaboration of a legal dogmatics different in style and in substance, which, by reimagining society in a coherent way, starting from disprivileged poles of present argumentation, can construct an objectively tenable body of 'deviationist doctrine'. This view may, however, be idiosyncratic. I take it that Balkin's thesis of ideological relativism (Balkin, 1987a; 1987b), according to which the global critique of any ideology would have to be framed through a different ideology which in turn is equally susceptible to a countercritique, is probably a more representative view. All that then follows is that there can be different approaches to legal decisions and to legal doctrine which can be equally rational and equally legitimate as forms of argumentation. If so, the error of the 'formalism' and 'objectivism' as excoriated by Unger are less than he suggests – it is not that mainstream argumentation has to be itself incoherent or lacking in moral intelligibility, but that it oversteps itself to the extent that it in turn suggests that alternative theses as to the meaning and interpretation of disputed areas of law must be either irrational or otherwise illegitimate.

Stripped down to a claim about the political and/or ideological quality of mainstream legal dogmatics when concerned with fundamental issues of interpretation and of coherence or value in law, the CLS position is a lot less radical than the grander programmatic presentations suggest. The thesis that even the best-drawn laws or lines leave some penumbra of doubt, and that this calls for an exercise of a partly political discretion to settle the doubt, is not particularly new; it is but the common currency of modern legal positivism. The claims about ideology can be matched fairly closely in the concluding chapter of Hans Kelsen's *Pure Theory of Law* (1967). The idea that legal principles may found rival and mutually exclusive prima facie rights between which judges must choose on inevitably consequentialist grounds is even to be found in my own *Legal Reasoning and Legal Theory* (1978). Yet my feeling is that all this positivistic stuff is itself included in the rejected mainstream and not deemed 'Critical' at all.

It is certainly good advice to scholars and practitioners that they should always be ready to turn any question upside down and to see whether underplayed principles cannot be played up to create a seriously arguable counter to the view which one has initially entertained. The danger of mere dogmatism in legal dogmatics comes from a failure to take seriously the possibility that another view might be argued just as well as one's own initial one and insightful CLS writings at the level of concrete doctrine rather than general programmatics demonstrate this.

A crucial point, though, is that one ought not to miss or underestimate the significance of line-drawing or *determinatio* as already discussed. The law really does and really can settle issues of priority between principles by fixing rules, and even when problems of interpreting rules arise, those focus on more narrowly defined points than if the matter were still at large as one of pure principle. Fixing rules can be done either by legislation or by precedent; most commonly, in modern systems, by the two in combination. It is one of the gifts of law to civilisation that it can subject practical questions to more narrowly focused forms of argument than those which are available to unrestricted practical reason (cf. Finnis, 1980; Alexy, 1989; MacCormick, 1978, pp. 108–19, 129–51).

Further, it is for many situations an oversimplification (as Fuller has shown) to see questions just in terms of paired polar oppositions of principle (though pairing of polar opposites always has pedagogical and often has argumentative and rhetorical utility). Moreover, the mere presence of two or more principles which favour differing solutions in a concrete case is not of itself proof that the question remains rationally open as one of law. Arguments from coherence and from what Ronald Dworkin (1986, pp. 240–8, 283–5) calls 'fit' can often work so as to show a decisive preferability for one position over another, and, even where matters remain somewhat in balance at that level, the value judgments operative in consequentialist arguments can be pretty compelling in some legal settings (they are rarely as monovalent as Posnerian law and economics suggests, though).

Again, we come to the issue of an understanding of practical reasoning both in its legal and in its general forms. The weakness of the theory (to which I also formerly subscribed) that any issue which involves a choice between rival theories or ideologies is undecidable objectively is that it is itself a claim at the level of practical reason, and therefore one which ought to be challenged or sustained case by case. As a global thesis about the undecidability of questions, it is itself a highly implausible reading of the materials (cf. Dworkin, 1986, pp. 271–4). What now seems to me better to say is that there quite often arise really difficult and finely balanced questions of law. At the level of law *simpliciter*, these lack a determinate solution dictated by the materials. We have a simple conflict of legal prima facie rights or duties. But the law does then require deciders to have recourse to general practical reasoning. What that means is that only certain kinds of arguments have rational persuasiveness here. There is no reason to doubt that quite often the relative weight of the arguments may be such as to close the legally open issue. If in a given case they do not, the issue is then one of pure decision (subject to any presumptions that are applicable in case of uncertainty) at the best intuitive judgment of the authorised decision-maker. That the decision has been refined through so many levels of argument makes it arbitrary only in a Pickwickian sense. That it is also political is what no-one can or should doubt.

WHAT ABOUT LEGAL DOGMATICS?

Once we have accepted all that should be accepted out of the general CLS theory about legal indeterminacy and omnipresent contradiction, it becomes clear that a flat dismissal of the totality of traditional mainstream scholarship is impossible. My argument on this is that the proper task of legal scholarship in the form of doctrine or dogmatics is the 'rational reconstruction' of legal materials (MacCormick and Summers, 1991).

In law, in the social sciences and indeed in the natural sciences, the scholar or researcher is confronted by a vast body of material or of experimental or observational data. The materials and/or data may seem confused and disorderly, partly or potentially conflicting, gappy in places. As 'materials' or 'data', they already represent some kind of a more or less deliberate selection out of the totality of experience. The task of scholarship or science is then to take these selected items and put them back together, to *reconstruct* them in a way that makes them comprehensible because they are now shown as parts of a well-ordered though complex whole. This requires explanatory principles establishing criteria of what counts as well-ordered and rational. To be sure, rational reconstruction is an intellectual process, involving a new imagining and describing of the found order, not literally a rebuilding of objects in the world.

In legal scholarship, rational reconstruction, or legal dogmatics, means the production of clear and systematic statements of legal doctrine, accounting for statute law and case law in terms of organising principles, relating actual or hypothetical decisions both to their factual bases and to governing norms elaborated out of the authoritative materials. Legal doctrine produced in this way degenerates into mere casuistry where it purports to reconcile and work in every single case and statute into some grand scheme; there has to be some discrimination between the parts that belong in the coherent whole and the mistakes or anomalies that do not fit and ought to be discarded or abandoned or at least revised.

The work of legal dogmatics is sometimes dismissed as mere transcription, with the scholar simply acting as no more than scribe to the judge or legislator. But this is a total misunderstanding. For it calls for the exercise of creative intelligence and disciplined imagination to master the large and always changing bodies of material involved, to grasp them all together, and to reconstruct them all together into systematised and coherent wholes articulated out of complex and internally articulated parts.

It might be noted that this activity presupposes but does not itself elaborate an ontology.[2] There have to be reasons why the materials of the law count as such, independently of the activity of rational reconstruction of the materials that do count. Legal facts are institutional facts (not 'plain facts'), but they are so independently of particular reconstructions and partial transformations of them. This objective underpinning is essential to the firmly intersubjective factuality or objectivity of the materials on which the legal scholar's work is done. Even anomalous cases or statutes are real decisions and real laws, whose effects must be taken into account at the same time as they may be put to one side as anomalous, or not reconcilable with the main doctrinal schema reconstructed out of the rest of the material.

The information with which the legal scholar works is, it must be repeated, episodic and fragmentary in character. Acts of legislation, regulations issued by officials, decisions handed down by judges, all are issued as occasion arises, that is, as politics, policy, or the accidents of litigation may require. Their topics and conclusions belong to various agendas of political parties, of governmental agencies, of public prosecutors, of pressure groups, of private litigants. Some are extremely general, some quite particular, most somewhere in between. It is not a priori particularly probable that new material as produced raw will show exactly on its face how it reconciles itself with the whole schema to which it is supposed to belong. Legal systems tend towards chaos almost as strongly as they tend towards system. Each attempt at legislative or adjudicative simplification is apt to generate a new complexity (Luhmann, 1985, pp. 161–6).

This is why one who seeks to produce a rationally coherent systemati-sation of legal material must have the capacity first to master in a raw form a huge mass of material and then to exercise imagination, intelligence and insight in order to bring it together into an intelligible whole. Normative order as order is not a natural datum of human society but a hard-won production of organising intelligence. The fact that the materials are themselves produced though rational activity, at least partly informed by previous dogmatic reconstructions, helps, of course; so indeed does the fact that there are many such reconstructions in the form of treatises, monographs and learned articles; but none of this in itself *creates* the intelligible wholeness of the doctrinal system. It is as nearly true the other way round – the maintenance of doctrinal integrity through the good practice of legal dogmatics is what makes possible intelligent legislation and well-grounded judicial decision-making.

This, I think, shows why the juristic job both is and is not political. It is not like setting up a committee or pressure group to change the law in some way. Indeed, it is not remotely like that kind of politics. It is, on the other hand, highly judgmental, and the value judgments involved in the ordering of legal material include judgments of moral and political value. Moreover, it is intensely political in its effects. In a modern state, the continuing intelligibility and operability of law depends crucially on its continuing servicing by academic commentators as well as by practitioners and judges. It would therefore be a self-defeating act to take part in the project of the doctrinal construction of law as a coherent object of thought if one were not persuaded at least on balance that legal order as such has some value. For my part, I think that, faults and all, it has; that is, I subscribe, with all necessary qualifications, to what I call the 'ethics of legalism'.

In the setting of debates around the theme of 'closure or critique', this conclusion may suggest a tendency on my part toward the pole of 'closure'. But in fact I think that the imperative to see coherence in law is better interpreted as a guiding ideal than an ever fully accomplished fact. The law is not in actuality a closed system. It is, at the very least, 'cognitively open', to borrow an idea from Niklas Luhmann. Norm-atively, it is notoriously open-ended in hard cases. The act of interpretation, whether in doctrinal reconstruction, in advocacy or in adjudication, commonly confronts an open question. Operative interpre-tation in decision-making must always close the open question for the particular case. But the precedent thus established becomes itself the object of interpretation thereafter. The basis of interpretation is opinion –

one's opinion as to the best sense that can be made of the available materials in the light of legal and social values, acceptable modes of argumentation, and the like. Upon this, reasonable opinions can and do differ. If the law is to be thought of as a chain novel, let us think of it as a novel like *The French Lieutenant's Woman* – that is, a novel with alternative endings.[3]

NOTES

1. These terms are taken from the American Uniform Commercial Code (articles 2–508 and 2–714). For discussion of the use of broad standards within the UCC, see Z. B. Wiseman (1987), 'The limits of vision: Karl Llewellyn and the merchant rules', *Harvard Law Review* 100, 465.
2. Dworkin's discussion of 'External Scepticism', though thoroughly convincing in itself for the purpose for which it is deployed in *Law's Empire* (pp. 78–85 and 266–7), does nevertheless dodge the issue of what exists (pompously, the issue of 'ontology'). This is an aspect of the poverty and imprecision of what he says about the pre-interpretive stage of interpretation.
3. This is a slimmed-down version of a similarly entitled paper published in the *Oxford Journal of Legal Studies* for 1991. I profited greatly from friendly criticisms during a seminar in the University of Warwick in February 1991; but the final version has been yet further improved by rigorous pruning advised by the present editor.

REFERENCES

Alexy, R. (1989), *A Theory of Legal Argumentation* (transl. R. Adler and N. MacCormick), Oxford: Oxford University Press.
Balkin, J. M. (1987a), 'Taking ideology seriously', *University of Missouri at Kansas City Law Review* 55, 392–433.
——— (1987b), 'Deconstructive practice and legal theory', *Yale Law Journal* 96, 743–87.
Campbell, T. D. (1988), 'Ethical positivism', in S. Panou (ed.), *Theory and Systems of Legal Philosophy*, Stuttgart: Franz Steiner Verlag.
Dworkin, R. (1986), *Law's Empire*, Cambridge, Ma: Harvard University Press/ London: Fontana.
Finnis, J. M. (1980), *Natural Law and Natural Rights*, Oxford: Clarendon.
——— (1985), 'On "the Critical Legal Studies movement"', *American Journal of Jurisprudence* 30, 21–42.
Fuller, L. L. (1969), *The Morality of Law*, New Haven: Yale University Press.
Hart, H. L. A. (1961), *The Concept of Law*, Oxford: Clarendon.
Hohfeld, W. N. (1919), *Fundamental Legal Concepts*, New Haven: Yale University Press.
Kelman, M. (1987), *A Guide to Critical Legal Studies*, Cambridge, Ma: Harvard University Press.
Kennedy, D. (1976), 'Form and substance in private law adjudication', *Harvard Law Review* 89, 1685.

——— (1979), 'The structure of Blackstone's commentaries', *Buffalo Law Review* 28, 205.

Levenbook, B. B. 'The role of coherence in legal reasoning', *Law and Philosophy* 3, 355–74.

Luhmann, N. (1985), *A Sociological Theory of Law* (transl. E. King-Utz and M. Albrow), London: Routledge and Kegan Paul.

MacCormick, D. N. (1978), *Legal Reasoning and Legal Theory*, Oxford: Clarendon.

——— (1981), *H. L. A. Hart*, London: Edward Arnold.

——— (1982), *Legal Rights and Social Democracy*, Oxford: Oxford University Press.

——— (1984), 'Coherence in legal justification', in W. Krawietz et al. (eds), *Theorie der Normen*, Berlin: Duncker and Humblot.

——— (1985), 'A moralistic case for a moralistic law', *Valparaiso University Law Review* 20, 1–42.

——— (1989), 'The ethics of legalism', *Ratio Juris* 2, 184–93.

MacCormick, D. N. and Summers, R. S. (1991), *Interpreting Statutes: a Comparative Study*, London: Dartmouth.

Nerhot, P. (ed.) (1990), *Law, Interpretation and Reality*, Dordrecht: Kluwer.

Unger, R. M. (1986), *The Critical Legal Studies Movement*, Cambridge, Ma: Harvard University Press.

Wiseman, Z. B. (1987), 'The limits of vision: Karl Llewellyn and the merchant rules', *Harvard Law Review* 100, 465.

9

The Law Wishes to Have a Formal Existence

STANLEY FISH

ACHIEVING PLAIN AND CLEAR MEANINGS

The law wishes to have a formal existence. That means, first of all, that the law does not wish to be absorbed by, or declared subordinate to, some other – non-legal – structure of concern; the law wishes, in a word, to be distinct, not something else. And second, the law wishes in its distinctness to be perspicuous; that is, it desires that the components of its autonomous existence be self-declaring and not be in need of piecing-out by some supplementary discourse; for, were it necessary for the law to have recourse to a supplementary discourse at crucial points, that discourse would be in the business of specifying what the law is, and, consequently, its autonomy would have been compromised indirectly. It matters little whether one simply announces that the principles and mechanisms of the law exist ready-made in the articulations of another system or allows those principles and mechanisms to be determined by something they do not contain; in either case, the law as something independent and self-identifying will have disappeared.

In its long history, the law has perceived many threats to its autonomy, but two seem perennial: morality and interpretation. The dangers which these two pose are, at least at first glance, different. Morality is something to which the law wishes to be related, but not too closely; a legal system whose conclusions clashed with our moral intuitions at every point so that the categories *legally valid* and *morally right* never (or almost never) coincided would immediately be suspect; but a legal system whose judgments perfectly meshed with our moral intuitions would be thereby rendered superfluous. The point is made concisely by the Supreme Court of Utah in a case where it was argued that the gratuitous payment by one party of the other party's mortgage legally obligated the beneficiary to repay. The court rejected the argument, saying 'that if a mere moral, as distinguished from a legal, obligation were recognized as valid consideration for a contract, that would practically erode to the vanishing point the necessity for finding a consideration'.[1] That is to say, if one can infer directly from one's moral obligation in a situation to one's legal obligation, there is no work for the legal system to do; the system of morality has already done it. Although it might seem (as it does to many natural law theorists) that such a collapsing of categories recommends itself if only on the basis of efficiency (why have two systems when you can make do with one?), the defender of a distinctly legal realm will quickly answer that since moral intuitions are notoriously various and contested, the identification of law with morality would leave every individual his or her own judge; in place of a single abiding standard to which disputing parties might have recourse, we would have many standards with no way of adjudicating between them. In short, many moralities would make many laws, and the law would lack its most saliently desirable properties, generality and stability.

It is here that the danger posed by morality to law, or, more precisely, to the rule (in two senses) of law intersects with the danger posed by interpretation. The link is to be found in the desire to identify a perspective larger and more stable than the perspective of local and individual concerns. Morality frustrates that desire because, in a world of more than one church, recourse to morality will always be recourse to someone's or some group's challengeable moral vision. Interpretation frustrates that desire because, in the pejorative sense which it usually bears in these discussions, interpretation is the name for what happens when the meanings embedded in an object or text are set aside in favour of the meanings demanded by some angled, partisan object. Interpretation, in this view, is the effort of a morality, of a particular, interested agenda, to extend itself into the world by inscribing its message on every available space. It follows, then, that, in order to check the imperial ambitions of particular moralities, some point of resistance to interpretation must be found, and that is why the doctrine of formalism has proved so attractive. Formalism is the thesis that it is possible to put down marks so self-sufficiently perspicuous that they repel interpretation; it is the thesis that one can write sentences of such precision and simplicity that their meanings leap off the page in a way that no-one – no matter what his or her situation or point of view – can ignore; it is the thesis that one can devise procedures that are self-executing in the sense that their unfolding is independent of the differences between the agents who might set them in motion. In the presence (in the strong Derridean sense) of such a mark or sentence or procedure, the interpretive will is stopped short and is obliged to press its claims within the constraints provided by that which it cannot override. It must take the marks into account; it must respect the self-declaring reasons; it must follow the route laid down by the implacable procedures, and if it then wins it will have done so fairly, with justice, with reason.

Obviously, then, formalism's appeal is a function of the number of problems that it solves, or at least appears to solve: it provides the law with a palpable manifestation of its basic claim to be perdurable and general; that is, not shifting and changing, but standing as a point of reference in relation to which change can be assessed and controlled; it enables the law to hold contending substantive agendas at bay by establishing threshold requirements of procedure that force those agendas to assume a shape that the system will recognise. The idea is that once a question has been posed as a *legal* question – has been put into the proper *form* – the answer to it will be generated by relations of entailment between that form and other forms in the system.

As Hans Kelsen put it, in a book aptly named *The Pure Theory of Law*, 'The law is an order, and therefore all legal problems must be set and solved as order problems. In this way legal theory becomes an exact structural analysis of positive law, free of all ethical-political value judgments.'[2] Kelsen's last clause says it all: the realms of the ethical, the political, and of value in general are the threats to the law's integrity. They are what must be kept out if the law is to be something more than a misnomer for the local and (illegitimate) triumph of some particular point of view.

There are at least two strong responses to this conception of law. The first, which we might call the 'humanistic' response, objects that a legal system so conceived is impoverished, and that, once you have severed procedures from value, it will prove enormously difficult, if not impossible, to relink them in particular cases. Since the answers generated by a purely formal system will be empty of content (that, after all, is the formalist claim), the reintroduction of content will always be arbitrary. The second response, which we might call 'radical' or 'critical', would simply declare that a purely formal system is not a possibility, and that any system pretending to that status is already informed by that which it purports to exclude. Value, of both an ethical and political kind, is already inside the gate, and the adherents of the system are either ignorant of its sources or are engaged in a political effort to obscure them in the course of laying claim to a spurious purity. In what follows, I shall be elaborating a version of the second response, and arguing that however much the law wishes to have a formal existence, it cannot succeed in doing so, because – at any level from the most highly abstract to the most particular and detailed – any specification of what the law is will already be infected by interpretation and will therefore be challengeable. Nevertheless, my conclusion will be not that the law fails to have a formal existence but that, in a sense which I shall explain, it always succeeds, although the nature of that success – it is a political/rhetorical achievement – renders it bitter to the formalist taste.

We may see what is at stake in disputes about formalism by turning to a recent (July 1988) opinion delivered by Judge Alex Kozinski of the United States Court of Appeals for the Ninth Circuit.[3] The case involved the desire of a construction partnership called Trident Center to refinance a loan at rates more favourable than those originally secured. Unfortunately (or so it seemed), language in the original agreement expressly blocked such an action, to wit that the '"[m]aker shall not have the right to prepay the principal amount hereof in whole or in part" for the first 12 years'.[4]

Trident's attorneys, however, pointed to another place in the writing where it is stipulated that '[i]n the event of a prepayment resulting from a default ... prior to January 10, 1996, the prepayment fee will be ten percent'[5] and argued that this clause gives Trident the option of prepaying the loan provided that it is willing to incur the penalty as stated. Kozinski is singularly unimpressed by this reasoning, and, as he himself says, dismisses it 'out of hand',[6] citing as his justification the clear and unambiguous language of the contract. Referring to Trident's contention that it is entitled to precipitate a default by tendering the balance plus the ten per cent fee, Kozinski declares that 'the contract language, cited above, leaves no room for this construction',[7] a judgment belied by the fact that Trident's lawyers managed to make room for just that construction in their arguments. It is a feature of cases like this that turn on the issue of what is and is not 'expressly' said that the proclamation of an undisputed meaning always occurs in the midst of a dispute about it. Given Kozinski's rhetorical stance, the mere citation (his word, and a very dangerous one for his position) of the contract language should be sufficient to end all argument, but what he himself immediately proceeds to do is argue, offering a succession of analyses designed to buttress his contention, that 'it is difficult to imagine language that more clearly or unambiguously expresses the idea that Trident may not unilaterally [more is given away by this word than Kozinski acknowledges] prepay the loan during its first 12 years'.[8] If this were in fact so, it would be difficult to imagine why Kozinski should feel compelled to elaborate his opinion again and again. I shall not take up his points except to say that, in general, they are not particularly persuasive and usually function to open up just the kind of interpretive room that he declares unavailable. Thus, for example, he reasons that Trident's interpretation 'would result in a contradiction between two clauses of the contract' whereas the 'normal rule of construction ... is that courts must interpret contracts, if possible, so as to avoid internal conflict'.[9] But it is no trick at all (or at least not a hard one) to treat the two clauses so that they refer to different anticipated situations and are not contradictory (indeed, that is what Trident's lawyers do): in the ordinary course of things, as defined by the rate and schedule of payments set down in the contract, Trident will not have the option of prepaying;

but in the extraordinary event of a default, the prepayment penalty clause will then kick in. To be sure, Kozinski is ready with objections to this line of argument, but those objections themselves trace out a line of argument and operate (no less than the interpretations which he rejects) to fill out the language whose self-sufficiency he repeatedly invokes.

In short (and this is a point that I shall make often), Kozinski's assertion of ready-made, formal constraints is belied by his efforts to stabilise what he supposedly relies on, the plain meaning of absolutely clear language. The act of construction for which he says there is no room is one that he is continually performing. Moreover, he performs it in a way no different from the performance which he castigates. Trident, he complains, is attempting 'to obtain judicial sterilization of its intended default',[10] and the reading which its lawyers propose is an extension of that attempt rather than a faithful rendering or what the document says. The implication is that *his* reading is the extension of nothing, proceeds from no purpose except the purpose to be scrupulously literal. But his very next words reveal another, less disinterested purpose: 'but defaults are messy things and they are supposed to be ... Fear of these repercussions is strong medicine that keeps debtors from shirking their obligations.'[11] And he is, of course, now administering that strong medicine through his reading, a reading that is produced not by the agreement, but by his antecedent determination to enforce contracts whenever he can. The contrast, then, is not (as he attempts to draw it) between a respect for what 'the contract clearly does ... provide'[12] and the bending of the words to an antecedently held purpose, but between two bendings, one of which by virtue of its institutional positioning – Kozinski is, after all, the judge – wins the day.

Except that it does not. In the second half of the opinion, there is a surprise turn, one that alerts us to the larger issue that Kozinski sees in the case and explains the vehemence (often close to anger) of his language. The turn is that Kozinski rules for Trident, setting aside the district court's declaration that the clear and ambiguous nature of the document leaves Trident with no cause of action and setting aside, too, the same court's sanction of Trident for the filing of a frivolous lawsuit. In so doing, Kozinski is responding to Trident's second argument, which is that 'even if the language of the contract appears to be unambiguous, the deal the parties actually struck is in fact quite different' and that 'extrinsic evidence' shows 'that the parties had agreed Trident could prepay at any time within the first 12 years by tendering the full amount plus a 10 percent prepayment fee'.[13] Kozinski makes it clear that he would like to reject this argument and rely on the traditional contract principle of the parol evidence rule, the rule (not of evidence but of law) by which 'extrinsic evidence is inadmissible to interpret, vary or add to the terms of an unambiguous integrated written instrument'.[14] He concedes, however, that this rule has not been followed in California since *Pacific Gas & Electric Co v. G. W. Thomas Drayage & Rigging Co*[15] a case in which the state supreme court famously declared that there is no such thing as a clear and unambiguous document because it is not 'feasible to determine the meaning the parties gave to the words from the instrument alone'.[16] In other words (mine, not the court's), an instrument that seems clear and unambiguous on its face seems so because 'extrinsic evidence' – information about the conditions of its production, including the situation and state of mind of the contracting parties, etc. – is already in place and assumed as a background; that which the parol evidence rule is designed to exclude is already, and necessarily, invoked the moment that writing becomes intelligible. In a bravura gesture, Kozinski first expresses his horror at this doctrine ('it ... chips away at the foundation of our legal system')[17] and then flaunts it by complying with it.

> While we have our doubts about the wisdom of *Pacific Gas*, we have no difficulty understanding its meaning, even without extrinsic evidence to guide us ... we must reverse and remand to the district court in order to give plaintiff an opportunity to present extrinsic evidence as to the intentions of the parties.[18]

That is, 'you say that words cannot have clear and constant meanings and that, therefore, extrinsic evidence cannot be barred; I think you are wrong and I hereby refute you by adhering strictly to the rule that your words have laid down'.

But of course he has not. The entire history of the parol evidence rule – the purposes that it supposedly serves, the fears to which it is a response, the hopes of which it is a repository – constitutes the extrinsic evidence within whose assumption the text of the case makes the sense that Kozinski labels 'literal'. When he prefaces his final gesture (the judicial equivalent of 'up yours') by saying 'As we read the rule', he acknowledges that it is *reading* and not simply receiving that he is doing.[19] And to acknowledge as much is to acknowledge that *Pacific Gas* could be read differently. Nevertheless, the challenge that Kozinski issues to the Traynor court is pertinent; for what he is saying is that the question of whether or not it is possible to produce 'a perfect verbal expression'[20] – an expression that will serve as a 'meaningful constraint on public and private conduct'[21] – will not be settled by the pronouncement of a court. Either it is or it is not; either a court or a legislature or a constitutional convention can order words in such a way as to constrain what interpreters can then do with them, or it cannot. The proof will be in the pudding, in what happens to texts or parts of texts that are the repository of that (formalist) hope. The parol evidence rule will not have the desired effect if no-one could possibly follow it.

That this is, in fact, the case is indicated by the very attempt to formulate the rule. Consider, for example, the formulation found in section 2–202 of the Uniform Commercial Code.

> Terms with respect to which the confirmatory memoranda of the parties agree or which are otherwise set forth in a writing intended by the parties as a final expression of their agreement with respect to such terms as are included therein may not be contradicted by evidence of any prior agreement or of a contemporaneous oral agreement but may be explained or supplemented
>
> a) by course of dealing or usage of trade (Section 1–205) or by course of performance (Section 2–208); and
>
> b) by evidence of consistent additional terms unless the court finds the writing to have been intended also as a complete and exclusive statement of the terms of the agreement.[22]

One could pause at almost any place to bring the troubles lying in wait for would-be users of this section to the surface, beginning perhaps with the juxtaposition of 'writing' and 'intended', which reproduces the conflict supposedly being adjudicated. (Is the writing to pronounce on its own meaning and completeness, or are we to look beyond it to the intentions of the parties?) Let me focus, however, on the distinction between explaining or supplementing and contradicting or varying. The question is: how can you tell whether a disputed piece of evidence is one or the other? And the answer is that you could only tell if the document in relation to which the evidence was to be labelled one or the other declared its own meaning; for only then could you look at 'it' and then at the evidence and proclaim the evidence either explanatory or contradictory. But if the meaning and completeness of the document were self-evident (a wonderfully accurate phrase), explanatory evidence would be superfluous and the issue would never arise. And on the other hand, if the document's significance and state of integration are not self-evident – if 'it' is not complete but must be pieced out in order to become what 'it' is – then the relation to 'it' of a piece of so-called extrinsic evidence can only be determined after the evidence has been admitted and is no longer extrinsic. Either there is no problem or it can only be solved by recourse to that which is in dispute.

Exactly the same fate awaits the distinction between 'consistent additional terms' and additional terms that are inconsistent. 'Consistent in relation to what?' is the question; the answer is 'consistent in relation to the writing'. But if the writing were clear enough to establish its own terms, additional terms would not be needed to explain it (subsection b, you will remember, is an explanation of 'explained or supplemented'), and if additional terms are needed there is not yet anything for them to be consistent or inconsistent with. The underlying point here has to do with the distinction – assumed but never examined in these contexts – between inside and outside, between what the document contains and what is external to it. What becomes clear is that the determination of what is 'inside' will always be a function of whatever 'outside' has already been assumed (I use quotation marks to indicate that the distinction is inter-pretive, not absolute). As one commentary puts it, 'questions concerning the admissibility of parol evidence cannot be resolved without considering the nature and scope of the evidence which is being offered', and 'thus the court must go beyond the writing to determine whether the writing should be held to be a final expression of the parties' ... agreement'.[23]

Nowhere is this more obvious than in the matter of *trade usage*, the first body of knowledge authorised as properly explanatory by the code. Trade usage refers to conventions of meaning routinely employed by members of a trade or industry, and is contrasted to *ordinary usage*, that is, to the meanings that words ordinarily have by virtue of their place in the structure of English. The willingness of courts to regard trade usage as legitimately explanatory of contract language seems only a minor conces-sion to the desire of the law to find a public – i.e., objective – linguistic basis, but in fact it is fatal, for it opens up a door that cannot be (and never has been) closed. In a typical trade usage case, one party is given the opportunity to 'prove' that the words of an agreement do not mean what they seem to mean because they emerged from a special context, a context defined by the parties' expectations. Thus, for example, in one case it was held that, by virtue of trade usage, the shipment term 'June-Aug.' in an agreement was to be read as excluding delivery in August;[24] and in another case the introduction of trade usage led the court to hold that an order for thirty-six-inch steel was satisfied by the delivery of steel measur-ing thirty-seven inches.[25] But if 'June-Aug.' can, in certain persuasively established circumstances, be understood to exclude August and 'thirty-six' can be understood as meaning thirty-seven, then anything, once a sufficiently elaborated argument is in place, can mean anything: 'thirty-six' could mean seventy-five, or, in relation to a code so firmly established that it governed the expectations of the parties, 'thirty-six' could mean 'detonate the atomic bomb'.

If this line of reasoning seems to slide down the slippery slope too precipitously, consider the oft-cited case of *Columbia Nitrogen Corporation v. Royster Company*.[26] The two firms had negotiated a contract by which Columbia would purchase from Royster 31,000 tons of phosphate each year for three years, with an option to extend the term. The agreement was marked by 'detailed provisions regarding the base price, escalation, minimum tonnage and delivery schedules',[27] but, when phosphate prices fell, Columbia ordered and accepted only one-tenth of what was speci-fied. Understandably, Royster sued for breach of contract, and was awarded a judgment of $750,000 in district court. Columbia appealed, contending that, in the fertiliser industry, 'because of uncertain crop and weather conditions, farming practices, and government agricultural programs, express price and quantity terms in contracts ... are mere projections to be adjusted according to market forces'.[28]

One would think that this argument would fail because it would amount to saying that the contract was not worth the paper it was printed on. If emerging circumstances could always be invoked as controlling, even in the face of carefully negotiated terms, why bother to negotiate? Royster does not make this point directly, but attempts to go the (apparently) narrower route of section 202. After all, even trade usage is inadmissible according to that section if it contradicts, rather than explains, the terms of the agreement; and, as one authority observes, 'it is hard to imagine a ... "trade usage" that contradicts a stated contractual term more directly than did the usage in *Columbia Nitrogen Corporation*'.[29] The court, however, does not see it that way. Although the opinion claims to reaffirm 'the well established rule that evidence of usage of trade ... should be excluded whenever it cannot be reasonably construed as consistent with the terms of the contract'[30] the reaffirmation undoes itself; for by making the threshold of admissibility the production of a 'reasonable construal' rather than an obvious inconsistency (as in '31,000 is inconsistent with 3,100'), the court more or less admits that what is required to satisfy the section is not a demonstration of formal congruity but an exercise of rhetorical skill. As long as one party can tell a story sufficiently overreaching so as to allow the terms of the contract and the evidence of trade usage to fit comfortably within its frame, that evidence will be found consistent rather than contradictory. What is and is not a 'reasonable construal' will be a function of the persuasiveness of the construer and not of any formal fact that is perspicuous before some act of persuasion has been performed.

The extent to which this court is willing to give scope to the exercise of rhetorical ingenuity is indicated by its final dismissal of the contention by Royster that there is nothing in the contract about adjusting its terms to reflect a declining market. 'Just so', says the court, there is nothing in the contract about this and that is why its introduction is not a contradiction or inconsistency. Since 'the contract is silent about adjusting prices and quantities ... it neither permits or prohibits adjustment, and this neutrality provides a fitting occasion for recourse to usage of trade ... to supplement the contract and explain its terms'.[31] Needless to say, as an interpretive strategy this could work to authorise almost anything, and it is itself authorised by the first of the official comments on section 202 (and why a section designed supposedly to establish the priority of completely integrated writings is itself in need of commentary is a question almost too obvious to ask): 'This section definitely rejects (a) any assumption that because a writing has been worked out which is final on some matters, it is to be taken as including all the matters agreed upon'.[32] Or in other words, just because a writing says something does not mean that it says everything relevant to the matter; it may be silent on some things, and in relation to those things parol evidence is admissible. But of course the number of things on which a document (however interpreted) is silent is infinite, and consequently there is no end to the information that can be introduced if it can be linked narratively to a document that now becomes a mere component (albeit a significant one) in a larger contractual context.

This conclusion might seem to be the one towards which I was moving in the course of presenting these examples, for surely the moral of *Columbia Nitrogen* and *Pacific Gas* (and countless others that could be adduced) is that the parol evidence rule is wholly ineffective as a stay against interpretive assaults on the express language of contracts and statutes. But the moral that I wish to draw goes in quite another direction, one that reaffirms (although not in a way that formalists will find comforting) the power both of the parol evidence rule and of the language whose 'rights' it would protect, to 'provide a meaningful constraint on public and private conduct'.[33] Certainly *Columbia Nitrogen* indicates that no matter how carefully a contract is drafted, it cannot resist incorporation into a persuasively-told story in the course of whose unfolding its significance may be altered from what it had seemed to be. But the same case also indicates that the story so told cannot be any old story; it must be one that fashions its coherence out of materials that it is required to take into account. The important fact is not that a court may succeed in getting around the parol evidence rule, but that it is the parol evidence rule – and not the first chapter of Genesis or the first law of thermodynamics – that it feels obliged to get around. That is, given the constraints of the institutional setting – constraints that help shape the issue being adjudicated – the court could not proceed on its way without raising and dealing with the parol evidence rule; consequently, the 'path' to the result which it finally reaches is constrained, in part, by the very doctrine that result will fail to honour.

In short the parol evidence rule is of more service to the law's wish to have a formal existence than one might think from these examples. The service that it provides, however, is not (as is sometimes claimed) the service of safeguarding a formalism already in place, but the weaker (although more exacting) service of laying down the route by which a formalism can be fashioned. I am aware, of course, that this notion of the formal will seem strange to those for whom a formalism is what is 'given' as opposed to something that is made. But, in fact, efficacious formalisms – marks and sounds that declare meanings to which all relevant parties attest – are always the product of the forces – desire, will, intentions, circumstances, interpretation – which they are meant to hold in check. No one has seen this more clearly than Arthur Corbin, who, noting that 'sometimes it is said that "the courts will not disregard the plain language of a contract or interpolate something not contained in it"',[34] offers for that dictum this substitute.

> If, after a careful consideration of the words of a contract, in the light of all the relevant circumstances, and of all the tentative rules of interpretation based upon the experience of courts and linguists, a plain and definite meaning is achieved by the court, a meaning actually given by one party as the other party had reason to know, it will not disregard this plain and definite meaning and substitute another that is less convincing.[35]

There are many words and phrases that one might want to pause over in this remarkable sentence ('relevant', 'tentative', 'experience', 'actually'), but for our purposes the most significant word is 'achieved' and, after that, 'convincing'. 'Achieved' is a surprise because, in most of the literature, a plain meaning is something that constrains or even precludes interpretation, while in Corbin's statement it is something that interpretation helps fashion. Once it is fashioned, the parol evidence rule can then be invoked with genuine force: you must not disregard this meaning – that is, the meaning that has been established in the course of the interpretive process – for one that has not been so established. 'Convincing' names the required (indeed the only) mode of establishing, the mode of persuasion, and what one is persuaded *to* is an account (story) of the circumstances ('relevant' not before, but as a result of, the account) in relation to which the words of the agreement could only mean one thing. Of course, if an alternative account were to become more rather than less convincing – perhaps in the course of appeal – then the meanings that followed from *its* establishment would be protected by the rule from the claims of meanings to which the court had not been persuaded. As Corbin puts it in another passage, 'when a court says that it will enforce a contract in accordance with the "plain and clear" meaning of its words ... the losing party has merely urged the drawing of inferences ... that the court is unwilling to draw'.[36] That is, the losing party has told an unpersuasive story, and consequently the meanings that it urges – i.e., the inferences that it would draw – strike the court as strained and obscure rather than plain.

There are, then, two stages to the work done by the parol evidence rule: in the first, its presence on the 'interpretative scene' works to constrain the path that interpreters must take on their way to telling a persuasive story (an account of all the 'relevant' circumstances); then, once the story has been persuasively told, the rule is invoked to protect the meanings that flow from that story. The phrase that remains to be filled in is 'persuasive story'. What is one and how is it, in Corbin's word, 'achieved'? The persuasiveness of a story is not the product merely of the arguments it explicitly presents, but of the relationship between those arguments and other, more tacit, arguments – tantamount to already in-place beliefs – that are not so much being urged as traded on. It is this second, recessed, tier of arguments – of beliefs so much a part of the background that they are partly determinative of what will be heard as an argument – that does much of the work of fashioning a persuasive story and, therefore does much of the work of filling in the category of 'plain and clear' meaning. What kinds of arguments or (deep) assumptions are these? It is difficult to generalise (and dangerous, since generalisation would hold out the false promise of a *formal* account of persuasion), but one could say first of all that they will include, among other things, beliefs that one might want to call 'moral' – dispositions as to the way things are or should be as encoded in maxims and slogans like 'order must be preserved' or 'freedom of expression' or 'the American way' or 'the Judaeo-Christian tradition' or 'we must draw the line somewhere'. It follows, then, that whenever there is a dispute about the plain meaning of a contract, at some level the dispute is between two (or more) visions of *what life is or should* be like.

THE AMAZING TRICK

An unsympathetic reader of the foregoing pages might say that what I have shown is that what works in the law is what you can get away with, precisely the observation made by some members of the Critical Legal Studies movement in essays that point, as I have, to the contradictions that fissure legal doctrine. The difference between those essays and this chapter lies in the conclusions that follow (or are said to follow) from the analysis. The conclusion often (but not always) reached by Critical Legal Studies proponents is that the inability of legal doctrine to generate logically consistent outcomes from rules and distinctions that have a clear formal basis means that the entire process is at once empty and insidious. The process is empty because its results are entirely ad hoc – lacking firm definitions or borders, the concepts of doctrine can be manipulated at will and in any direction one pleases – and the process is insidious because these wholly ad hoc determinations are presented to us as if they had been produced by an abstract and godly machine. Here is a representative statement from a well-known essay by Clare Dalton that anticipates many of my own arguments.

> ... we need ... to understand ... how doctrinal inconsistency neces-
> sarily undermines the force of any conventional legal argument, and
> how opposing arguments can be made with equal force. We need
> also to understand how legal argumentation disguises its own
> inherent indeterminacy and continues to appear a viable way of
> talking and persuading.[37]

By 'doctrinal inconsistency', Dalton means, first, the inability of doctrine
to keep itself pure – as she points out the poles of supposedly firm
oppositions are defined in terms of one another and thus cannot do the
work that they pretend to do – and, second, the presence in doctrine of
contradictory justificatory arguments that are deployed by lawyers and
jurists in an ad hoc and opportunistic manner. That is why 'opposing
arguments can be made with equal force': given the play in the logic of
justification, the facts of a case can, with equal plausibility, be made to
generate any number of outcomes, no one of which is deduced from a firm
base of principle. Nevertheless, Dalton's complaint continues, the law's
apologists present these outcomes as if they issued from a procedure that
was as determinate as it was impersonal.

To this I would reply, first, that doctrinal inconsistency undoes conventional argument only when the arguments are removed from the local
occasion of their emergence and then put to the test of fitting with one
another independently of any particular circumstances. But since it is
only in particular circumstances that arguments weigh or fail to weigh, the
inconsistency which Dalton is able to document is not fatal and is
embarrassing only if the context is not law and its workings, but philosophy and its requirements. Law, however, is not philosophical (except
when it borrows philosophy's arguments for its own purposes) but
pragmatic; and, from the pragmatic standpoint, the inconsistency of
doctrine is what enables law to work. Dalton inadvertently says as much
when, in the same sentence, she denies force to conventional argument
because of its inconsistency, and then complains that conventional argument, again because of its inconsistency, has too much force. This is not
so much a contradiction as it is a distinction (not quite spelled out)
between two kinds of force, one good and one bad. The good force is the
force of determinate procedure, and that is what the law lacks; the bad
force is the force of rhetorical virtuosity, and that the law has in shameful
abundance. But the rhetorical nature of law is a shameful fact only if one
requires that it operate algorithmically, and that is the requirement (of
which there are hard and soft versions) of the position which Dalton
rejects. By stigmatising the law's rhetorical content, she makes herself
indistinguishable from her opponents, for, like them, she measures the
law by a standard of rational determinacy; it is just that where they give the
law high marks, she finds it everywhere failing.

My point is that while Dalton's description of the law is exactly right, it is a description of strengths rather than weaknesses. When Dalton observes that the law's normative statements are so vaguely formulated ('fairness', 'what justice requires', 'good faith') that the moment of 'normative choice' is deferred 'until an individual judge is required to make an individual decision',[38] all she means is that while the law's normative formulations specify the vocabulary and conceptual 'neighbourhood' of decision-making, they set no limits to what a judge can do with that vocabulary on the way to reaching a plausible (in the sense of recognisably legal) result. In the absence of a mechanical decision procedure, there is ample room for judicial manoeuvring (although, as I have shown, that manoeuvring is itself far from free), and if the 'individual decision' is strong enough – if the story which it tells seems sufficiently seamless – it will have constituted the norm that it triumphantly invokes as its justification. That is the trouble, Dalton might respond: the law is at once thoroughly rhetorical and engaged in the effacing of its own rhetoricity. Exactly, I would reply, and isn't it marvellous (a word intended none-evaluatively) to behold. It may be true that 'we have no reliable, and therefore no legitimate, basis for allocating responsibility between contracting parties',[39] but while the legitimacy is not ready-made in the form of some determinate system of rules and distinctions, it is continually being achieved by the very means which Dalton rehearses in such detail.

Consider, for example, her discussion of the interplay between the doctrines of consideration and reliance. She has been retelling the story of *Second Restatement* sections 71 and 90 (one defining contract obligation in terms of consideration, the other concerning 'Contracts without Consideration') and notes the avoidance both in the *Restatement* and in the cases that invoke it of 'the knotty questions of how their coexistence should be imagined'.[40] The mechanisms of avoidance, as she describes them, include the sequential application of the doctrines so that each of them seems to be preserved and a clash between them is forever deferred; the stipulating of different measures of recovery in a way that suggests a distinction that an analysis of the cases does not support; and the elaboration of different vocabularies that cause 'reliance rhetoric to sound different from consideration rhetoric', although when the occasion demands, the two vocabularies can draw together and begin 'to appear indistinguishable'.[41] Impressive as this is, it is only a partial catalogue of the mechanisms at the law's disposal, mechanisms that allow a distinction that cannot finally be maintained to be reinforced and, at other times, relaxed and, at still other times, conveniently forgotten. The story is an amazing one, and Dalton accurately characterises it as 'the story of how what appears impossible is made possible'.[42]

It is, in short, the story of rhetoric, the art of constructing the (verbal) ground upon which you then confidently walk. Reviewing a case that displays the law's virtuosity at its height, Harry Scheiber exclaims:

> One is reminded of a dazzling double-feint, backhand flying lay-up shot by a basketball immortal. Only in slow motion replay does one comprehend the whole move; and only then does one realize that defiance of gravity is an essential component of it![43]

Scheiber calls this the law's 'amazing trick', the trick by which the law rebuilds itself in mid-air without ever touching down. It is a trick that Dalton and others decry, but it is the trick by which law subsists, and it is hard to imagine doing without it. The alternatives would seem to be either the determinate rationality that every critical legal analysis shows to be impossible, or the continual exposure of the sleights of hand by means of which the 'amazing trick' is performed. But if the latter alternative were followed, and every legal procedure turned into a debunking analysis of its enabling conditions, decisions would never be reached and the law's primary business would never get done. Perhaps this is the result we want, but somehow I doubt it, and therefore I tend to think that the law's creative rhetoricity will survive every effort to deconstruct it.

I cannot conclude without speaking briefly to three additional points. First of all, my account and defence of the law's rhetoricity – of the strategies by which it generates outcomes from concerns and perspectives which it ostentatiously disavows – should not be taken as endorsing those outcomes. Although much of legal theory is an effort to draw a direct line between some description of the law's workings and the rightness (or wrongness) of particular decisions, it has been my (antitheoretical) point that 'rightness' is automatically conferred on any decision that the system produces, that is to say, any decision that follows from the persuasive marshalling of certain arguments. As soon as an argument has proven to be persuasive to the relevant parties – a court, a jury – we say of it that it is right, by which we mean that it is now the law (nothing succeeds like success), that it is *legally* right. Of course, we are still free to object to the decision on other grounds, to find it 'wrong' in moral terms or in terms of the long-range health of the republic. In that event, however, our recourse would not be to an alternative form of the legal process but to alternative arguments that would be successful – that is, persuasive – within the same general form. In my view, the legal process is always the same, an open though bounded, forum where forensic battles are contingently and temporarily won; therefore, preferred outcomes are to be achieved not by changing the game but by playing it more effectively (and what is and is not 'more effective' is itself something that cannot be known in advance). In short, even if the cases I discuss were to be decided differently, were to be reversed or overturned, the routes of decision would be as I have described them here.

This brings me to my second point. It might seem that, by saying that the legal process is always the same, I have made the law into an ahistorical abstraction and endowed it with the universality and stability that my argument so often denies. However, this objection (which I raise myself because others will certainly raise it) turns on a logical quibble and on the assumption that one cannot at the same time be true to history and contingency and make flat categorical statements about the way things *always* are. But what I am saying is that things always are historical and contingent; that is, I am privileging history by refusing to recognise a check on it – a determinate set of facts, a monumentally self-declaring kind of language – and it is only a philosophical parlour trick that turns this insistence on historicity into something ahistorical. The alternative to my account would be one in which the law's operations were grounded in a reality (be it God or a brute materiality or universal moral principles) independent of historical process, and it seems curious to reason that, because I do not allow for that reality, I am being unhistorical. To be sure, the possibility that such an independent reality may reveal itself to me tomorrow remains an alive one, but it is not a possibility that can weigh on my present understanding of these matters, nor would it be the case that the act of ritually acknowledging it would be doing anything of consequence. Nevertheless, there is a sense in which this chapter is not historical: it does not do historical *work*; that is, it does not chart in any detail any of the differently contingent courses that the law has taken in the areas which it has marked out for its own. That work, however, is in no way precluded by my thesis and, indeed, the value of doing it is greatly enhanced once that thesis is assented to; once contingency (or ad-hocness or makeshiftness or rhetoricity) is recognised as constitutive of the law's life, its many and various instantiations can be explored without apology and without any larger (that is, grandly philosophical) rationale.

This brings me to my final point. Assuming, for the sake of argument, that I am right about the law and that it is in the business of producing the very authority it retroactively invokes, why should it be so? Why should law take *that* self-occluding and perhaps self-deceiving form? The short answer is that that is the law's job, to stand between us and the contingency out of which its own structures are fashioned. In a world without foundational essences – the world of human existence; there may be another, more essential one, but we know nothing of it – there are always institutions (the family, the university, local and national governments) that are assigned the task of providing the spaces (or are they theatres) in which we negotiate the differences that would, if they were given full sway, prevent us from living together in what we are pleased to call civilisation. And what, after all, are the alternatives? Either the impossible alternative of grounding the law in perspicuous and immutable abstractions, or the unworkable alternative of intruding that impossibility into every phase of the law's operations, unworkable because the effect of such intrusions would be so to attenuate those operations that they would finally disappear. That leaves us with the law as it is, something that we believe in because it answers to, even as it is the creation of, our desires.

NOTES

1. Manwill v. Oyler, N Utah 2d 433, 361 p. 2d 177 (1961).
2. 1967, 2nd (revised and enlarged) German ed. (transl. M. Knight), Berkeley: University of California Press, p. 192.
3. Trident Center v. Connecticut General Life Insurance Company, 847 F. 2d 564 (9th Cir. 1988).
4. Ibid., 566.
5. Ibid.
6. Ibid.
7. Ibid., 567.
8. Ibid., 566.
9. Ibid.
10. Ibid., 568.
11. Ibid.
12. Ibid., 567 n. 1.
13. Ibid., 568.
14. Ibid.
15. 68 Cal. 2d 33, 442 P. 2d 641 (1968).
16. Trident Center v. Connecticut General, 568 (citing 69 Cal. 2d 38).
17. Ibid., 569.
18. Ibid., 569–70.
19. Ibid., 569.
20. Ibid. (citing 69 Cal 2d 37).
21. Ibid., 569.
22. Ibid. *Uniform Commercial Code* (1967) 10th ed., St Paul, Mn: West Publishing, p. 71.
23. Gordon D. Schaber and Claude D. Roher (1984), *Contracts in a Nutshell*, 2nd ed., St Paul, Mn: West Publishing, p. 243.
24. Warren's Kiddie Shoppe, Inc. v. Casual Slacks, Inc., 120 Ga. App. 578, 171 S.E. 2d 643 (1969).
25. Dekker Steel Co v. Exchange National Bank of Chicago, 330 F. 2d 82 (1964).
26. 451 F. 2d 3 (1971).
27. Ibid., 9.
28. Ibid., 7.
29. Steven Emanuel and Steven Knowles (1987), *Contracts*, Larchmont, New York: Emanuel Law Outlines, p. 160.
30. Columbia Nitrogen v. Royster Company, 451 F. 2d 3 (1971), 9.
31. Ibid., 9–10.
32. *Uniform Commercial Code*, 71.
33. *Trident Center*, 569.
34. Corbin (1952), *Corbin on Contracts*, one-volume edition, St Paul, Mn: West Publishing, p. 496.

35. Ibid., p. 497.
36. Ibid., p. 515.
37. Clare Dalton (1985), 'An essay in the deconstruction of contract doctrine', *Yale Law Review* 94, 1007.
38. Ibid., p. 1035.
39. Ibid., p. 1066.
40. Ibid., p. 1084.
41. Ibid., p. 1091.
42. Ibid., p. 1087.
43. Harry Scheiber (1984), 'Public rights and the rule of law in American legal history', *California Law Review* 72, 236–7.

REFERENCES

Corbin, A. (1952), *Corbin on Contracts*, St Paul, Mn: West Publishing.

Dalton, C. (1985), 'An essay in the deconstruction of contract doctrine', *Yale Law Review* 94, 1007.

Emanuel, S. and Knowles, S. (1987), *Contracts*, New York: Emanuel Law Outlines.

Kelsen, H. (1967), *The Pure Theory of Law* (transl. M. Knight), Berkeley: University of California Press.

Schaber, G. D. and Roher, C. D. (1984), *Contracts in a Nutshell*, St Paul, Mn: West Publishing.

Scheiber, H. (1984), 'Public rights and the rule of law in American legal history', *California Law Review* 72, 217.

10

Sociological Perspectives on Legal Closure

ROGER COTTERRELL

In this chapter, legal closure refers to the multifaceted but ubiquitous idea that law is, in some way, radically autonomous, self-reproducing or self-validating in relation to an environment defined as 'extralegal'. The idea is multifaceted because it can be applied to whatever the word 'law' is treated as identifying – an intellectual discipline, a professional practice, a discourse, a normative or communicative system, or a field of knowledge or experience. And it is ubiquitous in the sense that it seems to have embedded itself in many different kinds of legal philosophy and intellectual practice. To adopt an idea of legal closure is to claim that law is self-standing and irreducible or has an independent integrity which is normally unproblematic, natural or self-generated, not dependent on contingent links with an extralegal environment of knowledge or practice.

Legal closure, therefore, implies diverse but interconnected understandings of law. The purpose of this chapter is to defend the utility of a sociological perspective, or set of perspectives, on what will be termed here normative and discursive closure. My aim is not to show that conceptions of normative or discursive legal closure are misguided in the particular contexts in which these conceptions have been developed, but that they can be reconsidered in a broader sociological perspective. Such a perspective ultimately denies that law is adequately understood as a 'closed' system, knowledge-field, intellectual discipline or discourse. But it recognises the social conditions that may make law so appear, or which seem to impel the 'legal' to seek to achieve 'closure' in a variety of ways.

LEGAL CLOSURE AND LEGITIMATION

Viewed sociologically, legal closure can be treated primarily as a means by which various forms of legal or political practice attempt to enhance their own legitimacy. Ideas of legal closure are part of the means by which an appeal to 'the legal' provides legitimacy in a variety of empirical settings. First, legal closure helps to support the legitimacy of the office of *judge* as quite other than that of a political or administrative decision-maker. The confident marking-off of what is within the enclosure of law from what is outside makes possible a reliable knowledge of what can and cannot properly be said in judgments if judicial authority is to be preserved and enhanced. This is not just a matter of knowing the law – of understanding the criteria that mark particular rules as legally 'valid' and identify precedents as 'binding'. It is also a matter of understanding what kinds of argument and phrasing, what styles of analysis and connections of ideas will be viewed as proper; as examples of correct and praiseworthy judicial practice. It is a matter of knowing what lines divide imaginativeness from unsoundness, skill and creativity in reasoning from idiosyncrasy, robustness from carelessness. Of course, these concerns are those of any lawyer who wishes to have his ideas respected within his professional world. But, for the judge, the arena in which all of this must be done is, in many cases, more exposed than that of other lawyers; and more is at stake, since a specifically 'legal' authority is maintained by every sound publicised judgment and undermined by every unsound one.

Second, legal closure may underpin aspects of the *legal practitioner's* legitimacy, as a kind of pale reflection of the judicial situation. An understanding of what lies within and what is to be considered outside the distinct realm of law provides important elements of the lawyer's professional conception of 'relevance'; of what will count as professional knowledge and good legal arguments. However, it is not necessary to adopt a view of law as radically closed off from an extralegal environment in order to practise it confidently. Political (or at least policy) arguments, appeals to moral values, emotional rhetoric and economic calculation may all have well-understood parts to play in the construction of forensic arguments and in the interpretation or prediction of judicial decisions. Nevertheless, for certain purposes, professional claims of special expertise are significantly underpinned by the idea that there is a distinctive, autonomous legal knowledge; or a special logic of law to be understood only through specialised training and experience; or, more broadly, that there is a certain indefinable style of thought, a manner of marshalling and of working with ideas, which constitutes 'thinking like a lawyer'. Legal closure, the presumed separation of legal ways as radically distinct, irreducible and self-validating, may provide powerful support for legal professional status and legitimacy. This is so, even though it is possible for lawyers to practise law without subscribing to any view that the realm of legal knowledge, legal methods or legal reasoning is distinctive or autonomous.

Third, legal closure may provide legitimacy for the *academic lawyer's* claim to expertise as teacher and expositor of law. In a relatively vocational environment, this may be a direct reflection of the legal practitioners' claims of expertise; a matter of knowing what can be taught to create proper lawyers. Elsewhere, the exposition of law has often been predicated on the assumption or assertion that legal ideas can be organised into an integrated, distinctive, autonomous system of interrelated rules. This system may be treated as gaining much of its intellectual validity from its internal coherence, and the reconciliation of apparent doctrinal contradictions. The most orthodox styles of legal exposition have actually been organised around the effort *to create* legal closure; to portray legal doctrine or discourse as integrated, intellectually and normatively autonomous (at least to a considerable extent), and possessing a self-generated validity though its systematic and logical character. Claims about the autonomy of legal studies are also made on the basis of assumptions about or efforts to demonstrate distinct analytical methods, forms of reasoning, subject matter, theory or objectives of legal studies.

Nevertheless, much legal exposition in no way relies upon such models of legal closure. It treats law as open, extremely diverse in its subject matter and regulatory forms, dependent on moral or political sources of evaluation and validation, often contradictory, implicated in an indeterminate range of extralegal considerations, and to be taught not as an autonomous body of knowledge, set of skills or manner of reasoning, but as the focus of broad interdisciplinary endeavour. The law teacher, not necessarily as committed to a distinct legal professional identity as the legal practitioner, and less committed also to the preservation of legal authority than the judge, may have less need than either of them for the aids to legitimation which a conception of legal closure may offer.

Finally, consider the position of an individual *citizen*, a legal layperson. It might be thought that such a person would have least concern for the kinds of legitimating functions that legal closure may offer. This is so, but subject to an important caveat. Legal closure may underpin, to a significant degree, the citizen's perception of security as an inhabitant of a normatively ordered, moral and political environment free from arbitrariness and uncontrolled discretion, or protected from 'naked politics'. In this setting, legitimacy of the social and political order is provided, at least partly, through *legality* (see e.g. Luhmann, 1985, pp. 199–206; cf. Cotterrell, 1983). It is guaranteed through popular perception of rule-governed, predictable procedures, radically distinguished from extralegal arbitrariness or unfettered discretion (Tyler, 1990). That is, it relies on belief in the rule of law, itself dependent on the possibility of firmly distinguishing law from 'non-law' in the organisation of social and political relationships. The legitimation which legal closure provides links inseparably the security of the citizen with the legal title to rule held by those who govern.

From a sociological perspective, must legal closure be viewed only in terms of these legitimating strategies and functions? Clearly not. It is also necessary to explore the empirical conditions of existence of law (as normative order, discourse, institutions or practices), which make conceptions of legal closure plausible. A sociological approach should seek to consider what social and political conditions are represented by conceptions of legal closure. From such a standpoint, conceptions of legal closure are most usefully understood as ideological – that is, they represent certain partial perspectives on legal experience as if these constituted the totality. Sociologically, law is to be seen as an aspect of social life, implicated in social relations and structures in connection with which 'the legal' refers only to a certain facet or field of experience, variously identified. It is not even useful to think of law as a distinct intellectual discipline, except insofar as this refers to an actual collective allegiance of practitioners or scholars to something which they call 'law'. Its forms of knowledge, methods and practices are the outcome of a disparate range of demands created by innumerable historical contingencies.

Considered as a field of experience, law in the broadest sense is a myriad of diverse practices loosely arranged around certain continually reformulated practical problems of government and social control. As means of adjustment to ever-changing political and social conditions, these practices are contingent and likely to be transient, unstructured, pragmatic and frequently inconsistent. Yet unending efforts are made to subject many of them to systematic organisation and rationalisation so as to form the basis of legal professional, bureaucratic and governmental expertise and codified systems of knowledge and technique. In this way, the task of creating law in the more specific sense of a finite body of professional, rationally ordered normative knowledge is pursued. And, as in the case of other fields of intellectual practice, the intimate relationship between knowledge and power may make possible the illusion of closure in this intellectual field of law. Legal practices gain power, influence and authority to the extent that they appear to be expressions or applications of a unified, autonomous body of knowledge of doctrine (Cotterrell, 1986).

NORMATIVE CLOSURE

Many conceptions of legal closure assume, imply or assert that law is to be radically distinguished from the 'extra legal' or 'non-legal' by certain identifiable normative characteristics which give it its particular prescriptive character and concerns. *Procedure* is often considered the key. For example, in distinguishing legality from administrative expediency, procedural categories of natural justice or due process of law help to map the terrain of legality within administration and informal dispute resolution. More generally, procedure defines the creation of law, allowing the identification of legislation and other new law as the outcome of specific events marking the transition of a bill to an Act of Parliament, or the coming into force of a new order or regulation. In the USA, the once influential 'process' school of scholarship emphasised the essence of legal craftsmanship in processes of legal development rather than in the substance of legal outcomes (see especially Hart and Sacks, 1958). Process, as a field of integrity, protected law from being devoured by political partisanship (Wechsler, 1959).

Law and non-law may also be considered radically separated by the hallmarks of *legal form*. For Franz Neumann, the distinguishing mark of law is found in the fusion of *ratio* and *voluntas*, the insistence that the sovereign's will is to be expressed in the rational form of general rules. To be law, political regulation must assume a form other that of particularised regulation or broad discretion. In Neumann's case, this assertion of the radical separation of law from 'non-law' has the political purpose of making possible a clear identification of the legal pathology of the Weimar and Nazi regimes (Neumann, 1986, chs 15 and 16; Neumann, 1944, pp. 440–58) and, in particular, the pernicious character of *Generalklauseln*. But the emphasis on a fundamental defining form of law is pervasive in much legal philosophy, often introduced with the clear intention of radically separating a realm of 'the legal' from an environment of disorder or unreason. Thus, Fuller's criteria of legality (Fuller, 1969, ch. 2), though often referred to as constituting a 'procedural' conception of law, essentially attempt to elaborate what is entailed in the idea of law if it is assumed that law must take the specific form of rules. One aspect of this approach (though ultimately a subordinate one) is to deny the name of law to certain barbaric regulatory systems, such as that of Nazi Germany (Fuller, 1958). Even in the case of Hart's model of rules as the core of the legal, a model presented as disinterestedly analytical, the rule form distinguishes law from discretion and helps to ground a belief in the doctrine of the rule of law by insisting that a settled core of legal meaning in rules can be securely distinguished from a penumbra of disputed interpretation to be handed over to politics or policy (Hart, 1961, ch. 7).

Significantly, all of these types of normative closure are fragile and qualified. Hart's legal rules are only a category of social rules, distinguished from others by relatively flexible empirical criteria of obligation and significance. Fuller insists that the existence of law is a matter of degree, and, in his later works, is much concerned to examine the empirical conditions that make specific legal forms and institutions viable. Neumann's examination of legal form is specifically intended to show its contingent historical character; its fragility and changeability in its close relationships with political, economic and social conditions. Again, an emphasis on process criteria of the legal has tended to lead either to explorations of process in terms of specific empirical conditions or, where process has been claimed to have independent, autonomous merit, the process approach has sometimes been criticised as naive or sterile (see Miller and Howell, 1960; and more generally White, 1973). Principles of natural justice may appear in broader perspective not as an irreducible essence of legality, but as moral considerations of fair treatment which for political reasons of good government, social justice and administrative expediency deserve protection and enforcement in many specific contexts.

In general, therefore, these attempts at normative closure of law appear to fail because the postulates of the distinctively legal ultimately can be demonstrated to depend upon particular historical contingencies or conditions. Thus they appear as a foundation of shifting sands on which the edifice of law is built. Attempts at closure fail because the normative essence of the legal turns out to express or depend upon extra-legal considerations. Certainly, the need to designate the legal field for the purposes of analysis and legal practice is not to be denied. But the effort to describe an essence of the legal analytically separate from – rather than empirically dependent upon – specific social environments seems to lead to a reification of law. Legal forms and processes are treated as natural, expressing some thing-like essence of the legal, rather than recognised as the consequence of specific, contingent social conditions.[1]

A sociological view cannot be content to dismiss conceptions of normative closure in law as mystification. Law does present itself in certain perennial forms, and through certain distinctive procedures. If law is to be understood empirically as a social phenomenon with social causes and effects, the social origins and consequences of these specific normative characteristics of law demand analysis. The literature of the sociology of law already contains important if still inadequately developed resources for this. In particular, it remains necessary to build on Max Weber's studies of modern legal formalism, including his analyses of relationships between formal legal rationality and the conditions of bureaucratic administration, of connections between formal rationality in modern law and the claims to legitimacy made by modern government, and of enduring tensions between formal and substantive rationality in modern law.

Much has changed, however, since Weber wrote early in the twentieth century. Legal positivism, which may be said to provide the foundation for almost all significant modern claims of *normative* legal closure, was recognised by Weber as the basis of legal modernity when he wrote of the disintegration of natural law conceptions as a foundation of law's legitimacy in modern conditions; of modern law having lost its 'metaphysical dignity' and being revealed as no more than the product or the technical means of compromises of conflicting interests (Weber, 1978, pp. 874–5). Subsequent writers on law in society have done little to displace Weber's diagnosis of the condition of modern western law. But what Weber could not see was the continuing decline in the consistency of modern rational legal forms as the century has progressed. Thus general rules have increasingly been supplemented and supplanted by particularised, mechanical and discretionary regulation (Cotterrell, 1992, pp. 161–6), so that the conception of formal legal rationality has been reduced to the idea that any kinds of regulation (orders, precedents, rules, guidelines, technical specifications, authorisations, definitions, broad discretions, and so on) can be produced within law provided that their official provenance can be traced to certain formal sources of governmental authority. Law has lost its metaphysical dignity in a more fundamental way than even Weber seemed to contemplate. The idea of legal closure, which makes possible a practical and reliable identification of what is legally valid and binding, now seems to have to allow law to encompass the most diverse, unrelated, unsystematic and – in a specific sense – unprincipled regulation, made up of the technical minutiae of innumerable, disparate and ever-changing governmental directives.

A further major theoretical source for sociological examination of normative legal closure is in Pashukanis's now neglected Marxist legal theory, and some of the writings which have built upon it. A major virtue of Pashukanis's work is that it treats an examination of the distinctiveness of legal form as central to a sociological understanding of law; law is to be identified and explained as a social phenomenon in terms of its irreducible form so that a kind of normative legal closure can be explained sociologically. Pashukanis sees the concept of formal equivalence in legal relations – the formal equality of legal subjects or legal persons – as the essence of law. Law is to be understood in terms not of rules but of juridical relations between persons treated as formally identical for the purposes of those relations (Pashukanis, 1978, ch. 3).

Unlike Weber, whose analysis of law's contribution to capitalism is highly ambiguous, Pashukanis makes specific and fundamental theoretical connections between legal form and capitalist social relations, in fact treating them as inseparable and thereby creating what many critics have considered a mechanistic and reductive account of law. But, as Norrie (1982) has pointed out, Pashukanis does not confuse form and function of law. His analysis can be seen as an effort to explain the social conditions under which a distinctive modern legal form emerged and the contribution which that form makes to the fundamental structure of social relations in a capitalist society. Pashukanis's analyses do not necessarily require the conclusion, which he himself reached, that legal form is specific *only* to capitalist social formations; nor is it necessary to prejudge the possible variations of legal form and the functions it may serve in contemporary conditions.

The most valuable aspect of Pashukanis's work may be the hints that it contains of problems that affect legal forms reflecting capitalist social relations, in circumstances where the state, for various reasons, needs to control, direct or modify those relations, or intervene in the processes of their reproduction.[2] To this extent, Pashukanis points to specific tensions in the forms of modern law which are generally less clearly recognised in the Weberian tradition. Claims about the decline of what has been conceptualised, under Pashukanis's influence, as *Gesellschaft* law (Kamenka and Tay, 1975) are paralleled by observations of the bureaucratisation of the 'autonomous' legal system (Unger, 1976) and of the invasion of the legal form of bourgeois law by the political imperatives of corporate society (Neumann, 1957). The most serious limitation of Pashukanis's work, however, is surely its inability to treat legal forms as other than exceptional insofar as they do not reflect the relations of equivalence or the logic of commodity relations that his theory makes central. One might say that he treated legal form *too* seriously, essentialising it, so that the idea of legal closure, instead of being an object of sociological inquiry, came to ensnare his sociology of law.

DISCURSIVE CLOSURE

Because normative closure postulates specific features of law which identify and descriptively distinguish it, sociological approaches to law usually have little difficulty in relativising such claims of closure. But assertions of what can be called discursive closure pose a different order of problems and challenge the explanatory aspirations of the sociology of law in a fundamental way. By discursive closure I mean a conception of law as a distinct discourse, possessing its own integrity, its own criteria of significance and validation, its own means of cognition and of constituting the objects of which it speaks. This conception of legal discourse typically goes along with the claim that discourses are incommensurable; that truth or validity criteria, established by a discourse, function within it without reference to the status of those criteria outside that discourse; that there are no metadiscourses which make it possible to adjudicate on the relative merits of truth or validity claims of different discourses (see e.g. Rorty, 1980). Hence, according to this conception, a sociological perspective on legal closure cannot address the significance of legal closure for *law*; that is, for the discourse of law. It can only observe, from a distance, so to speak, the character of another discourse. Sociological characterisation cannot be shown to be better or worse than, only different from, the characterisation which participants in legal discourse themselves adopt. The challenge for a sociological perspective on legal closure is, thus, to show, first, that a sociological discourse about law is possible if law is, itself, a distinct discourse; and, secondly, that a sociological characterisation of legal closure is relevant to participants in any such legal discourse.

Several forms of discursive legal closure are exemplified by modern legal philosophy. Hans Kelsen's pure theory of law is significant in this context for its insistence on the distinctiveness and irreducibility of different modes of cognition. For Kelsen, a science of law constructs its own objects, and presents legal reasoning as a realm of thought and understanding wholly apart from sociological observation: 'in so far as it is the method or form of understanding through which the object (the given) is determined, the antithesis of causal and normative sciences rests just as much on a difference in the direction of understanding as on a difference in the object of understanding'.[3] Kelsen admits that a sociology of law is possible, but this would be a sociology of behaviour in legal contexts and of its ideological determinants, including the ideology of justice (Kelsen, 1957, p. 271). Sociological investigations would be wholly distinct from those framed by a science of law, since legal science is concerned with norms and not with empirical causes and consequences.

The Kelsenian idea of a science of law suggests that the realm of norms remains an object of cognition. The pure theory of law is a means of conceptualising the normativity of law, of structuring a science of law in terms of a logic of norms. Because law, for Kelsen, can still be described in terms of its form (norms) and their relationships (imputation), his work does not seem to render impossible, and may even facilitate, the adoption of a sociological perspective on legal science; one which would seek to explain the social conditions that make possible the forms of legal thought characterised in pure or ideal form by Kelsen. Again, Weber's examination of the modern conditions of rationality in many spheres of modern experience is highly relevant to such a project. Far from being essentially a theorisation of links between law and capitalism, Weber's sociology of formal legal rationality can probably best be considered part of a lifetime study of the fate of humanity in the modern world (Hennis, 1988), a fate bound up with the contradictions of rationality and the complexities of its expression and application.[4]

Weber's conception of diverse value spheres – his diagnosis of the 'ethical irrationality of the world' or the conflicting, independent and irreconcilable rationalities of different areas of life (see Weber, 1948) – mirrors in a significant way Kelsen's insistence on a firm link between philosophical relativism and political pluralism. Kelsen justifies democracy as the device by which continuing processes of tolerant compromise can be made possible in a world of irreconcilable modes of cognition and evaluation (Kelsen, 1955). Thus, for him, the 'closure' of law to politics or morality makes possible the preservation of an 'empty', neutral legal science capable of building the autonomous structures of compromise available to mediate between conflicting values and interests. Ultimately, the effort to maintain legal closure through a theoretical project such as Kelsen's can be portrayed as one kind of response to the moral and political conditions of contemporary life, in which, as Weber emphasised, absolute universal values are no longer available to regulate complexity. But Weberian sociology of law seems to indicate that law's structures of reason are always *contingent, timebound and contested*; there is no warrant to claim that, even in modern conditions, law has actually become an autonomous 'value sphere', despite the powerful impetus which these conditions might give to efforts to secure law's closure.[5]

Because Kelsen discusses law and the possibility of a science of law in descriptive fashion, he creates objects which a sociological analysis can locate in some broader context of social existence. Such an analysis does not in any way deny the importance of legal science as Kelsen describes it, but suggests that the significance and character of this science can be better – because more broadly – understood in a sociological perspective. The situation is different, however, with an approach such as Ronald Dworkin's, which treats law as entirely a matter of discourse and in no way a matter of distinctive normative criteria. Thus, Dworkin denies that 'the very meaning of the word "law" makes law depend on certain specific criteria' and that our 'rules for using "law" tie law to plain historical fact' (Dworkin, 1986, p. 31). Law is best thought of as the conversation of participants in an endless collective enterprise of interpretation; in other words, a discourse. Dworkin does not consider – like the early Foucault or the literary theorist Stanley Fish – that this discourse entirely constructs its own objects of knowledge. For Dworkin, there still remain historical legal materials to be interpreted, so that interpretation must somehow 'fit' what is interpreted. Nevertheless, it is far from clear what the criterion of 'fit' entails in Dworkin's legal theory (see e.g. Cotterrell, 1989, pp. 178–80). The whole thrust of his current legal philosophy is to treat law as entirely constituted by interpretation; as a discourse within which all criteria of the legal are determined by discourse itself.

What is the nature of this Dworkinian discourse of law? It is a discourse in which all participants are engaged in a search for the 'best reading' of legal doctrine, the reading that will make best sense of the patterns of moral and political communication in which paticipants in legal talk are involved. The search for the best reading presumes that a correct interpretation of legal doctrine is possible; it assumes the *possibility* of discursive unity and forces all legal participants who wish to challenge this unity to do so only by engaging in the effort to demonstrate it. Law is properly understood as having an underlying, immanent or overall rationality and moral integrity capable of being elaborated through law's own discursive methods. The possibility that law is a field of experience consisting of fragmentary, diverse and fundamentally inconsistent forms of talk and practice is marginalised. The Dworkinian idea of 'integrity' as a hallmark of best legal interpretive practice, and the associated idea that there can be 'right answers' to all legal disputes, further symbolise the claim that legal discourse is ultimately coherent and comprehensive, generating resources for a comprehensive legal interpretation of reality. Dworkinian legal discourse generates its own closed world, observing morality, politics and society only in its own discursive terms.

A legal sociologist is given two choices by this approach: either accept the Dworkinian characterisation of law's discursive realm and share in legal knowledge as a participant in this discourse; or else remain an outside observer unable to speak of 'law' as such, since law is accessible only as and through legal discourse. If legal sociologists resist being co-opted within this project of exploring the integrity of law's discursive empire, law's closure appears to condemn legal sociology to inhabit an external discourse, unrelated to and unable to embrace, invade or interact with law.

The dilemma is, however, false. It remains a very open question how far law can be considered an integrated and independent discourse. This is not to deny the specific character and contexts of legal reasoning and the processes by which legal knowledge is generated and validated within the interpretive communities of law. These communities correspond roughly to those categories of judges, practitioners, legal scholars and teachers, and citizens whose possible interests in legal closure or legal 'integrity' were noted at the beginning of this chapter. It is possible that they might be united, for some purposes and to some extent, in a single legal community, as Dworkin seems to suggest (Dworkin, 1986, ch. 6). Even so, it seems realistic to recognise numerous sub-communities and that the intellectual practices of law may not constitute a discursive unity. The structure and conditions of existence of law's interpretive communities can be examined sociologically. The question is whether legal discourse and sociological discourse remain distinct, unable to invade each other.

Can the legal discourse of a whole political community as portrayed by Dworkin be thought of as having even *potential* moral or intellectual integrity and autonomy? Or does it, in fact, consist only of diverse, loosely and contingently related rhetorics and rationalities drawn from *realpolitik*, moral conviction, arguments of economic efficiency, techniques of textual interpretation and criticism, and many other sources? It seems that no convincing reasons for adopting the former view and rejecting the latter have yet been provided by legal philosophers. But if law can be seen sociologically as a field of experience in which actors explain to themselves and others the meaning, structure or significance of this field and their situation within it in terms of *all or any* of these sources, a sociological perspective on the kind of discursive closure suggested by Dworkin's view of law as interpretation will tend to portray it as mystification.

The claim would be that Dworkin postulates a community which either does not exist or is so loosely conceived that the word 'community' lacks substantial meaning.[6] Such a sociological view might insist that the processes of legal interpretation with which lawyers work can be better illuminated by examining the conditions enabling certain interpretations to prevail over others in law's various interpretive communities, and ordering those communities in hierarchies of social and political significance seemingly unrecognised in Dworkin's theories. These conditions can only be understood in the broad context of empirical examination of legal practices and legal politics.

AUTOPOIESIS

In one recent sociological movement in legal theory, the idea of law's discursive closure has been seen as the consequence of the character of law as a communication system. Autopoiesis theory, developed in relation to law by Niklas Luhmann and Gunther Teubner, postulates a form of legal closure as radical as any to be found or implied in the literature of legal philosophy. In Luhmann's formulation, law as a social system of communication is cognitively open but normatively closed. Law receives communications of information from, for example, natural science (perhaps medical knowledge) or economics (efficiency information), but it attributes or denies significance to these communications in accordance with its *own* system imperatives and only by transforming them into its own normative terms. Closure 'consists in the fact that all operations always reproduce the system' (Luhmann, 1988, p. 15). Teubner declares that 'legal discourse invents and deals with a juridical "hyperreality" that has lost contact with the realities of everyday life and at the same time superimposes new realities on everyday life', and that 'law becomes autonomous from general societal communication' (1989, p. 742). It has become increasingly a self-referential system. Thus, legal doctrine on the relationship between corporations and legal personality is neither superior nor inferior to social scientific theory about relationships between organisation and collective action. Inhabiting different discourses, these are merely incommensurable knowledges (Teubner, 1989, pp. 743–4).

In Teubner's most recent writings, the radical autonomy of legal discourse has been expressed, perhaps somewhat confusingly, in terms of law's capacity as a social system or as an institution to 'think' independently from the minds of individual actors. This means that 'law autonomously processes information, creates worlds of meaning, sets goals and purposes, produces reality constructions – and all this quite apart from the world constructions in lawyer's minds' (Teubner, 1989, p. 739). Autopoiesis theory thus accepts the idea of law as a discourse or system of communication creating its own objects, truth criteria and canons of validity, while receiving information from and transferring information to its environment (conceived as other systems, such as those associated with politics, science, economy or the psyche). Luhmann's and Teubner's versions of autopoiesis theory seek to conceptualise discursive or system closure sociologically in terms of the conditions of existence of autopoietic systems as well as in terms of their structure and means of self-reproduction. The emergence of self-referential systems is seen as a response to the growing complexity of societies. The separation of social subsystems makes it possible to reduce, through specialisation and differentiation, the organisation and information overload problems that otherwise accompany complexity.

At least in Teubner's case, the development of legal autopoiesis theory was inspired by problems in the sociology of law. The need to explain the causes of failure to shape society through law and law through social science, or to account for the unpredictability and unintended effects of legal action, led to an attempt to examine legal closure in terms of system imperatives. All this represents a necessary effort in legal sociology to take ideas of legal closure seriously. But it is significant that Teubner, perhaps more clearly than Luhmann, has recognised that the achievement of self-referentiality or system closure in law is a relative and even problematic matter. Hence it is appropriate to talk of the *tendency* to autopoietic system reproduction and closure, rather than its achievement. Teubner at least refers to the 'dynamics of social evolution' (in other words, a continuing present process) in which 'self-referential relations are multiplying within the legal process'.[7]

Equally, Teubner's concern is now increasingly with the problem of conceptualising relations between systems; in particular between law and its environment – that is, its observation of other autopoietic systems or discourses. Given the conception of system self-referentiality and closure which legal autopoiesis theory holds, the theory seems to adopt a correlative conception of an *absence* of theoretically definable relations between law and its environment. Law does not interact with the environment but is subject to and creates 'interference' in connection with it (Teubner, 1985). The most important problem for autopoiesis theory is now to try to find ways of conceptualising the extremely complex and varied ways in which this interference may occur.[8]

Autopoiesis theory is the most sophisticated attempt so far to explain, in social scientific terms, such familiar notions in legal philosophy as law which 'regulates its own creation' or law as a 'gapless' system or a legal 'heaven of concepts'. But the theory seems to fuse questions about discursive closure (questions about the nature of ideological thought and practices) with issues relating to the conditions of existence and character of specific social systems of communication (empirical issues about constraints and imperatives arising from dominant interests within organisations and collectivities and affecting the decisions and outlook of members or shaping roles within institutions). There is no doubt that ideology and organisational interests are closely interrelated. Nevertheless, some analytical separation of them might make it easier to keep in focus the possibility that, even in a formalised, seemingly closed legal system, it is not "the system" which thinks or communicates, but individual actors (lawyers, judges, citizens, etc.) whose thinking and communicating creates and sustains the system. The constraints upon or conditions and possibilities of their thought and action are capable of being explained in terms of structures of ideology – for example, professional ideologies, legal ideology and political ideologies. These constraints, conditions and possibilities also relate to structures of discipline, reward, opportunity and repression created by dominant interests within organisations, occupational groups and interpretive communities of many kinds.

In its effort to take discourses or abstract communication systems seriously, a sociological perspective should avoid the temptation to reify them. Even autopoietic metaphors may be dangerous to the extent that they portray a world over which individuals have not only lost control but in relation to which they might also absolve themselves of responsibility, so it seems, for autonomous action. It is important to recognise the full extent to which, in modern conditions, subject-centred reason has been confined, repressed, trivialised and debased in innumerable ways; but it may be possible to do this without actually reducing the sociological status of the individual theoretically to that of a construct or carrier of various social systems, whose human autonomy is retained only as a 'psychic system' (cf. Teubner, 1989, p. 741; 1991, p. 37).

CLOSURE AND DISCLOSURE

If it is asked what the status of autopoietic legal theory is in relation to the discourse of law which it presupposes and examines, it seems likely that its exponents would claim that it inhabits the discourse of science, which itself is to be understood as an autopoietic communication system. As a form of legal sociology, it seeks scientific explanation of a sector of the social world. Hence, this is no challenge to the position seemingly represented by those, like Dworkin, who assert that, from the standpoint of legal discourse, 'external' perspectives such as those offered by legal sociology can offer no elucidation of law itself. Indeed, autopoiesis theory would seem merely to confirm this position in its insistence on the closed character of self-referential social systems of communication. Accordingly, a legal sociologist adopting this kind of perspective on legal closure will presumably state honestly that his standpoint is that of social science, offering a different and distinct knowledge from that of participants in legal discourse; neither better nor worse, or stronger nor weaker, because incommensurable.

Whether one can go beyond this limited position in asserting the power of sociological perspectives on discursive legal closure is the vital question. Numerous writings in contemporary philosophy and social theory assume or assert the incommensurability of discourses, the non-existence of any metatheory or metadiscourse which could somehow adjudicate between the truth claims of different discourses, the failure of correspondence theories of knowledge, and the survival only of pragmatic relativism (see e.g., Dews, 1987; Rajchman and West (eds), 1985). In postmodern conditions, we are said to be fated to engage in endless ungrounded conversation. We can it seems only assert knowledge claims lacking and denying all authority beyond the conditions of argument giving them 'local' meaning within a discourse. Such claims must be refused any more fundamental significance as transdiscursive truth.

The possibility remains, however, that discourses are not as self-sufficient, secure and integrated as they are sometimes made to appear. It was suggested earlier that the discourse of law which Dworkin explores and celebrates may be much more fragmented and morally or intellectually vulnerable than the confident 'empire' that he sees. At the same time, the *assertion* that law constitutes an integrated and autonomous sphere of intellectual practice serves important legitimating functions and therefore is strongly maintained. Sociology, if it takes all social experience for its province, must also embrace the examination of the social foundations of all disciplines and discourses, including its own. Thus, its fundamentally reflexive self-conscious, self-contextualising character makes it unlike the political-inellectual practices of law and capable, by its nature, of examining the social foundations of legal knowledges and practices; it can even contribute knowledge necessary to participants in legal discourses when, for various reasons, law is forced by crises of confidence to attempt to become, itself, self-critical and self-contextualising (Cotterrell, 1986). Law, lacking the inherently reflexive character of sociology and necessarily presenting itself in normal conditions as authoritative and normatively secure, may, at times of uncertainty, actually need the perspective on its practices which a sociological standpoint can offer.

It would seem that, for Dworkin, the preferred and probably necessary standpoint for understanding law is that of an active participant in legal reasoning. But the claim of legal sociology is that a sociological perspective can be more inclusive and more illuminating than that of such a participant, because it embraces particular participant perspectives but goes beyond them, recognising their diversity, interpreting and preserving them within a widening vision of law in society. In relation to conceptions of *normative* closure, sociological perspectives can contextualise the lawyer's claims of closure in ways that further clarify their significance. In relation to *discursive* closure, it is unnecessary, or certainly premature, to conclude that law is a unified discourse in relation to which any sociological perspective on legal practice must remain external. On the contrary, sociological perspectives suggest explanations for the contingency and diversity of law's discourses. The most appropriate strategy for sociological studies of law is to explore the conditions and limitations of the varieties of legal closure; ceaselessly contextualising and relativising law's knowledges, exploring the conditions of their truth claims and, through a permanently self-critical, reflexive sociological perspective, attempting to open possibilities for productive confrontations between discourses (cf. Cotterrell, 1986).

In such a project, sociology is not presented as a metadiscourse or as the purveyor of a metatheory transcending existing divides between discourses. Indeed, it should not be presented as an existing *unity* at all. That would be to mirror the ideology of legal closure. Sociology of law entails only the never-ending effort and aspiration to transcend partial perspectives on legal experience. In my view, the reflexivity inherent in the development of sociological inquiry makes such an effort worthwhile and such an aspiration feasible. There is no 'true' or complete view to be gained by such means; only the possibility of more comprehending and comprehensive ones – capable of incorporating, without denying or trivialising, more specific participant perspectives. The sociology of law should treat legal closure as a significant underpinning of some of these specific perspectives on legal experience.[9]

NOTES

1. Among modern legal philosophers, Lon Fuller has made the most sustained and serious attempts to recognise and remedy these inadequacies in the analysis of legal forms and procedures. See especially Winston (ed.) (1981, section 2).
2. On this, Pashukanis's (1980) discussion of state controls during the First World War in Britain and other capitalist states contains much of interest.
3. Kelsen, quoted by Alida Wilson in Tur and Twining (eds) (1986, p. 53).

4. The work of the Frankfurt School and, most notably in recent times, Jürgen Habermas can be considered the most direct continuing expression of these concerns.
5. See Weber (1978, pp. 880–95). The search for 'purity' or closure eventually leads Kelsen to a theory of norms or normativity, rather than of law as such; as though law gets left behind, or the focus is switched beyond the legal to something 'purer'. Cf. Kelsen (1991). It is significant also that insofar as Hart's (1961, pp. 55–6) 'internal aspect' of rules indicates a distinct realm of normative discourse, this discourse is not restricted to law.
6. Cf. Dworkin (1989, p. 496), where 'political community' is treated as synonymous with 'nation' or 'state'.
7. Teubner (1989, p. 742); and see Teubner (1988). Luhmann seems to accept the idea of the functional indispensability of system closure. Thus, he states that legal system 'autonomy is not a desired goal but a fateful necessity': see Luhmann (1986, p. 112).
8. Recently, Teubner has talked in terms of a system having a 'real contact' with its environment, not in the sense of filtering inputs from it, but in the sense that expectations within the system may create a sensitivity to the external environment (*une sensibilité interne au monde extérieur*), impelling the system to ask 'yes/no' questions of that environment. Adjusting itself in the light of the answers, the system then continues to carry on its own processes in its own way: see Teubner (1991, p. 38). Luhmann (1986, p. 114) refers to the legal system requiring external 'limitation and guidance – but not determination! – of choice'.
9. I am grateful to Alan Norrie, Gunther Teubner and Bob Fine for comments on earlier versions of this paper.

REFERENCES

Cotterrell, R. B. M. (1983), 'Legality and political legitimacy in the sociology of Max Weber, in D. Sugarman (ed.), *Legality, Ideology and the State*, London: Academic Press.
———— (1986, 'Law and sociology: notes on the constitution and confrontations of disciplines', *Journal of Law and Society* 13, 9.
———— (1989), *The Politics of Jurisprudence: A Critical Introduction to Legal Philosophy*, Philadelphia: University of Pennsylvania Press. London: Butterworths.
———— (1992), *The Sociology of Law: An Introduction*, 2nd ed., London: Butterworths.
Dews, P. (1987), *Logics of Disintegration: Post-Structuralist Thought and the Claims of Critical Theory*, London: Verso.
Dworkin, R. (1986), *Law's Empire*, Cambridge, MA: Harvard University Press London: Fontana.
———— (1989), 'Liberal community', *California Law Review* 77, 479.
Fuller, L. L. (1958), 'Positivism and fidelity to law', Harvard Law Review 71, 630.
———— (1969), *The Morality of Law*, revised ed., New Haven: Yale University Press.
Hart, H. M. and Sacks, A. M. (1958) *The Legal Process: Basic Problems in the Making and Application of Law*, Tentative ed., Cambridge Ma.: Harvard Law School.

Hart, H. L. A. (1961), *The Concept of Law*, Oxford: Oxford University Press.

Hennis, W. (1988), *Max Weber: Essays in Reconstruction*, transl. K. Tribe, London: Allen and Unwin.

Kamenka, E. and Tay, A. E.-S. (1975), 'Beyond bourgeois individualism: the contemporary crisis in law and ideology', in E. Kamenka and R. S. Neale (eds), *Feudalism, Capitalism and Beyond*, London: Edward Arnold.

Kelsen, H. (1955), 'Foundations of democracy', *Ethics* 66, 1.

—— (1957), *What is Justice?: Justice, Law and Politics in the Mirror of Science*, Berkeley: University of California Press.

—— (1991), *General Theory of Norms*, transl. M. Hartney, Oxford: Oxford University Press.

Luhmann, N. (1985), *A Sociological Theory of Law*, transl. E. King-Utz and M. Albrow, London: Routledge and Kegan Paul.

—— (1986), 'The self-reproduction of law and its limits', in G. Teubner (ed.), *Dilemmas of Law in the Welfare State*, Berlin: Walter de Gruyter.

—— (1988) 'The Unity of the Legal System', in G. Teubner (ed.), *Autopoietic Law: A New Approach to Law and Society*, Berlin: Walter de Gruyter.

Miller, A. S. and Howell, R. F. (1960), 'The myth of neutrality in constitutional adjudication', *University of Chicago Law Review* 27, 661.

Neumann F. L. (1944), *Behemoth: The Structure and Practice of National Socialism*, New York: Octagon reprint, 1983.

—— (1957), 'The change in the function of law in modern society', in H. Marcuse (ed.), *The Democratic and the Authoritarian State: Essays in Political and Legal Theory by Franz Neumann*, Glencoe, Ill.: Free Press. London: Collier-Macmillan.

—— (1986), *The Rule of Law: Political Theory and the Legal System in Modern Society*, Leamington Spa: Berg.

Norrie, A. (1982), 'Pashukanis and the "commodity form theory": a reply to Warrington', *International Journal of the Sociology of Law* 10, 419.

Pashukanis, E. B. (1978), *Law and Marxism: A General Theory*, transl. B. Einhorn, London: Ink Links.

—— (1980), 'Economics and legal regulation' in P. Beirne and R. Sharlet (eds), *Pashukanis: Selected Writings on Marxism and Law*, London: Academic Press.

Rajchman, J. and West, C. (eds) (1985), *Post-Analytic Philosophy*, New York: Columbia University Press.

Rorty, R. (1980), *Philosophy and the Mirror of Nature*, Princeton: Princeton University Press. Oxford: Basil Blackwell.

Teubner, G. (1985), 'Social order from legislative noise?: Autopoietic closure as a problem for legal regulation', Colloquium paper, European University Institute, Florence.

—— (1988), 'Evolution of autopoietic law', in Teubner (ed.), *Autopoietic Law*, Berlin: Walter de Gruyter.

—— (1989), 'How the law thinks: toward a constructivist epistemology of law', *Law and Society Review* 23, 727.

—— (1991), 'La théorie des systèmes autopoiétiques: Interview de Gunther Teubner réalisé par V. Munoz-Darde et Y. Sintomer', *Journal M*, no 44, February–March.

Tur, R. and Twining, W. (eds) (1986), *Essays on Kelsen*, Oxford: Oxford University Press.

Tyler, T. R. (1990), *Why People Obey the Law*, New Haven: Yale University Press.

Unger, R. M. (1976), *Law in Modern Society: Toward a Criticism of Social Theory*, New York: Free Press. London: Collier-Macmillan.

Weber, M. (1948), 'Religious rejections of the world and their directions', in H. H. Gerth and C. Wright Mills (eds), *From Max Weber: Essays in Sociology*, London: Routledge and Kegan Paul.

——— (1978), *Economy and Society: An Outline of Interpretive Sociology*, transl. E. Fischoff et al., Berkeley: University of California Press.

Wechsler, H. (1959), 'Toward neutral principles in constitutional law', *Harvard Law Review* 73, 1.

White, G. E. (1973), 'The evolution of reasoned elaboration: jurisprudential criticism and social change', *Virginia Law Review* 59, 279.

Winston, K. I. (ed.) (1981), *The Principles of Social Order: Selected Essays of Lon L. Fuller*, Durham, NC: Duke University Press.

11

Closure and Critique in Feminist Jurisprudence: Transcending the Dichotomy or a Foot in Both Camps?

NICOLA LACEY

The enterprise of feminist jurisprudence represents a distinctive testing ground for issues of closure and critique in legal theory. This is because the very possibility of feminist jurisprudence has been questioned, not just by anti-feminists, but also, and most powerfully, by feminist scholars themselves (Smart, 1989; Thornton, 1986). In this chapter, I shall reflect on why the issue of feminist jurisprudence is problematic for contemporary feminism. I shall argue that this debate touches on some deep sources of ambivalence in feminist thought, and that these sources raise fundamental theoretical questions which are related to the supposed dichotomy between closure and critique. I shall begin by giving an outline of the cases for and against a feminist jurisprudence; I shall then move on to make some general comments on the debate and to identify a danger of theoretical slippage in discussions of some central problems of strategy and principle. In the final section, I shall draw some analogies between the debate about feminist jurisprudence and recent discussions in political and social theory. I shall suggest that while there are clear reasons for ambivalence about the appropriate location for feminist scholarship on the closure/critique axis, developments in social theory should lead us to question the idea of closure and critique as a dichotomy or a pair of mutually exclusive approaches to the analysis of social practices. In particular, I shall argue that a reading of some recent communitarian and 'pragmatist' literature can provide some useful tools for feminist thought in approaching if not resolving the question of the grounding for feminist critique.

Throughout, I shall be working with a broad conception of feminism as any set of political ideas and commitments which explicate gender as a crucial factor in the constitution of social relations, and as a hierarchical structure by means of which women are subordinated. It is axiomatic, on this view of feminism, that gender is politically problematic, rather than merely of explanatory significance. Clearly, much more could be said of the variety of feminisms which have developed out of the second wave of the women's movement, but I hope that this inclusive conception will be sufficient to underpin the limited project of this chapter. Some preliminary remarks are also called for about the notions of closure and critique around which my argument is structured. The idea of critique is widely used in legal and social theory, often without any great analytical precision. Indeed, the use of the description 'critical' by those of us who see our work as politically radical or of the left has sometimes caused resentment among those who, reasonably enough, point out that any self-respecting intellectual enterprise must see itself as critical. In what follows, I shall be using the term 'critique' broadly to identify projects within legal theory which are specifically concerned to go beyond the superficial appearance of legal practices and discourses and to question, unsettle and expose to careful scrutiny not only current laws and their organisation but also the claims to authority and legitimacy which legal officials, law-makers, legal practices and theories express on law's behalf.

The idea of closure, on the other hand, implies claims of authority which are *grounded* in some way. I want to distinguish between legal closure on the one hand and philosophical closure on the other. By legal closure, I mean the claim to autonomy and specificity made by law or on law's behalf. The claims that there are right (legal) answers to questions of law, and that legal reasoning is a specific form of reasoning distinct from ethical or other forms of practical reasoning, would be good examples of ideas which presuppose or claim legal closure. This is a rather different matter from the question of philosophical closure, which has been a particular preoccupation in ethics. Here, too, the issue is one of the *grounding* of claims, but the debate is more abstract and metaphysical. Should we regard philosophical arguments as being grounded in, legitimated by, some transcendent order of truth or reality? Or are they grounded only in human practices and traditions which are historically specific and contingent? As we shall see, each of these kinds of closure raises questions to which feminist analysis can make a useful contribution. But they also raise important and difficult methodological questions for feminism. The closure/critique axis in legal and social theory therefore seems a promising focus of inquiry from a feminist point of view.

ARGUMENTS FOR AND AGAINST A FEMINIST JURISPRUDENCE

Several arguments have been used to support the idea that feminist legal scholars should engage in the development of a feminist jurisprudence. Perhaps most obviously, it may be argued that feminist analysis and critique of laws and legal institutions is itself inevitably a theoretical enterprise which merits the denomination 'jurisprudence'. Furthermore, many of the 'standard' jurisprudential questions are of explicit or implicit relevance for feminist enterprises. On the one hand, feminism poses certain distinctive theoretical questions of and about law: why are women excluded from certain areas of law; what happens when women are included; how does law construct the female subject in language; how can law be changed better to reflect women's interests and experience? These explicitly feminist questions of legal theory are located within broader categories of legal theoretical enterprise: sociological jurisprudence, discourse theory, the analysis of law's ideological functions. More controversially, it could be argued that feminist legal theory inevitably begs questions about the definition of law and the legal sphere which have been the stuff of analytical jurisprudence. Feminisms which move beyond a liberal framework to develop a more radical critique generally reject and regard as theoretically flawed the very enterprises of 'objective' analysis and of normative jurisprudence which claim to reflect the ethical 'view from nowhere'. These arguments detect, among other things, a strong tendency towards legal closure in orthodox constructions of the jurisprudential enterprise. Yet there are strong reasons to assert that jurisprudence encompasses critical and interpretive tasks which are quite in tune with feminist theoretical thinking.

A second reason for thinking that feminists should engage in jurisprudence has to do with the power of orthodox theoretical thinking about law and the legal sphere. For example, the traditional stance of analytical jurisprudence, with its common emphasis on legal closure – the autonomy of law – has been a crucially important focus for feminist critique of the pretended 'objectivity' and 'neutrality' of 'the legal point of view'. Yet feminist scholars have in fact engaged in rather little direct debate with traditional jurisprudence, perhaps out of a conviction that it is too antediluvian to merit explicit attention, or out of an anxiety that such a debate would inevitably be constructed in terms of an agenda set by orthodoxy. This is unfortunate, given that many of the beliefs about neutrality and autonomy criticised by feminists are bolstered by the traditional jurisprudential texts which constitute the core of many jurisprudence courses. It also arguably weakens the feminist position by giving rise to a tendency to lump all 'traditional jurisprudence' together, condemning it in undifferentiated terms as 'positivist', 'essentialist', 'gender-blind', 'masculinist' or 'objectivist'. Traditional jurisprudence, of course, encompasses a variety of theoretical projects and positions, which raise different kinds of problems from a feminist perspective, and not all of which are inevitably prone to either legal closure or gender-blindness. A critical feminist jurisprudence which took on particular jurisprudential doctrines and positions might well strengthen the case for the general propositions which feminists wish to assert.

Third, feminist legal scholarship's emphasis upon the importance of careful analysis and critique of particular legal practices could be read as contributing to a shift away from a monolithic, universalising conception of the jurisprudential project, centred around a number of abstract questions such as 'what is law?' or 'what is distinctive about legal reasoning?', towards a more concrete and particularistic conception of jurisprudence. Should we allow orthodox scholars to appropriate the concept of jurisprudence, marginalising the more 'applied', political theoretical enterprises around law, or should we rather assert the status of this work as properly within the scope of jurisprudence?

Finally, the most straightforward way in which feminist legal scholarship may engage in jurisprudence is in terms of a liberal feminism mainly concerned to develop an 'immanent critique' of laws and legal practices. In other words, this feminist approach takes jurisprudence and the legal sphere on their own terms, and then holds up their actuality to contrast them with their own professed standards and ideals. This is the kind of analysis which argues for formal legal equality and equality of opportunity for women in law, and which has met with a substantial degree of success in many legal systems in modern times. Yet it is at precisely this point that ambivalence about feminist jurisprudence begins to surface, for the majority of feminist scholars working in this area today want to press beyond a liberal analysis to a more radical critique.

The case against a feminist jurisprudence has been put most powerfully by Carol Smart. Smart notes the attractions of feminist jurisprudence:

> The idea of a feminist jurisprudence is tantalizing in that it appears to hold out the promise of a fully integrated theoretical framework and political practice which will be transformative, unlike the partial or liberal measures of the past. ... It promises a general theory of law which has practical applications. Because it appears to offer the combination of theory and practice, and because it will be grounded in women's experience, the ideal of a feminist jurisprudence appears to be a way out of the impasse of liberal feminist theories of law reform. (Smart, 1989, p. 66)

But she sees the idea as giving rise to two problems:

> We should ... consider whether the quest for a feminist jurisprudence is not falling into the trap of ... the 'androcentric standard' whereby feminists find they enter into a game whose rules are predetermined by masculine requirements and a positivistic tradition ... We need also to consider whether implicit in this quest is the tendency to place law far too much into the centre of our thinking. (ibid., pp. 67–8)

To take the latter point first, 'grand' feminist theorising about law has, on this view, served women badly. While Smart certainly does not reject abstract theory itself, she is critical of the way in which the debate in and around the work of writers such as Gilligan (1982) and MacKinnon (1987; 1989) has too often remained at an abstract level, trapped within theoretical dichotomies such as equality versus difference, public versus private, which are partly of its own creation. Smart's other argument might be taken to suggest a more fundamental objection to 'grand' theory. What are the 'masculine requirements' which taint the very notion of feminist jurisprudence? One view could be that the very project of abstract theorisation is unsatisfactory and indeed to be regarded with suspicion by feminists and other radicals. For the move from concrete to abstract becomes a means of assimilating and hence disguising the varied experiences of legal subjects; factors such as race and gender are rendered invisible by the move to abstraction; the voices of people of colour, poor people, women and other powerless groups are silenced.

Smart wants to distinguish, however, between 'grand' and 'abstract' theory, her objection being to the former rather than the latter. On this view, 'grand' theory is that which 'totalises' or 'universalises' – which claims to generate truths of general applicability. Any 'total' theory of or about law may lead subtly to a 'totalising' theory which represses difference, and even to 'totalitarian' thinking and practice; any 'normative' theory may lead towards 'normalisation' and hence to repression. Alternatively, such 'grand' theory may succeed only in offering accounts of the phenomena which it purports to explain at so high a level of abstraction that they become banal or simplistic. The main burden of Smart's argument is that legal theory as it traditionally conceives itself is ideological and hence effective in underpinning the very power of law: its claims to truth, impartiality and objectivity, its place high up in the hierarchy of knowledges, which have been so damaging to women and other oppressed groups. Legal theory, in other words, participates in a strong form of legal closure which is inimical to a recognition of the politics of law.

INTERPRETING THE DEBATE

It would, of course, be possible to interpret the debate about feminist jurisprudence as a trivial disagreement which turns on semantics. This would, I think, be a mistake. For the debate touches on a number of fundamental theoretical and political issues which are salient in contemporary feminism, and the very reason why the question of feminist jurisprudence is so problematic is connected to these deeper questions.

Most obviously, there is the question of what kind of theoretical enterprise feminism should engage in, and how far it should concern itself with law in the first place. Is the very idea of a feminist theory of law one which implicitly acknowledges legal closure, the autonomy of the legal realm – a closure which is ultimately disempowering to feminism, whose main task is political critique? Is the idea of a feminist theory of law simply a contradiction in terms? Do we really have the power to construct the debate in our own terms – or is the jurisprudential enterprise inevitably loaded towards masculinist concepts and male interests, so that the construction of a feminist jurisprudence, in Audre Lorde's famous phrase, is a futile attempt to destroy the master's house with the master's tools (Lorde, 1984)? Even worse, does the project of constructing a feminist theory of law commit the almost unmentionable sin of essentialism, participating in the idea that law has some fixed 'essence', as opposed to being open to social and political reconstruction (Smart, 1989, p. 69)? If legal theory does contain an irreducible core of essentialism, is this inevitable, or defensible on strategic grounds (Fuss, 1989)?

Second, there is a set of questions about the place in feminism for normative, reconstructive or utopian thinking, as opposed to negatively critical or 'deconstructive'[1] thinking. Does the idea of feminism as critique mean that we are always 'trashing' – exposing sexism, bias, lack, absence – or is it the job of feminist legal scholars also to prescribe – to suggest legal reforms – or to imagine other possible legal worlds and processes, or indeed worlds without law? And if, as many feminists believe, there is this positive, reconstructive aspect to the feminist enterprise, does it need some kind of grounding or foundation (Benhabib, 1987, 1990; Fraser, 1989; Harding, 1990)? This shades into a third important question, and brings the issue of philosophical closure into the argument. We must ask whether feminist thought should continue to be located firmly in the post-enlightenment modernism in whose terms (rights, calls for equality and so on) we have become familiar with feminist claims being couched. Alternatively, it might be argued that the critical potential of modernism and liberalism have been exhausted and must now give way to a postmodernist, resolutely critical mode which utterly rejects philosophical closure and opens up legal discourse to the 'play of difference', to the multiple possibilities raised by deconstructive critique. Yet even this way of putting the question is misleading, for it suggests that deconstruction, discourse theory, postmodernist fragmentation and relativism necessarily go hand in hand. While it is certainly true that this relationship is a familiar one, Drucilla Cornell (Cornell, 1990) has suggested that one can combine a deconstructive project with an ethical feminism which seems to belong firmly in the modernist tradition.[2] Ultimately, this brings us back to the question of what kind of theory feminism can and should engage in, refined in terms of possibly multiple combinations of modernist and postmodernist, critical and reconstructive, discourse-oriented and materialist, essentialist and social-constructionist projects. Should these dichotomies themselves be regarded as having any validity, and what combinations of project may be theoretically defensible or politically productive?

Fourth, the questions already raised connect with a further important feminist preoccupation: that of the relationship between theory and practice. Feminism has generally been fiercely committed to the idea that theory and practice form inseparable parts of the political project: theory which is neither informed by the issues thrown up by practice nor likely to contribute to feminist praxis has been seen as an irrelevant and even elitist preoccupation, of no real theoretical or political validity. This commitment to the interrelation of theory and practice which feminism shares with many other radical discourses of course relates to feminist ambivalence about 'grand' and, in some feminisms, all abstract theory, and marks a tendency in feminist thought which is resistant to philosophical closure. But recent debates have thrown up, as I shall try to show, some intractable questions about the political and strategic defensibility of engaging in action informed by theory which falls short of feminist ideals: in Cornell's words, deciding to work for, for example, legal equality, while still knowing that this is something that one will never be prepared to *settle for* (Cornell, 1990, p. 689).

Fifth, the debate about feminist jurisprudence touches on important questions about the relationship of law to other institutions and structures of power. Is law a *relatively* autonomous field, change in which really holds out the hope of material gains for women? Or is law radically implicated with other powerful discourses and institutions in the social, political, cultural and economic realms? This question has a crucial bearing on the potential efficacy of feminist legal strategies. Finally, the debate about feminist jurisprudence raises questions about the relationship between feminism and other social critiques which present themselves as progressive – work in critical race theory, Critical Legal Studies, Marxist theory, poststructuralist and postmodernist analysis. In a sense, then, there is an important issue about closure within feminism – both in terms of how autonomous it is as a critical analysis, and in terms of how far it presupposes a foundationalist meta-ethics. The increasing recognition in modern feminist thought of the diversity and fragmentation of social experience and hence of the need to listen to the insights of women situated in a variety of locations relative to the many powerful sites of social oppression – class, race, sexuality – raises important and exciting questions about the power of a critique which draws on several sources of enlightenment and a common methodology. At the same time, the spectre of total fragmentation seems to threaten feminism's mission to speak in the voice of political outrage or advocacy – practice which at least superficially seems to pull feminism back in the direction of philosophical closure.

Thus the questions about feminist jurisprudence touch on some fundamental philosophical and political questions. These questions are closely connected with debates around issues of closure and critique at the levels of both legal and social theory, to which I now turn.

Some of the concrete problems around which the debate about feminist jurisprudence has been centred seem as intractable as they do, not just because of the complexity of the theoretical and political questions involved, but also because of a degree of slippage between those different questions. I shall illustrate this contention with some examples.

What Is 'Grand Theory'?

The debate about the problematic nature of 'grand' theory seems to me to be underdeveloped, with the result that some versions of the argument are in danger of abandoning important feminist legal theoretical projects along with analytical jurisprudence, 'viewpointless' normative jurisprudence and crudely monolithic feminist theories. It is open to feminists to construct the jurisprudential project in interpretive and critical ways which are friendly to feminism and certainly not 'grand' in the relevant sense. Indeed, Carol Smart's critique of the 'quest for a feminist jurisprudence' itself employs concepts such as 'patriarchy' and 'phallogocentrism' which are themselves highly theorised ideas, just as much of her work shows a strong commitment to engage in theoretical tasks of conceptualisation and analysis. Foucaultian discourse theory and Derridean deconstruction could be said to be every bit as 'grandly theoretical' as any jurisprudential theory so far attempted. They too are universalistic at least at the level of method, and to the extent that they seek our attention they inevitably claim a persuasiveness which participates in some kind of validity claim. Of course, we may well want to criticise critical theories as themselves unduly abstract, apolitical or inaccessible. But it seems unarguable that they have generated theoretical ideas which have been found to be powerful in developing feminist critiques of law (Rhode, 1990). This having been said, the question of just what makes a 'grand theory' 'grand' still needs clearer specification if we are to accept it as a generally negative denomination. And in seeking that clarification, we should be sensitive to the fact that, irrespective of the kinds of truth claims which they assert, the progressiveness and illuminating potential of theories is heavily context-dependent. For example, natural law theory's influence on liberation theology and positivism's basically constructionist stance and its critique of the authoritarian model of law and state implicit in some natural law theory constitute contributions with which many feminists would be sympathetic.

There are at least three elements to the idea of 'grand' theory as a pejorative. The first objection is to theories which have pretensions to assert Truth (with a capital T!) (Smart, 1989, pp. 71–2, 85–6; Rorty, 1991). This may be 'true' of all theories except for the most thoroughly deconstructive ones, but it is a relatively trivial 'truth'. For comprehensive theories of law can easily be reinterpreted as offering partial perspectives or insights – interpretations rather than 'truths'. In other words, while theories inevitably make an implicit claim to 'truth' or 'validity', it is up to us, the critical audience, to reconstruct the status of their claims, and in doing so to take on board such insights as they have rather than rejecting them in a wholesale way. If the core of the idea of grand theory lies in the status of its truth claims, this is perhaps something which feminism need not fear in any general way. For it may be argued that the very multiplicity of and controversy among 'grand' theories purporting to have access to Truth or give us the last word on reality are undermining to that status in a fairly effective way. The interpretivist reconstruction of such theories does indeed seem to be an important feminist move, but this should not rule out feminist jurisprudence. Furthermore, while *law*'s pretensions to Truth or objective validity are clearly a central object of critique in feminist theory, it is not clear that feminist *jurisprudence* necessarily has to engage in the same pretensions. In this sense, the burden of Smart's argument concerns feminist engagement with *law* rather than with *legal theory*.

The second theme which can be identified in the objection to 'grand' theory is to theories which are monolithic in the sense that they seek to reduce all aspects of women's oppression to one or two basic factors such as sexuality or, as in the case of early Marxist feminism, a particular conception of class. This is indeed an important defect of some theories, but it does not apply to all theories which purport to have a broad scope. The search for a 'universal' theory of law does not necessarily imply that it must be 'universalising' or 'totalising'; it may in fact be eclectic, complex, pluralistic. For example, Tove Stang Dahl interprets the feminist jurisprudential project in a pluralistic and positive way, identifying a number of sites and modes of legal subordination of women, and engaging in a project of reconceptualisation of legal categories along feminist lines (Stang Dahl, 1986). Her particular reconceptualisation is, I think, problematic, but much of her methodology is instructive (Lacey, 1989; Fraser and Nicholson, 1990; for instances of this kind of theory-building in social and political theory, see Connell, 1987; Walby, 1990).

Finally, a third objection is to the (high) degree of abstraction of 'grand' theories. Again, this seems to me to be an important objection given that the move from concrete to abstract can indeed serve as a cover for the marginalisation or suppression of varying perspectives: abstraction can indeed serve totalisation. Yet this must be a question of degree. *Any* use of theoretical terms inevitably involves conceptualisation and hence a degree of abstraction; indeed, this is an inevitable feature of the use of language. As we have already seen, Smart and other feminist theorists themselves clearly affirm the necessity for legitimacy of abstraction in the theoretical enterprise. The three aspects of 'grand' theory, then, need to be looked at separately in the case of any candidate for the category.

Against 'Grand' Theory or against 'Centre-ing' Law?

It seems to me that the central object of Carol Smart's critique is not so much the idea of grand theory but rather her second concern – the importance which the project of feminist jurisprudence implicitly accords to law as a site of women's oppression and, most importantly, for feminist activism and reform. Smart has powerful arguments about the limitations of law as a feminist strategy. To the extent that we accept them, these arguments give us powerful political reasons not to expend too much energy on reconstructive legal theory. This is a very different issue from that of the status of theory itself. But Smart's political argument can be questioned. Her explicit acceptance of the importance of the critical project implicitly recognises, as the title of her book suggests, the importance of law as a means of entrenching, expressing and maintaining women's oppression. If law can be powerful in these ways, does not legal critique and change hold out some prospect of progress for women, even if not a panacea? The view that law is a relatively unimportant site for feminist intervention, and that we should be cautious in engaging with it, is itself informed by a set of theoretical views about the relative significance of different sites and modes of power, among which Smart emphasises the importance of law's claims to Truth and its high position in the 'hierarchy of knowledges' (Smart, 1989, ch. 1). But this argument is not in itself sufficient to support the 'de-centre-ing' of law in feminist theory and practice; this conclusion only follows if it is clear that *other* discourses or institutions exist or can be created which make a weaker claim to Truth than does law. Yet obvious possibilities such as institutions within the political sphere themselves engage in effective marginalising strategies which make them problematic in terms of feminist practice.

The Problem of Induction from Theory to Practice

Whether or not it is appropriate to take a *general* position on the need for feminists to 'de-centre' law in our approach to theory and practice, we need to avoid another potential slippage in the debate about feminist jurisprudence and legal reforms. This is a shift from a general argument about the need to 'de-centre' law to a specific, and often powerful, critique of particular inductions from theory to practice in feminist legal scholarship. Perhaps the best example here is the debate around MacKinnon's and Dworkin's famous attempt to legislate

against pornography by means of an ordinance which, among other
things, sought to give individual women a civil right of action for the
harms done to them by pornography as sex discrimination via the sexual
objectification of women (MacKinnon, 1987, Part III; 1989, chs 7 and
11). Smart, among others, has cogent criticisms of MacKinnon's induction from theory to practice (Smart, 1989, ch. 6; Lacey, 1989): her
monolithic theory, which identifies sexuality as the ultimate site of
women's oppression and male power, directs her to a political strategy
which brings with it significant risks. In the first place, it is likely to lead
feminists into dangerous political alliances with groups which oppose
pornography for reasons which are antipathetic to feminist ideals. Second, it gives judges and law enforcement officers – neither of them groups
widely thought to be sympathetic to feminist perspectives – the power to
interpret relatively open-ended legal formulations, and thus potentially to
distort the feminist aspects of the legislation. This critique has two
dimensions: first, there is an argument about the kind of theory which
MacKinnon develops – a monolithic, 'grand' feminist jurisprudence
which seeks to reduce all aspects of women's oppression to one dimension, and which treads dangerously close to a biologistic essentialism. The
practical implication of this must be something close to total hopelessness
in terms of the prospects for feminist progress. On the other hand, there
is a critique of MacKinnon's political strategy: even if we agreed with her
analysis, would we want to affirm this particular kind of reformism?

Of course, this brings us back to the questions of the relation between
theory and practice and between principle and strategy. The distinction
which I have drawn between the two aspects of the critique of MacKinnon
raises the converse possibility that even though we disagreed with her
analysis, we might still see sense in her legal strategies. For example,
despite its strategic dangers already discussed, one potential advantage of
the anti-pornography campaign might well have been a contribution to
opening up the legal process in a way which enables women to use it –
both in the sense of having effective access to it, and in the sense of
recognising the rights and claims which it instantiates as responding to
women's needs and therefore thinking of law as something which can be
empowering to women as well as to men. More straightforwardly, I would
argue that MacKinnon's campaign to have sexual harassment recognised
as a legal wrong has been an important and in many ways effective
feminist strategy.

I want to emphasise this distinction, because I think that it is most
unlikely, given the centrally *political* impetus of feminism, that feminist
lawyers will give up hope of the possibility of modest progress through
legal change. What is more, it would be very unfortunate if we did give it
up. As Smart herself argues, it would be a mistake to regard all legal

reformist strategies as equally flawed. What we need is not an abandonment of the legal/political project, but rather the development of more
sophisticated understandings of legal practices, their strengths as well as
their evident and important limitations. This would include a theoretical
understanding of how law relates to other powerful institutions and
discourses. Doubtless this is an inelegantly electric view, but I would
contend that feminist politics around law have room not only for critical
analysis of the status quo but also for both pragmatic/strategic and
utopian thinking and action. If I am right, it follows that we must be alive
to the differences between strategy and ideal, and of the different ways in
which they must be assessed.

FEMINISM, LAW AND CRITIQUE

I have suggested that several of the problems which have surfaced in the
debate about feminist jurisprudence have seemed more intractable than
they need to because of a slippage in argument between questions of
theory and those of practice and strategy. However, many of these points
do not tell against a thoroughly critical stance which 'de-centres' and even
eschews not only the project of reconstruction via legal reform but also the
very idea of feminism as concerned with political prescription or reconstruction. In her most recent work, Carol Smart (Smart, 1990; 1992)
follows through the implications of the rejection of abstract theorisation
as totalising and potentially repressive, and makes a persuasive case for
the position not only that feminism will be better served by a
postmodernist critique, but also that this is the only theoretically sound
position to be adopted. The relationship between feminism and
postmodernism and of feminist attitudes to philosophical closure are, of
course, among the most important questions of contemporary social
theory (Lovibond, 1989; Nicholson (ed.), 1990). In the legal sphere,
postmodernism and deconstruction raise crucial issues of theory and
practice: given feminism's irreducibly political underpinning, can a radically critical project sustain the kind of politics, including the ideal of
reconstruction, which has so long been accepted as a part of feminism?

Drucilla Cornell has recently argued that feminist legal scholars can and
should combine a politically motivated deconstruction with an 'ethical
feminism' which argues for the reconstruction of the legal sphere (Cornell,
1990; 1991).[3] Cornell's brand of deconstruction is rooted in psychoanalytic
concepts which, she argues, escape the biological essentialism and strong
social determinism which characterise many feminist theories. Cornell's
position is particularly interesting in that we can see it as a vivid metaphor for
what is perhaps the most difficult question for contemporary feminism:
whether to break free of its modernist ties and step over into the kind of
thorough postmodernism which Smart advocates, or whether to reject such

a move as threatening a disintegration of feminism through the deconstruction of the very categories – woman, gender – which inform it. Doubtless this point should not be overplayed: feminist theory and practice has never taken the category 'woman' as a given, but has struggled to reconstruct notions of femininity in ways which have both sought to and in fact changed the meaning of what it is to be a woman, and the possible ways of living femininity. In this sense, feminist reliance on the notion of woman may be seen as a necessary, strategic and non-dangerous form of weak essentialism (Fuss, 1989; the idea is criticised in Cornell, 1991, pp. 179–83). Yet there is a sense in which the very feminist project assumes some degree of continuity among women's oppressions, and the rejection of this basic idea might be thought to threaten feminism with the spectre of disintegration. Does the kind of move which Smart advocates lead us towards exciting new possibilities, or to a politically frightening, or perhaps irresponsible, relativism? We could see Cornell's approach as 'a foot in both camps' – or we may see it as a transcending of the modernism/postmodernism dichotomy. After all, many commentators have questioned just how far 'postmodernism' represents a genuine rupture with Enlightenment thinking, as opposed to one final immanent critique of modernism itself (Bordo, 1990; Fraser, 1989, chs 1–3; Hartsock, 1990; Huyssen, 1990).

Cornell is certainly not alone in rejecting the idea that we must opt either for a thorough postmodern critique or a less radical modernist reconstructive project which participates in philosophical closure. Roberto Unger, for example, combines critique of legal doctrine with a commitment to utopian thinking about the possibilities for social recon-struction – for different social and legal practices and worlds (Unger, 1986; 1987). We need not accept that the salvaging of the reconstructive project depends on a commitment to transcendent foundationalism. Indeed, this would be to resurrect rather than to undermine the closure-critique dichotomy. Arguably, Unger's utopianism, like the leaps of political imagination advocated by thoroughgoing social constructionists like Rorty, emphasises the opening-up of different possibilities, of experi-mentation and the celebration of fluidity and variety, in a way which is more resonant with postmodern thinking than with the kind of transcen-dental normative ethics of modernist political, moral and legal philoso-phers (Rorty, 1989). This appears to be much the kind of project envisaged by Cornell when she argues that we should be pointing to the possibility of 'a new choreography of sexual difference'. Indeed, Rorty argues that we lose nothing in embracing wholeheartedly contingency and an ironic attitude, since the promises of transcendental grounding have never been more than a chimera offered by abstract philosophy. This need not lead us to abandon the use of normative language; it merely entails that we reconstruct the meaning of apparently realist/objectivist truth claims as statements made 'as if' there were some independent reality to which we are appealing, rather than as making such claims.

As Susan Williams suggests in her response to Cornell's article (Williams, 1990), the turn to communitarianism in recent social theory may offer something of a halfway house between the transcendental universalist approach and the radical relativism which seems to be embraced by some postmodernist theories and which arguably threatens to cut the political ground from under feminism's feet (Nussbaum, 1990, chs 8 and 15; see particularly pp. 228–9). The definition of communitarianism is problematic, for the idea has emerged from a critique of liberalism developed by a number of theorists who have overlapping concerns but whose views are far from identical and who do not all identify themselves as communitarians. The main writers in question are MacIntyre (1981; 1988; 1990), Sandel (1982), Taylor (1985; 1989), Unger (1987) and Walzer (1983; 1987). In their writings two main themes may be distinguished. The first is methodological and could be described as the social-constructionist theme. Communitarians reject the idea of political philosophy as an objective, non-socially-grounded project which proposes values and frameworks which are of universal validity. They replace this conception with a view of social theory as socially grounded and as interpretive. Emerging from this methodological stance, communitarians have argued that both human identity and values are socially constructed. This exposes as a social construct the liberal idea of an abstract, disembodied individual who bears rights, needs and interests which are independent of any particular social situation. Moreover, the facts of human sociality and interdependence render the presocial conception of individual personhood inappropriate as a starting point for political theory.[4] This kind of interpretivist methodology rejects a strong idea of philosophical closure, or one that is necessarily inimical to critique. While communitarian political argument is clearly grounded in the sense of finding its foundation in certain concrete social practices, it does not pretend to transcendent or objective foundations.

The second theme which emerges from these writers' work might be called 'value-communitarianism'. Communitarians have been critical of liberalism's unwillingness or inability to develop an adequate account of what might be called 'communitarian values' – public goods and collective values such as solidarity and reciprocity as opposed to the individual-oriented values encapsulated in liberal conceptions of rights and freedom (Lacey, 1992). Clearly, the second theme is related to the first: a recognition of the inevitable sociality of human life renders appropriate a focus on collective values and public goods and renders problematic a focus on a 'presocial' conception of the individual. The

need to develop a sophisticated account of public goods and collective
values, and to focus on questions of public culture and collective
provision, follows quite naturally from a recognition of human interdependence and the constitutive role of community ties and values in the
creation of human identity.

Communitarians, then, start from the premise that all social theory is
basically interpretive – grounded in specific social discourses and practices. It must therefore find its critical foothold in our experience and
understanding of prevailing cultural codes, conventions and discourses;
our attempts to make sense of our lives and, crucially, to apply a critically
reflexive attitude to our complex experiences. Feminist politics, like all
politics, must be grounded in the insights which come from diverse,
fragmented human experience of social life lived across a number of
'interpretive communities'. The attractions of this view are evident as a
corrective to the kind of 'grand' theory to which postmodernism objects:
the transcendental claim to absolute truth which is monolithic and highly
abstract, thus insensitive to the diversity of human experience. Could this
be a way to explode the closure/critique, foundationalist/anti-foundation-
alist, modernist/postmodernist dichotomies in social theory? Certainly, it
looks promising: communitarian interpretivism as a methodology for
social theory at once spawns critique and engages in a weak form of
closure (or even essentialism). The alternative critical discourses and
strategies of resistance which it generates are located or 'grounded' in
human experience and consciousness and validated by the culture from
which they emerge, rather than any transcendental pretension to
ahistorical, asocial truth.

But to acknowledge that interpretivist methodology in some sense
transcends the dichotomy is not to say that it is unproblematic from the
point of view of feminist politics. For one question which is absolutely
central to feminist politics has yet to be addressed adequately by not only
communitarianism but also other poststructuralist social theories which
employ a similarly interpretivist, practice-oriented methodology. This is
the question of how the critical insights which result from human experience attain the kind of status which accords political power. Interpretivism opens up the idea of a society in which different communities
assert their competing or complementary points of view; it welcomes
pluralism. But it leaves open the possibility (indeed the probability) that
the perspectives which command assent, change or action are those
emanating from the most powerful communities. It has little to say, as yet,
about how marginalised groups are to attain political power. This may
simply be an inevitable political problem, but we should guard against the
danger that a communitarian interpretivism may translate into a rationalisation of the status quo – in other words, into conservatism (Frazer and

Lacey, 1993; Okin, 1989, ch. 3). This is particularly true of those forms of communitarianism such as MacIntyre's which have failed to emphasise the notion of critical reflexivity in the assessment of practices, and correspondingly less so of the work of writers like Taylor, who give more thought to this question.[5] Clearly, further theoretical work needs to be done to relate the insights of the communitarians in political theory and developments in poststructuralist and other forms of critical social theory to the specific debates within feminist and other critical legal theory which we have been exploring in terms of the closure/critique dichotomy. I hope that I have said enough here at least to demonstrate the potential fruitfulness of such work, and to suggest that holding to the closure/ critique dichotomy may lead to an impoverished conception of the possibilities for feminist legal theory.

CONCLUDING THOUGHTS

If we were to think of law and theories of law as a type of game of whose structure and substance we are critical, we could think about the debate about feminist jurisprudence as torn between the options of trying to get into the team to have a better chance of changing the structure of the game or of engaging in strategic rule-breaking; of simply withdrawing to create and play a different game altogether; of watching on the sidelines and allowing ourselves the luxury of throwing the occasional rotten tomato from a safe distance; or some combination of these three. I have suggested that although the theoretically pure approach may well be the second, there will often be tactical and strategic reasons for engaging in the first and the third, and that we need a careful analysis in each case of just what the dangers and advantages of a pragmatic strategy are likely to be. The idea of 'de-centre-ing' law is an attractive one to the extent either that there are other established practices, intervention in which would be likely to be more politically productive, or that the creation of alternative, autonomous practices offers, in the long run, the possibility of political progress as opposed to further marginalisation. But a combined strategy may often be less politically compromising than we fear. The development of alternative, resistant discourses is certainly a central project of feminism, but its political impetus must also lead feminists to engage with currently powerful discourses and institutions. It is far form clear that institutions such as politics, conventional morality, the family and religion are any more hospitable to feminist intervention, critique and reconstruction than is law. As feminist lawyers and legal scholars, it seems reasonable to assert that feminist theoretical projects around law, which need not amount to 'grand theorising', will assume both an intellectual and political priority in our practice. In developing feminist approaches to law, we certainly have to be wary of a too hasty closure around the concept of law. But the recognition that contingent and constructed structures and institutions are nonetheless powerful means that the project must proceed.

On the questions of closure and critique, we must return to the distinction drawn early on in the chapter between legal and philosophical closure. As far as the former is concerned, any feminist theoretical project around law will inevitably reject the idea of law as an autonomous structure generating claims to truth which are insulated from political critique. Feminism, in common with other critical approaches in social theory, will always be concerned to undermine, to expose as false, law's pretended autonomy, objectivity and neutrality. As far as philosophical closure is concerned, however, we have to conclude that much feminist theory is still hovering over the alleged divide between modernist and postmodernist projects, uncertain whether to jump one way or another or to reject the dichotomy itself. Many feminists continue to fear that the move to postmodernism may cut our political ground form under us, may reduce our perspective to 'just one view among others' – including that of sexism – and may deny us the basis for speaking in terms of anger and advocacy. We therefore hesitate on the boundary, fearful of the political consequences of fragmentation and relativism, and even sceptical of the emergence of postmodernism at just the moment when feminist modernist critiques seemed to be gaining some power (Di Stefano, 1990). The temptation both to assert the moral high ground as our own, and simultaneously to cut it away from under ourselves as theoretically unsound, remain strong opposing tendencies in contemporary feminism. Ultimately, I would argue that the reasons for resisting the closure/ critique, modernism/postmodernism dichotomies in legal and social philosophy are strong. Feminist legal theorists such as Carol Smart and Drucilla Cornell have asserted and demonstrated in different ways the *political* power and status of critique, and it seems highly unlikely that feminism will or should give up its utopian and reconstructive dimension, whatever its epistemological basis is taken to be. In this context, the most persuasive feminist work represents neither a real transcendence of the closure/critique dichotomy, nor the unsatisfactory compromise suggested by the idea of a foot in both camps. It rather rejects the conceptual straitjacket which a rigid closure/critique dichotomy seeks to impose, and questions the need to understand closure and critique in strongly dichotomised terms. Perhaps the best lesson we can learn from the debate about feminist jurisprudence is the importance of feminism's power to question and reshape the categories of traditional theoretical debate. We should not abandon the concept of jurisprudence to orthodoxy, but claim it for our own as part of a transformative feminist practice.

NOTES

1. The idea of deconstruction is now widely and somewhat loosely used in critical social theory. At Suzanne Gibson's suggestion, I have tried to avoid using the term except where it is meant in the very specific sense developed by Jacques Derrida, with an emphasis on binary oppositions and on strategies of displacement and reversal, destabilising what is by confronting it with the Other which it excludes yet on which it depends. This sense of deconstruction has, of course, been influential in a wide range of literary, psychoanalytic and social theory. But, especially in Anglo-American work, the term 'deconstruction' often refers to a much wider practice. I have referred to what I take to be this wider idea of 'deconstruction' simply as 'critique'.

2. This chapter was written before the publication of Cornell's *Beyond Accommodation* (Cornell, 1991). In this book, Cornell makes it clear that she aligns herself, with some reservations, with postmodernism. More generally, it would of course be a mistake to conflate the 'textual turn' in contemporary social theory with a general postmodernist rejection of the possibility of coherent metanarratives. For example, the work of Pierre Bourdieu (Bourdieu, 1977) combines a focus on discourse, social constructionism and rejection of universalism with a decisive rejection of the postmodernism of other French social theorists such as Derrida and Lyotard: see also Robbins (1991).

3. In her most recent work (Cornell, 1991), Cornell identifies the 'ethical moment' of deconstruction as the imperative to attend to difference which is implicit in the deconstructive move to unearth the repressed 'Other' (see note 1). A proper assessment of this full statement of her position cannot be given here. *Beyond Accommodation* certainly provides the most persuasive and thorough application of deconstruction to feminist legal theory yet attempted, although questions remain about whether Cornell's psychoanalytic account of the repressed 'feminine imaginary' indeed escapes a form of essentialism.

4. For many of the communitarians, this kind of approach is exemplified in modern political philosophy by the work of John Rawls and in particular by his conception of the 'original position' as a neocontractarian legitimating device for his theory of justice (Rawls, 1971). It is interesting to note that, while not accepting many of the arguments that the communitarians have developed about his conception of the person, Rawls has made significant concessions, both methodologically and substantively, to communitarian ideas in his more recent work: see particularly Rawls (1980; 1985).

5. By 'critical reflexivity' I mean the capacity of persons to question, assess, reflect critically upon (even) those practices and beliefs which are dominant in their culture and which play a constitutive role in their identities and conceptions of the good. This involves the capacity to stand aside to some extent from the practices in question – but not to the extent needed to achieve the radically detached stance envisaged by much universalistic philosophy: see Frazer and Lacey (1993); Passerin d'Entrèves (1990, pp. 82–8); Walzer (1987).

REFERENCES

Andrews, R. M. (1993), *Punishment: Meanings, Purposes, Practices*, New York: Peter Lang Publishing.

Benhabib, S. (1987), 'The generalised and the concrete Other', in Benhabib and Cornell (eds) (1987).

Benhabib, S. and Cornell, D. (eds) (1987), *Feminism as Critique*, Oxford: Polity Press.

Benhabib, S. (1990), 'Epistemologies of postmodernism: a rejoinder to Jean-Francois Lyotard', in Nicholson (ed.) (1990).

Bourdieu, P. (1977), *Outline of a Theory of Practice*, transl. R. Nice, Cambridge: Cambridge University Press.

Connell, R. W. (1987), *Gender and Power*, Oxford: Polity Press.

Cornell D. (1990), 'The doubly-prized world: myth, allegory and the feminine', *Cornell Law Review* 644.

Cornell D. (1991) *Beyond Accommodation: Ethical Feminism, Deconstruction and the Law*, London: Routledge.

Di Stefano, C. (1990), 'Dilemmas of difference: feminism, modernity and postmodernism', in Nicholson (ed.) (1990).

Fraser, N. (1989), *Unruly Practices: Power, Discourse and Gender in Contemporary Social Theory*, Oxford: Polity Press.

Fraser, N. and Nicholson, L. (1990), 'Social criticism without philosophy', in Nicholson (ed.) (1990).

Frazer, E. and Lacey, N. (1993), 'Feminism, MacIntyre and the concept of practice', in Horton and Mendus (eds) (1992).

Fuss, D. (1989), *Essentially Speaking: Feminism, Nature and Difference*, London: Routledge.

Gilligan, C. (1982), *In a Different Voice*, Cambridge, Ma: Harvard University Press.

Harding, S. (1990), 'Feminism, science and the anti-Enlightenment critiques', in Nicholson (ed.) (1990).

Hartsock, N. (1990), 'Foucault on power: a theory for women?', in Nicholson (ed.) (1990).

Horton, J. and Mendus, S. (1992) *After MacIntyre*, Oxford: Polity Press.

Huyssen, A. (1990), 'Mapping the postmodern', in Nicholson (ed.) (1990).

Lacey, N. (1989), 'Feminist legal theory', *Oxford Journal of Legal Studies* 9, 383.

Lacey, N. (1993), 'Punishment: a communitarian approach', in Andrews (ed.) (1993).

Lorde, A. (1984), *Sister Outsider*, New York: The Crossing Press.

Lovibond, S. (1989), 'Feminism and postmodernism', *New Left Review* 12.

MacIntyre, A. (1981), *After Virtue*, London: Duckworth.

MacIntyre, A. (1988), *Whose Justice, Which Rationality?*, London: Duckworth.

MacIntyre, A. (1990), *Three Rival Versions of Moral Enquiry*, London: Duckworth.

MacKinnon, C. (1987), *Feminism Unmodified*, Cambridge, Ma: Harvard University Press.

MacKinnon, C. (1989), *Toward a Feminist Theory of the State*, Cambridge, Ma: Harvard University Press.

Nicholson, L. (ed.) (1990), *Feminism/Postmodernism*, London: Routledge.

Nussbaum, M. (1990), *Love's Knowledge*, Oxford, Oxford University Press.

Okin, S. M. (1989), *Justice, Gender and the Family*, New York, Basic Books.

Passerin d'Entrèves, M. (1990), 'Communitarianism and the question of tolerance', *Journal of Social Philosophy* 77.

Rawls, J. (1971), *A Theory of Justice*, Oxford: Oxford University Press.

Rawls, J. (1980), 'Kantian constructivism in moral theory', *Journal of Philosophy* 515.

Rawls, J. (1985), 'Justice as fairness: political not metaphysical', *Philosophy and Public Affairs* 223.

Rhode, D. (1990), 'Feminist critical theories', *Stanford Law Review* 42, 617.

Robbins, D. (1991), *The Work of Pierre Bourdieu*, Milton Keynes: Open University Press.

Rorty, R. (1989), *Contingency, Irony and Solidarity*, Cambridge: Cambridge University Press.

Rorty, R. (1991), 'Feminism and pragmatism', *Radical Philosophy* 59, 3.

Sandel, M. (1982), *Liberalism and the Limits of Justice*, Cambridge: Cambridge University Press.

Smart, C. (1989), *Feminism and the Power of Law*, London: Routledge.

Smart, C. (1990), 'Law, the sexed body and feminist discourse', *Journal of Law and Society* 17, 194.

Smart, C. (1992), 'The woman of legal discourse', *Social and Legal Studies* 29.

Stang Dahl, T. (1986), *Women's Law: An Introduction to Feminist Jurisprudence*, Oslo: Norwegian University Press.

Taylor, C. (1985), *Philosophy and the Human Sciences*, Cambridge: Cambridge University Press.

Taylor, C. (1989), *Sources of the Self*, Cambridge: Cambridge University Press.

Thornton, M. (1986), 'Feminist jurisprudence: illusion or reality?', *Australian Journal of Law and Society* 3, 5.

Unger, R. M. (1986), *The Critical Legal Studies Movement*, Cambridge, Ma: Harvard University Press.

Unger, R. M. (1987), *Social Theory: Its Situation and Its Task*, Cambridge: Cambridge University Press.

Walby, S. (1990), *Theorising Patriarchy*, Oxford, Basil Blackwell.

Walzer, M. (1983), *Spheres of Justice: A Defence of Pluralism and Equality*, Oxford: Basil Blackwell.

Walzer, M. (1987), *Interpretation and Social Criticism*, Cambridge, Ma: Harvard University Press.

Williams, S. (1990), 'Feminism's search for the feminine: essentialism, utopianism and community', *Cornell Law Review*, 700.

Several of the arguments in this chapter originated in a presentation which Suzanne Gibson and I made to a seminar on Closure and Critique held at Warwick University in the Summer of 1991. I should like to thank Suzanne for helping me to formulate these ideas, in our discussion in preparation for the Warwick seminar and in her written comments on a draft of the paper. I am also grateful to Alan Norrie, Deborah Rhode and Carol Smart for their constructive comments on drafts of the paper, and to the participants at the Warwick Seminar, particularly Linda Luckhaus and Ann Stewart, for their helpful responses to the presentation and comments about how some of its ideas might be developed.

Index